Dmitrii Miliutin

DMITRII MILIUTIN

and the Reform Era
in Russia

FORRESTT A. MILLER

Vanderbilt University Press
1968

FOR NICHOLAS RIASANOVSKY

Acknowledgments

THE DEBTS owed by any author are extensive. Mine are especially so. Professor Charles Jelavich, now of Indiana University, first suggested the topic to me and through the Center for Slavic Studies at the University of California at Berkeley provided me with the necessary material support. Part of this work was included in my doctoral dissertation at Berkeley directed by Nicholas Riasanovsky to whom I owe more than I can ever repay. The research was conducted in a range of libraries: the Doe Library at Berkeley, the Library of Congress, Butler Library at Columbia University, and the New York Public Library. The Joint University Libraries at Vanderbilt University have been both kind and co-operative in obtaining materials for me for which my gratitude is extended to its director, Dr. David Kaser, and his staff. Two summer grants from Vanderbilt University enabled me to travel to the Helsinki University Library which proved invaluable.

The personal debts I have contracted are even more extensive. In addition to the above, I would like to thank Professors Martin Malia and Oleg Maslennikov of the University of California, Professors Herbert Weaver and Robert H. Birkby of Vanderbilt University, Professor Norman Wilensky of the University of Florida, Professor Paul M. Sonnino of the University of California at Santa Barbara, and countless others. Mr. Robert Emmitt of the Vanderbilt University Press has contributed mightily to the ultimate publication of my manuscript and has patiently forborn the eccentricities of the author. Last, but not least, I must acknowledge the help of my wife Suzanne, whose moral support has seen me through, and of my two children, Bradford and Kristina, who have allowed me sufficient moments of peace to finish.

Forrestt A. Miller

Contents

Dmitrii Miliutin

1

The Profile of a Reformer

THE PASSAGE of a century has left unanswered many questions about the Great Reforms of Russia, and within the limits of our knowledge are perhaps no darker corners than those occupied by the personalities of the reformers themselves. For the most part, we lack adequate understanding, either of their individual motives, the means by which they made their influence felt, their relations with one another as well as with those who opposed them, or the degree to which they realized the goals they themselves had established. Dmitrii Alexeevich Miliutin was one of the most important of these reformers and with his brother Nicholas headed a loose confederation or "party" which was responsible within the upper bureaucracy for the formulation of many aspects of the reform.

The Great Reforms took place between the years 1861 and 1874, with the tempo most intense during the first three or four years, when one legislative act followed closely on the heels of another. After this, only occasional reforms were passed, most of them extensions or adjustments of legislation already implemented. The great exception was the Universal Military Conscription Statute of 1874, which broke new ground and, because it was linked closely with the security of the Empire, proved to be one of the most durable of all the Reforms.

The keystone of the Great Reforms was the emancipation of the enserfed peasantry announced in a manifesto on February 19, 1861. Other

3

reforms followed in quick succession: the recasting of the courts and the administration of justice, the creation of autonomous and popularly elected local organs of government, the mitigation of censorship of the press, the granting of autonomy to institutions of higher education.

Important as these reforms were, they were only a beginning—a first step in the larger project of recasting Russia's anachronistic institutions and creating a more modern and viable society. Each reform was like a young plant that needed loving attention, pruning, and fertilization to insure its growth and maturity. It was precisely in this phase that the reforms failed.

Alexander II himself was committed to little more than the legal emancipation of the serfs. He was often ambivalent and lacked resolve toward the accompanying reforms. The inconsistencies of his own personality made it difficult for him to pursue a single course of action. In addition to the hesitancy of the Emperor, the reforms themselves helped crystallize the active opposition of those elements that militantly resisted any change in the existing structure of Russian society. This was augmented in turn by the appearance from the late fifties onward of more radical and sometimes revolutionary groups that thoroughly frightened the defenders of the old order. These defenders often saw the reformers and the revolutionaries as the same and resisted moderate change with as much fervor as they resisted revolution.

This opposition centered largely within the land-owning gentry class, to which I shall refer later as the "planter party,"[1] which was well represented in the government of Alexander II by a number of forceful men who occupied most of the higher posts of the Empire. The Emperor himself identified closely with the gentry class and throughout the sixties and seventies found it difficult to press any policy in the face of its resistance. The Emperor's personal entourage usually comprised members of the gentry, and he was clearly attached to them by a bond of sympathy.

The reforms themselves were products of the efforts of a number of dedicated and highly intelligent men, many of whom, Miliutin included,

---

1. This term is artificial but is not without precedence in the literature of the period. See, for example, W. E. Mosse, *Alexander II and the Modernization of Russia*, p. 58 and *passim*. It is descriptive of the essence of the group referred to while it avoids the need to use more complex, hyphenated words which would make the text more cumbersome.

came from the gentry class. But these men were professional bureaucrats and thought in terms of the national good rather than narrow class interest. They were intensely aware that Russia's place among the powers was being increasingly threatened by her failure to progress internally. These reformers were not revolutionaries; they were, in fact, supporters of the autocracy of Alexander II and saw in the crown a means of Russia's salvation.

The men of reforms, however, never had the undivided attention and support of the Emperor; quite to the contrary, they were often more or less in disfavor. It is easy to speculate here on what might have been accomplished had they had greater influence, for the reformers were men who had both vision and the ability to see Russia as it was. Given their heads, they might have transformed the face of Russia and created a modern society without the convulsions that have since accompanied that nation's entry into the modern world, costing so much in human material and resources. Not only were they denied the opportunity of accomplishment during the reign of Alexander II, but two succeeding reigns saw undone much of what they had built. Alexander III tried to turn back the clock and ended once and for all the autocracy as the agency for political and social progress. The forces of change from this time forward lay outside the government and had to seek its overthrow in order to solve Russia's problems and to transform her into a modern society.

Miliutin's position as the Minister of War during these difficult years placed him in a key role in nearly every political or social question that arose. Reflecting the pragmatism of the practical man he was, Miliutin was also committed to Russia's progress and her evolution toward a more nearly perfect society. He was able to use his office and his unquestionable loyalty to the crown to further the goals of the reformers. Miliutin's career, particularly his service as Minister of War, made him one of the most controversial figures of his era. He became the bête noire of the defenders of the old order and of gentry class interests. His voice in the high councils of government often opposed friend and foe alike, depending upon the issue. Few doubted his ability; most appreciated his great contributions to the Russian nation. The great liberal professor, B. N. Chicherin, later wrote of Miliutin that

He alone in Russia was capable of accomplishing the great task that was then imminent, to reform the Russian army from bondage into freedom, to adapt it to the relationships and demands of a renewed society with radically changing conditions of life, but without depriving it of those high qualities which distinguish it from its former condition. He accomplished this by working indefatigably, by probing into every detail, by pursuing a single high goal to which he surrendered his entire soul.[2]

The broader implications of Miliutin's activities also found appreciation. Those who lived during the period of his activity and in the generation following recognized that they owed him a great debt. One of these, Prince A. D. Obolenskii, wrote that Miliutin

alone was the first actual Minister of Public Instruction; the illiterates of the seventies of the last century in Russia were indebted to him because he made Russia literate. The military reforms made the nation study just at the time when Count D. A. Tolstoy was impeding the development of literacy. He who reading these lines remembers pre-reform Russia, vividly sees what was and what became.[3]

The mark he made on his times went so far beyond the normal limits of the ministry he headed for twenty years that full appreciation of all that he did is difficult to achieve.

One critic observed that Miliutin was unable to value talent and preferred instead to have obedient people around him.[4] This may appear true on the face of it, but it is too simple. Miliutin as a reformer and an administrator probably did not want to have to refight every battle all the way down the chain of command; thus he tended to replace those who would be obstacles to the implementation of his hard-won reforms. In like manner, one cannot conceive of the War Minister surrounding himself in the higher echelons by those who were unalterably opposed to his attitudes and purposes. One might conclude, therefore, that this was not a flaw of character as charged but rather an outgrowth of the hard practical realities of Miliutin's struggle to gain acceptance for his policies. One unfortunate consequence was the failure to produce

2. Quoted in *Niva (Prilozheniia)*, No. 6 (1912), p. 295.
3. Professor M. Chubinskii, "Pamiati D. A. Miliutina," *Vestnik Evropy*, September 1912, p. 316.
4. E. M. Feoktistov, *Vospominaniia E. M. Feoktistova: Za kulisami politiki i literatury, 1848–1896*, p. 334.

a new generation of military thinkers with independent views and proven abilities. The search for a successor to Miliutin after his resignation demonstrated the awful truth that there was none of sufficient ability or experience to adequately replace him.[5]

Miliutin was a quiet, reserved man—some even thought him cold—quite in contrast to his more ebullient and outgoing brother Nicholas.[6] For a professional officer, he was remarkably devoid of any interest in honors and decorations, even taking his elevation to the rank of Count completely in stride and brushing aside the attempts of old friends to pay him honor by addressing him formally.[7] Visitors to the Miliutin home were always received in quiet dignity whatever their position in life. When Miliutin played host to some of his son's subaltern friends, these would be surprised to find the War Minister waiting on them, pouring their tea or offering them something from a plate, as if it were the most natural thing in the world.[8] But this quiet and pleasant manner hid a will of iron and a dedication to the progress of Russia.

His placing the ultimate good of his country over all else was often misunderstood by his contemporaries, who often professed to find in him a political radical. One friendly witness to Miliutin's character was the famous diarist, A. V. Nikitenko, who, while attending a gala breakfast early in 1856 at which Ia. I. Rostovtsev was host, met Miliutin for the first time:

I did not feel well and sat in a corner talking with one and then another. General D. A. Miliutin quite captivated me. He is a person with nobly formed thoughts, an enlightened intellect and wide learning. He perfectly understands the present state of affairs, the scantiness of our education, and the need for improvement.[9]

5. *Dnevnik D. A. Miliutina*, edited by P. A. Zaionchkovskii, 4 vols., IV., 80–83. Henceforeward referred to as *Dnevnik*. Miliutin was succeeded in office by General P. S. Vannovskii under whose administration the archconservative camarilla succeeded in undoing some aspects of Miliutin's reforms. Vannovskii proved much less sensitive to the real sources of strength of the Russian army vis à vis the armies of the west, and such reforms as he did undertake were minor and peripheral.
6. Feoktistov, p. 330. For an examination of the character and official career of Nicholas Miliutin, see Anatole Leroy-Beaulieu, *Un homme d'Etat Russe*.
7. A. F. Koni, *Na zhiznennom puti*, II, 278.
8. Feoktistov, p. 329.
9. A. V. Nikitenko, *Dnevnik*, 3 vols., I, 401.

But just a few years later when it became clear that Miliutin would soon become a minister, Nikitenko assumed a more negative attitude and looked upon him as a "partisan 'of the reds' and a defender of democratic principles."[10] This was going too far, but despite this he valued Miliutin as a friend until his own death.

If Nikitenko considered the War Minister a bit too radical, the attitude of the Minister of Internal Affairs, P. A. Valuev, was one of conviction that Miliutin had sold out to the "reds." Their first meeting, which took place in January 1861 while Miliutin was still Deputy Minister of War, did nothing to dissuade the very conservative Valuev from that attitude:

> I was with Miliutin, the Deputy Minister of War, with whom I was not previously acquainted. He has a pleasing personality, but as regards the peasant question, he obviously is under the influence of his brother.[11]

This first impression was fortified a few days later:

> Dmitrii Miliutin dropped in on me. He is almost "more red" or more galling than his brother. When I said to him that it is impossible to announce the emancipation at Shrovetide when everybody is drunk, he answered, "Just so, there would be greater profit to the Treasury and to the leaseholders."[12]

It is clear that the pompous Valuev, who had no sense of humor anyway, was not amused. He was able in subsequent years to appreciate Miliutin's abilities, but he felt that when it came to social matters the War Minister was "below his usual standard."[13]

Valuev and others like him could lump Miliutin with the liberal and radical left because Miliutin *appeared* to espouse many of the same things. But others, whose personal aspirations had been thwarted by the fundamental reforms undertaken by Miliutin or whose vanities had somehow been injured, became implacable personal foes of the War Minister. As the planter party coalesced within the higher strata of the bureaucracy, it began to fuse with the personal enemies of Miliutin in order to undermine and eventually overturn the common enemy. This powerful coalition helped to blunt the progress of the reforms and to turn them into

10. Nikitenko, II, 395.
11. P. A. Valuev, *Dnevnik P. A. Valueva, 1862–1876*, 2 vols., I, 60.
12. *Ibid.*, I, 61.
13. *Ibid.*, I, 162.

new channels. Miliutin suffered agonies at their hands, but he crowned his greatest period of suffering with his universal military conscription statute and, soon after this, the dispersion of some of his most dangerous enemies. Miliutin's unique qualifications as a reformer and his will to bear the strain imposed upon him were the products of a lifetime of preparation, reflection, and experience.

Dmitrii Miliutin was born June 28, 1816, in Moscow. His ancestors had come to Russia from Serbia during the seventeenth century and had become hereditary gentry during the eighteenth century as a reward for state service. Miliutin's father had inherited a factory encumbered by a heavy debt, and because of this and his own personality his life was never crowned by any personal success.[14] He undertook innumerable enterprises, but all ended to some degree in failure. But like the unforgettable Mr. Micawber, the father always had great trust in the future, hoping that "something would turn up."

His father's constant preoccupation with one or another of his business affairs drew the young Dmitrii more closely to his mother. His desire to please her gave him the drive to succeed in all his undertakings, large or small. This close relationship was significant in another respect: his mother was the sister of Count Pavel Dmitrievich Kiselev, a man of great wealth and influence during the reign of Nicholas I. The Emperor entrusted Kiselev with a wide variety of delicate tasks, ranging from settling matters in the Danubian principalities following the War of Greek Independence to seeking solutions for the complex peasant problem in Russia. Miliutin as a boy was always close to his uncle, and this relationship continued into his maturity.[15] Kiselev more than once helped keep the Miliutin family solvent, and later he materially aided individual members of the family in launching their careers.

Dmitrii Miliutin's early boyhood was quite typical of his class and time. He lived at first on the family estate at Titov in Kaluga Province, and despite the sinking fortunes of the elder Miliutin the family lived in

---

14. *Dnevnik*, I., 5, and *Vospominaniia general-fel'dmarshala grafa Dmitriia Alekseevicha Miliutina*, edited by G. G. Khristianin, pp. 24ff. This volume, published by the Kolchak government, is designated as Volume I, Books, 1, 2, and 3, although no further volumes were ever published. I am indebted to the late Boris Nicolaevsky for the use of his copy.

15. *Vospominaniia Miliutina*, pp. 10–24.

a grand manner.[16] As was usual with provincial gentry, Dmitrii's first ventures in education came under the supervision of private tutors who resided in the Miliutin home. His first was a Mesieur [*sic*] Valee, a Swiss who taught him from French and English novels. When he reached the age of eight, a Polish tutor, Nikolai Matveevich Zaruzhitskii, was brought from Moscow to teach Dmitrii, while Valee turned to the instruction of the younger brother, Nicholas.[17] Dmitrii early developed a special love for mathematics. His training in this subject was largely practical and included studies in geometry and surveying. By the age of ten the future War Minister had demonstrated his precocity by drawing a complete schematic plan of the family estate. He also began the study of Russian and world history. By the end of his first decade he had read the monumental *History of the Russian State* of N. M. Karamzin, a work which without doubt made a solid impact upon the mind of so intelligent a youngster.

Unfortunately, the idyllic life of Miliutin's early years could not last. The family fortunes, never in good straits, went even more sharply into decline, and the Miliutin family were forced to leave the rural solitude of Kaluga Province in 1827 and move to the more lively environs of Moscow. They took up residence in a house near their kinsmen, the Kiselevs, and settled down to a new way of life.[18] The change from the abundance of country life to the cramped barrenness of the city marked a low point in Miliutin's boyhood.

Moreover, the family was more deeply in debt, necessitating an interruption in the children's education. Noting the plight of his sister's family, P. D. Kiselev came to their aid; he first sent a thousand rubles, and eventually he was able to obtain for his brother-in-law a position in the Ministry of Internal Affairs which at least assured the family of a regular income.[19] With this improvement in their affairs, it again became possible for the children to continue their education, and Dmitrii and his brother Nicholas were accordingly enrolled in the Moscow Province *Gymnazium*. From there they went on to matriculate in the Pension of Moscow Uni-

16. *Ibid.*, p. 27.
17. *Ibid.*, p. 31.
18. *Ibid.*, pp. 38–40.
19. *Ibid.*, p. 41.

versity.[20] Dmitrii was an apt student, finishing his course of studies in 1832 with a silver medal. During this time he demonstrated an interest in a wide range of subjects, and he wrote and had published his first works.[21]

Miliutin's choice of the army as a career was an accident. One day after completing his course at the Pension he accompanied his father on a business call. The pair met Colonel M. A. Maikov, the Commander of the First Guards Artillery Brigade, who took an interest in Dmitrii and suggested that he enter the Brigade.[22] This event determined his career. In March 1833 he took a tearful farewell from his mother and entered the First Guards Artillery Brigade as a junker. Junkers, according to a system rooted in Prussian custom, were sons of hereditary nobility who entered the army as noncommissioned officers with the privilege of becoming officers after a term of service and an examination.

Miliutin's early impressions of military life stayed with him all his life and were no doubt quite influential in forming those attitudes which underlay much of his later reforming activity. The pedantic formalism of the army was most irksome to the young Dmitrii. Every morning he and his fellow junkers mustered in the barrack yard for lessons in standing at attention, marching, and drill with sabers and rifles. Besides these dry and tedious exercises, the junkers, as have soldiers since time immemorial, performed the drab housekeeping tasks required by their respective companies and at intervals mounted guard at the Imperial Court.[23] The general purposelessness of such training and its irrelevance to the duties of an armed force taught Miliutin a lesson he never forgot. Nevertheless, in September of 1833 he took and passed the necessary examinations to become an officer. After meeting a board of three generals for a final review in November, the young man received his commission and began a long and fruitful career.[24]

His first assignment as an officer in the Brigade was with the First Light Battery, where he furthered his education by learning new lessons in the sterility of contemporary military education. No attempt was made

20. *Ibid.*, p. 43.
21. *Ibid.*, pp. 44–49.
22. *Ibid.*, pp. 74–76.
23. *Ibid.*, pp. 81–87.
24. *Ibid.*, pp. 88–90.

to train soldiers by helping them understand their tasks and their significance. A half-century later, Miliutin recalled these first months of his
service as an officer in his memoirs:

I was charged with the teaching of arithmetic and an elementary knowledge
of artillery to the enlisted men in the Feuerwerker School of the Guards
Artillery. This school, having the task of preparing privates to become
gunners (*feuerwerker*), was located in the so-called Arakcheev barracks
behind Tavriz Park. . . . The structure of the school and its internal arrangement were extremely unattractive; the teaching was conducted mechanically,
so to speak, by rote. The poor soldiers, half-literate, poorly developed, learned
the answers to the questions by heart from notebooks.[25]

It should be remembered that this was in an elite guards brigade and that
the soldiers in it were from the more privileged orders of society. It may
be assumed that the training within other units was not conducted on
any higher level.

The drabness of his teaching assignment, however, inspired him to take
up scholarly pursuits in order to further his own incomplete education.
The need to keep his mind alert and active in so stifling an atmosphere
led him to read widely and to inquire into a great variety of subjects, but
he concentrated particularly on mathematics and physics. These studies
were soon to bear fruit when in 1836 Miliutin was admitted to the senior
or practical class of the War Academy which was a usual requirement for
assignment as a staff officer.

Here again the young officer was treated to a taste of the aridity of
the system of military education. The internal order of the Academy was
a reign of terror. The Director of the Academy, I. O. Sukhozanet, was a
martinet and a worthy disciple of Arakcheev. This uncompromisingly
strict general would not hesitate to blight the whole future of a young
officer for any slight breach of discipline. Sukhozanet, however, was
never unpleasant to Miliutin personally; quite the contrary, he took pains
to be most cordial. There could be no doubt in the young man's mind
that this attitude was motivated by the knowledge that he was the
nephew of so important a figure as P. D. Kiselev.[26]

As Miliutin approached the completion of the course at the War

25. *Ibid.*, pp. 90–91.
26. *Ibid.*, p. 121.

Academy, both his father and Kiselev questioned him concerning his intentions upon leaving the Academy. He expressed a desire to be posted to the staff of the Quartermaster-General (the General Staff) in the War Ministry. His rather blunt uncle, who was very possibly already aware of the nature of his future assignment, told him that he would likely be sent to a general headquarters within the armed forces and that he should consequently prepare himself so that he might become an instructor in the War Academy.[27] Miliutin finished the course in the Academy brilliantly, falling only eight points short of a perfect score of 560 in his final examinations, and was graduated with a silver medal.[28] He was then posted to the staff of the Independent Guards Corps.

His duties in his new position were sufficiently light to allow him to begin to develop his literary talents more fully. While still a student in the Moscow University Pension he had participated in a literary circle under the aegis of Constantine Aksakov,[29] and while still a boy he had had published his first literary ventures. These had been only schoolboy efforts, but now they took a more serious turn as he began to write to augment his meager salary.

His first venture in this new enterprise was to write articles for the *Entsiklopedicheskii Leksikon*, for which he received 1,667 assignat rubles or an equivalent to 476 silver rubles, a quite handsome sum for the times. His articles dealt chiefly with military and mathematical subjects. He disguised his authorship by signing each of them with an initial, usually a "D" or a "G." As time went on he wrote similar items for the *Voenno-entsiklopedicheskii slovar'* which he signed with the letters "A" and "B."[30] But these employments were temporary, and he soon found it necessary to find other work. This he found in a co-operative venture which proposed to publish a military journal in the War Academy. This periodical, *Voennyi Zhurnal*, was dedicated to the his-

27. *Ibid.*, p. 128.
28. *Ibid.*, pp. 129–130.
29. *Dnevnik*, I., 7. Miliutin was also motivated in his new literary activity by the sheer drabness of his new post which was teaching in a military school. He took up at this time the study of such subjects as mathematics and physics to augment his relatively limited formal education. His first publications included: *Opyt literaturnogo slovaria* (Moscow), 1831, and *Rukovodstvo k s'emke planov s primeneniem matematiki*.
30. *Vospominaniia Miliutina*, pp. 143–144.

torical study of higher tactics, strategy, and the lives of great generals
and was intended to be a handbook for the officers acting as professors
in the War Academy. Miliutin not only contributed articles to this journal
but also served as business manager.[31]

His association with this enterprise brought the future War Minister
to the attention of Colonel Prince N. S. Golitsin, who wanted to initiate
a course in military history in the War Academy. Miliutin and his friends
were invited by the colonel to work on various aspects of the program.
As a subject for his study, Miliutin drew the Thirty Years War. While
researching this project, he continued his other pursuits and began to
contribute as well to a new journal, *Voennyi Bibliotek*. These activities
consumed most of the year 1838, but the energetic young officer found
sufficient time to establish a working relationship with A. A. Kraevskii,
the editor of the important journal *Otechestvennye Zapiski*, and to
write two articles for him, although only one passed the censors and was
published.[32]

Throughout all this furious literary activity, Miliutin remained an officer on active duty, and with the passage of time and the greater recognition of his talents by his superiors he began to assume more responsibilities. In 1837 he was transferred to the Guards General Headquarters, and
in 1838 the Quartermaster-General of the Guards Corps selected him to
prepare the maps for the summer maneuvers of the Corps. During that
summer he participated in those exercises in the capacity of Division
Quartermaster of the Second Guards Light Cavalry.[33]

This period of furious activity, however, was brought to an end by two
events that sharply altered Miliutin's way of life. The first was the death
of his mother. Always close to her, the young man was stunned.[34] In
the wake of this personal tragedy, bored with the formalism of military
service in St. Petersburg, Miliutin volunteered for active service in the
Caucasus. His request was granted and in 1839 he departed for battle
duty in that region. As a member of the staff of the Chechenskii De-

31. *Ibid.*, p. 156.
32. *Ibid.*, p. 157. The first article, "Suvorov kak polkovodets," appeared in *Otechestvennye Zapiski*, No. 4, April, 1839. The rejected item was entitled "Russkie
polkovodtsy XVIII stoletiia."
33. *Vospominaniia Miliutina*, p. 158.
34. *Ibid.*, pp. 160ff.

tachment, Miliutin saw considerable action and was wounded while participating in an expedition to Aichul'go, the capital of the mountain insurgents.

This campaign served as another school for the future War Minister and also helped to bring his considerable talents to the notice of his superiors. The deficiencies of the military system forged by the pedantry of the Russian emperors and their favorites were glaringly present and were duly noted by Miliutin:

> From the first days of the campaign, I was struck by the many weak facets of our method of operations against the mountaineers. . . . What astounded me most of all were the disadvantageous conditions under which our troops were obliged to carry on the struggle.[35]

Dismayed by the conditions and the approach to the problem of pacifying the Caucasus, Miliutin committed his thoughts to paper in the form of a memorandum to his commander, Lieutenant General P. Kh. Grabbe, who highly approved. Grabbe was much taken by the brilliant young staff officer and wrote of him at the time:

> Staff-Captain Miliutin [is] one of the most distinguished officers of the army. With intelligence set off by real learning, he manifests a practical viewpoint. . . .[36]

Later, after Grabbe was relieved of his command, he wrote to his successor:

> I read with special satisfaction the review of the present situation in the Caucasus; it acquainted me with the above mentioned and it redoubled in me the desire to serve again with Miliutin. . . . He is yet too young but a place will be made for him.[37]

After a successful tour of duty, he returned to St. Petersburg in 1840 and asked for an extended leave to go abroad.

Miliutin spent more than a year traveling the length and breadth of

---

35. *Dnevnik*, I., 9.

36. *Ibid.*, I., 10. Grabbe's relationship with Miliutin continued in the years following their return to the capital. In 1849 and 50, Miliutin wrote a series of articles for the *Severnaia Pchela* on the campaign of 1839 in the Caucasus, consulting from time to time with Grabbe. See, "Iz dnevnika i zapisnoi knizhki grafa P.Kh. Grabbe (1849–52)," *Russkii Arkhiv*, No. 3 (1889), pp. 473 and 482.

37. *Vospominaniia Miliutina*, p. 427.

Europe, visiting nearly all her sovereign states. This trip contributed mightily to his intellectual development and without doubt contributed to his later realism in assessing the relative strengths of Russia and the western powers. His impressions were vivid and strong and provided the thoughtful young man with a great deal of raw material for his reflections.

He much regretted not having seen the Prussian army during his visit there, but he had been able to meet a number of Prussian officers. His chief reaction was that with their various affectations, pretensions, and pedantry, they differed from his compatriots only in that they were also well trained and prepared for their profession.[38] Miliutin apparently could stomach a little foppishness if officers were efficient.

He returned to Russia in 1841 and resumed his active status as an officer. But the tour had been of great educational value to him and had opened many new horizons. One of the most important of these was the new perspective he had gained regarding his own country:

the journey opened my eyes to the actual situation in the cultural relationships of Russia compared with western Europe. Loving my homeland sincerely, I was deeply grieved to see every step that we have strayed from the path laid down by the great Peter. In the judgments of foreigners about us, couched in terms of indulgent civility, clanged an arrogant acknowledgement of the superiority of the civilized European over the half-educated barbarian. When I happened to see on the stage or to read in a book some cariacaturization of Russian life, the lies and the exaggerations in these cariacatures did not outrage me as much as it grieved my consciousness that our behavior gives rise to views by foreigners that are so offensive to us.[39]

Even though he wrote this more than forty years later, it is clear that he still felt the sting of this experience. One cannot help seeing in this one of the reasons he was later to be so insistent upon clinical efficiency and high standards of competence. It was humiliating to find Russia wanting and an object of ridicule, and it was incumbent upon Russians to prove themselves as able as the western Europeans.

After his return from abroad, Miliutin again found his duties sufficiently light to allow him to continue his studies. Freshly inspired by his trip abroad and acutely aware of the vast gaps in his knowledge, he began to read voraciously in such subjects as political economy, international

38. *Ibid.*, p. 317.
39. *Ibid.*, pp. 414–415.

law, politics, military administration and strategy. He not only read, but he began to reflect upon many of these subjects and write down his thoughts. He explored such fields as the relationship of tactics to fortifications, and he devised a new systematic general course in the military sciences.[40] He did not limit his speculations to military subjects, however. For example, while abroad he had found those Slavs living within the Austrian Empire to be sympathetic toward Russia.[41] Perhaps reflecting upon his own Serbian ancestry, Miliutin became interested in the Slavic peoples and sought to study them systematically. His inquiries were sufficiently thorough for him to write up his notes and reflections under the title of "The Histories of the Peoples and Governments of Eastern Europe."[42] Twenty years later, he was again to turn to this question within the context of practical politics and the need to seek a solution to Russia's relationship to the Polish insurgents on the one hand and to Slavic minorities both within and without the Empire on the other.

Miliutin's consciousness of the general professional weakness of the officer corps led him to initiate a new project. He felt that one way to improve the quality of officers was to provide the means for them to continue their studies in military subjects. He therefore proposed the establishment of a new military journal to be published within the headquarters of the Guards Corps. His superiors approved the project but it was later vetoed by the War Ministry.[43] A decade later he was to take up this project again and help found the *Voennyi Sbornik*.

Despite this flurry of activity, Miliutin found time to be bored—or perhaps it was really personal loneliness. To erase some of the drabness of his existence, he began to spend Wednesday evenings at the home of General Michael Poncet (Ponce), where a circle of the general's friends habitually gathered. Miliutin had nothing in common with the members of this group; the real attraction was the general's daughter, Natalia. He was unable to overcome his shyness until almost the eve of his departure for another tour of duty in the Caucasus: he proposed, the young lady accepted, and they were promptly married.[44] The marriage was a long

---

40. *Ibid.*, p. 421.
41. *Ibid.*, p. 401.
42. *Ibid.*, p. 421.
43. *Ibid.*, pp. 421–422.
44. *Ibid.*, pp. 423ff.

and happy one, lasting from 1843 until 1912, when the two died only a few days apart.

Immediately after his marriage, Miliutin departed for the Caucasus. The new commander in that theater, General Gurko, had read the memorandum written by Miliutin when he had been in the Caucasus several years earlier and had resolved to have him on his staff. He appointed Miliutin to the post of Over-Quartermaster of the Caucasus Line and the Black Sea, a position that called for someone far superior to him in rank.[45] It nevertheless appears that he was not happy during his tour of duty; whether it was being away from his young bride or the fact that no real attempt was made to implement his suggestions for putting an end to the incipient war in the Caucasus is not clear. At one time he even gave serious consideration to giving up his military career.[46]

But with his subsequent return to St. Petersburg, life began to look much brighter. A vacancy had occurred in the War Academy and Miliutin was posted to fill it. He began lecturing in a course in military geography, but his restless mind after some consideration came to the conclusion that it was unthinkable to limit a specialized military science to a single subject. So many factors were involved that he undertook to design a new course taking into account all the variables other than geography that had to be assessed in military planning. The result was a new course in military statistics which sought to be more comprehensive and therefore more realistic. He summed up his new approach in the following terms:

This program in its main outlines encompassed three parts: in the first, [we] investigate from the military point of view statistical data which conditions the material means of a state, i.e., the territory, population, political structure, and finances. In the second are included the many facets in the structure of the armed forces of a state and its military installations. Finally, in the third part are studied the territorial conditions determining operations, whether defensive or offensive.[47]

Miliutin's approach was much closer to the modern concept of the general staff's role in making strategic assessments, except that he apparently

45. *Ibid.*, pp. 427–432.
46. *Dnevnik*, I., p. 13.
47. *Dnevnik*, I., pp. 13–14.

made no place for those abstract qualities of a nation which have come
to be called the "imponderables." Nevertheless, it clearly illustrates that
the future Minister of War had firmly grasped the significance of the new
kind of warfare developing during the nineteenth century: the wars between peoples, not merely states and armies.

Miliutin retained his chair in the War Academy for eleven years,
surrendering it only to return to the Caucasus in 1856. These years were
rich and full for him. During this period his children were born and
he reached the apogee of his literary career. Always a man with great
energy and a capacity for work, Miliutin wrote a variety of articles and
produced in 1847 his first major monographic work. This study, *Pervye
opyty voennoi statistiki*, appeared in two volumes and was largely the
fruit of his labors in the War Academy. The first volume dealt with the
German Confederation, while the second was concerned with Prussia
alone.[48]

The War Minister, Prince A. I. Chernyshev, in 1848 selected Miliutin
to continue the work begun by the military historian, A. I. Mikhailovskii-
Danilevskii, who had recently died. The writing of this history, a study
of Suvorov's campaigns in Switzerland and northern Italy during the
year 1799, consumed the next three years.[49] The work was highly successful. It established for Miliutin a place as a gifted historian and
earned him an honorary Doctorate of History and a corresponding
membership in the Academy of Sciences.[50]

The scope and variety of all these activities were not enough to satisfy
the restless appetites of Miliutin. In the years 1845 to 1848 he assumed
the additional task of directing the Third or Training Section of His
Highness' Supreme Headquarters for the Institutions of Military Education.[51] With this appointment, he began to take a hand in influencing
the development of military education and training, a task which was

48. *Dnevnik*, I., p. 14.
49. *Dnevnik*, I., 15.
50. *Ibid.*, I., pp. 16–17. The work earned high praise from such professional his-
torians as T. N. Granovsky who wrote of the work's "extraordinary clarity and
balanced view." Quoted in M. Borodkin, *Graf D.A. Miliutin v otzyvakh evo
sovremennikov*, p. 55.
51. I. S. Siminov, "Graf D. A. Miliutin i voenno-uchebnoe vedomstvo," *Pedagogicheskii Sbornik*, No. 2 (1912), pp. 157–158.

to occupy him in one form or another throughout the rest of his official career.

Of great significance to Miliutin's career was the fact that he was brought into this new post after having come to the special attention of the Grand Duke Michael Pavlovich, brother of the Emperor and the Commandant of the military schools, and General Ia. I. Rostovtsev, the man who was later to play so important a role in the initial studies leading to the emancipation of the serfs. Miliutin worked especially closely to the latter during his three years at this post and engaged with him in a comprehensive review of the general curriculum offered by the military schools. The fruits of their labors were contained in the formal general guide approved by the Emperor on December 24, 1848, "Precepts for the Education of Students of the Military Institutions of Education," and in other published programs.[52]

Within the limits of his own office, Miliutin was responsible for the drafting and publication of a "Handbook for the Camp Life: Practical Exercises of Students for Tactics, Artillery, Engineering, and Topography." He also had compiled and published a guide for the reading of military students, "The Normal Catalogue for the Libraries of Military Institutions of Education," intending it to be as much an aid for the teacher as for the pupil. Miliutin somehow managed to edit at the same time a fortnightly journal published by his office, *The Journal for the Teacher of Students of the Institutions of Military Education.* His collaborators in these activities were generally men of ability, many of whom were later selected by Miliutin after he became Minister of War to implement his comprehensive reforms in the field of education. Included were such people as E. Kh. Wessel who later headed the military schools under Miliutin's administration; the famous lexicographer, V. I. Dal'; the mathematician and later Vice-President of the Academy of Sciences, V. Ia. Buniakovskii; the philologist and folklorist, F. I. Buslaev; the pedagogue A. D. Galakhov; the physicist E. Kh. Lentz; the mathematician M. V. Ostrogradskii; and the historian I. P. Shul'gin.[53]

When in 1848 the Emperor entrusted the completion of the work

52. *Ibid.*, pp. 158–159. Cf. D. A. Skalon, general editor, *Stoletie voennogo ministerstva, 1802–1902,* 13 vols., X, Part III, 20. This work will henceforeward be referred to as *Stoletie.*
53. Siminov, pp. 158–159.

begun by Mikhailovskii-Danilevskii to Miliutin, he relieved Miliutin of his post as chief of the training section. But Miliutin had so made his mark that the Grand Duke Michael did not want to see his talents lost to the cause of military education and he therefore interceded through the War Minister to have Miliutin, now a colonel, appointed to the War Ministry as a member of the Educational Committee for the military schools.[54] For the next several years, Miliutin's contribution to military education was relatively muted, but the subject never strayed far from his consciousness. When the gross failures of the professional training of Russian officers became apparent during the Crimean War, he again became active in seeking basic reform.

After completing his history of Suvorov's campaigns in 1799, Miliutin began to gather material for a history of the war in the Caucasus,[55] but was interrupted by the outbreak of the Crimean War. As the crisis heightened before the outbreak of hostilities, the War Minister, Prince V. A. Dolgorukov, assigned him to special duties within the War Ministry, particularly to the task of making studies for operations against Turkey. In the fall of 1853, Miliutin was among those accompanying Nicholas I abroad to conferences at Olmütz and Potsdam. When the war materialized and fears developed that the war would not remain localized in the south, Miliutin spent long months making various studies on military problems affecting both actual and potential theaters of war. Besides these duties, he served as an editor preparing dispatches from the front for public release. In 1854, Miliutin composed a memorandum concerning the problems connected with the defense of the Baltic sea-coast which bore fruit in the establishment of a special Baltic committee charged with making appropriate arrangements for the defense of the area. In recognition of his manifold contribution to the war effort, Miliutin was advanced to the rank of Major-General and named to His Majesty's Own Suite.[56]

The loss sustained by Russia in the Crimean War helped to quicken the demands for reforms both in the civil and military spheres of Russian life. Moreover, the accession of a new Emperor, Alexander II, pro-

54. See the footnote in Siminov, pp. 160–161.
55. *Dnevnik*, I., 16.
56. *Ibid.*, pp. 16–17.

vided at least the temporary hope that new faces would be seen in responsible positions, helping the Empire to make adjustments more easily to changing conditions. Most military thinkers, however, were capable only of planning along traditional lines, and thus the years immediately following the end of hostilities saw only nominal changes in the general structure and quality of the armed forces.[57]

Miliutin clearly perceived that the problems of the army were closely related to failures in administration and leadership. In March 1856 he drafted a comprehensive study taking note of these failures, entitled, "Thoughts on the Deficiencies Existing in the Russian Military System and the Means for Their Elimination." This memorandum proposed a fundamental reorganization of the armed forces and the use of a cadre system. He wanted to retain in peacetime only a skeleton force which would be augmented in wartime by soldiers who had been trained during relatively brief periods of active service and had then been returned to their usual civilian occupations as reserves. But this plan was premature; serfdom still existed in Russia and it was virtually impossible to furlough conscripts once they were on active service.[58]

One project undertaken by Miliutin at this time did result in solid achievement. In June 1856 he submitted to the War Ministry over the signature of the Deputy Minister of War, General A. A. Katenin, a proposal to start a new military journal. The obvious limitations in the quality of the officer corps were in Miliutin's opinion a consequence of their lack of general education and training:

57. See particularly the contemporary assessment in O., "Obzor deiatel'nosti voennogo ministerstva," *Voennyi Sbornik*, No. 10 (1865), particularly pp. 201–204. Chief among the reforms of the period between the Crimean War and the assumption of the post of War Minister by Miliutin were the liquidation of the old system of military colonies, the end of the system of cantonists, and the reduction to fifteen years of the term of active service required of a recruit. The War Minister during most of this period was General N. O. Sukhozanet, an officer directly out of the Nicholas I mold who never really understood the need for any basic changes. See, for example, P. A. Zaionchkovskii, "Voennye reformy D. A. Miliutina," *Voprosy Istorii*, No. 2, 1945, p. 10. For some insight into the character of Sukhozanet, see P. K. Men'kov, *Zapiski P. K. Men'kova*, 3 vols., II., 302. Cf. N.D.N., "Obshchii obzor' Preobrazovanii po chasti ustroistva vooruzhennykh sil Rossii s 1856 po 1860 god," *Voennyi Sbornik*, Nos, 1, 2, 3 (1861).
58. *Dnevnik*, I., 17.

Never has it been felt to such a degree as at the present time, how necessary it is for a well-organized army to have educated officers, not only in [their] special capacities but in all branches of arms.[59]

So critical a deficiency, he believed, could not be allowed to continue without severely jeopardizing the security of the Empire. He therefore reasoned that "it now follows to seek out ways for learning to be propagated as much as possible to the great mass of Russian officers."[60]

He noted with regret that many officers on active service had neither the inclination nor the means to develop their minds. These men were only half educated and felt no need for any more. Apathy was only part of the problem; even if these officers wished to extend their educations, there were no facilities in existence and no funds to assist them. If they read at all, they had only literary magazines or they were limited to stories, novels, and the like. Not only did these do nothing to enhance the professional competence of these officers, but, as Miliutin noted, it was rare for anyone to attempt to cultivate any feeling or appreciation for the arts.

Miliutin proposed that a partial solution to the problem would be to publish a journal which would contain informative material of professional interest. Such a periodical would have to be relatively inexpensive to insure the widest possible circulation. Miliutin wanted to model its format on the liberal journal *Sovremmenik*[61] and to include an official section for important communications from the War Ministry. The unofficial segment would contain articles on current problems, military history, and general professional information.[62] The War Ministry found merit in Miliutin's suggestions and despite a number of delays, the new journal *Voennyi Sbornik* appeared in 1858 with N. G. Chernyshevskii as its first editor.

The general flux following the end of the Crimean War had its impact

59. Colonel N. Makeev, *N. G. Chernyshevskii - Redaktor 'Voennogo Sbornika'* (Moscow, 1950), pp. 30–31.

60. *Ibid.*, p. 31.

61. Colonel Makeev and other Soviet scholars make much of Miliutin's apparent acquaintance with Chernyshevskii at this time (see, *ibid.*, p. 55), but there is almost no evidence to suggest that either had any real influence on the other. The source of their views is to be found in A. Ia. Panaeva, *Vospominaniia*, pp. 222–224.

62. *Makeev*, pp. 33–34.

on the War Ministry, manifesting itself in a series of personnel and
policy changes during the spring of 1856. After Dolgorukov's demotion,
Miliutin surrendered many of his duties in the War Ministry to devote
himself exclusively to his academic and literary pursuits, retaining only
his membership in the Military Education Committee.[63] But Miliutin
already had other important tasks. Responding to the suggestions for
reform submitted by Count F. V. Rüdiger, the Commander of the Guards
and Grenadier Corps, the Emperor appointed on July 20, 1855, a special
commission under the chairmanship of Count Rüdiger, the Commission
for the Improvement of Military Elements. This commission had among
its members Ia. I. Rostovtsev and Dmitrii Miliutin and included as
one of its most important functions the need to review and reform the
army's system of officer procurement and training.[64]

Despite the obvious need for reform, little was really accomplished.
Rüdiger, the moving spirit, soon died; General Rostovtsev became en-
grossed in studies that preceded the emancipation of the serfs; and
Miliutin departed again for service in the Caucasus. The incipient war
in that area which had dragged on for a half century became especially
acute during the Crimean War when Russian troops were attempting to
conduct operations against Turkey, whose borders were contiguous with
the region. Miliutin in November of 1854 had submitted to the Emperor Nicholas his views on the pacification of the area, and in March
1856 this memorandum was circulated by the new Emperor among
several high officers to solicit their views. Among those reading Miliutin's
study was Field-Marshal Prince A. I. Bariatinskii, who was subsequently
appointed as the commander of the forces in the Caucasus. When the
latter received this appointment and was looking about for someone to
serve as his chief of staff, his choice ultimately fell upon Miliutin.[65] It
took some persuading to get Miliutin to accept the assignment. His
health had been poor, and he was reluctant to leave the regular life of

63. *Dnevnik*, I., 18.
64. "K istorii voenno-uchebnoi reformy Imperatora Aleksandra II-go, 1856–
1870," *Russkaia Starina*, No. 5, 1887, p. 351.
65. A. L. Zisserman, *Fel'dmarshal kniaz' Aleksandr Ivanovich Bariatinskii, 1815–
1879*, 3 vols., II., 10–11. Cf. V. A. Insarskii, "Zapiski Vasiliia Antonovicha Insar-
skogo," *Russkaia Starina*, No. 8 (1895), pp. 21–22.

St. Petersburg for the hazards and responsibilities of the Caucasus,[66] but at length he reluctantly consented to do so. Characteristically, once he had made the decision, he threw himself into this new challenge with all his energy. When he returned to St. Petersburg in the summer of 1860 after a successful campaign in the Caucasus, he stood on the threshold of his greatest challenges and his highest achievements. He was appointed Deputy Minister of War and was the heir apparent for the ministerial portfolio itself.

66. A. L. Zisserman, "Feld'marshal kniaz' A. I. Bariatinskii," *Russkii Arkhiv*, No. 1 (1889), p. 127.

2

Genesis of the Reform

D M I T R I I M I L I U T I N became the Minister of War with a mandate for reforming the land forces of the Russian Empire. The mandate was prompted by the incipient fiscal crisis following the Crimean War and the nature of Miliutin's own solutions to the perennial war in the Caucasus. The defeat of the army in the Crimea had not alone provided those who understood the deficiencies of the armed forces with sufficient leverage to institute basic reforms. The first five years following the Treaty of Paris saw only piecemeal attempts at solving the fundamental flaws in training and administration which helped to render the Russian army incapable of successfully prosecuting a modern war. Despite its deficiencies as an effective defense force, the army remained a terrible fiscal burden upon a nation bordering on bankruptcy. The correspondence of high officials of the Empire in this period reads like the accounts of thrifty housewives registering their needs and outlays down to the last half kopeck.[1]

The relative fiscal viability so painfully effected by the Emperor Nicholas's Minister of Finance, Count E. Kankrin, was wiped out by the extraordinary costs of the military action taken in defense of the Habsburgs and of the Crimean War. The role of Russia as a Great Power was made increasingly more difficult by the rapid economic expansion

1. See, for example, the correspondence in Zisserman, II., *passim.*

of the western European powers, a process denied to Russia by her ossified social system. The industrial revolution fed on free labor and investment capital, both in short supply in Russia. The net result was that the essentially agricultural economy provided a tax base not sufficiently elastic for the state to respond to the more complex, and hence more expensive, needs of a modern power. The deficit and debt by 1855 amounted to 56,440,000 rubles, and over the next decade the deficits totaled the enormous sum of 808,760,625 rubles. The years 1865 to 1868 alone added to this amount another 90,259,660 rubles.[2] The general rise in prices throughout Europe put agrarian Russia at a serious disadvantage, and at the same time that new programs such as railway construction provided new impositions upon the limited resources of the nation.

But the largest single consumer of the revenues of the state was the War Ministry. Soon after the end of the Crimean War, a committee in the Ministry of Finance studied the situation and concluded that the best opportunity for the state to reduce its expenditures lay in trimming the military and naval budgets. These, they felt, could be returned to their 1847 level of 71,923,300 rubles.[3] Accordingly, on April 9, 1857, the Emperor appointed a special commission composed of General-Adjutants Prince M. D. Gorchakov and N. N. Annenkov. This body really could do very little; its powers were too limited, and the materiel and stores needed by the army cost as much or more than ever. The real problem was that the army, which had been greatly expanded during the war, had no effective program for reducing its size in peacetime. As a consequence, the economies effected by this commission were insignificant. Without specifying where cuts could be made, the commission recommended that the military budget for 1858 be arbitrarily reduced by 7,100,000 rubles.[4] The War Ministry did in fact manage to reduce its demands upon the resources of the state, but only by taking the drastic step of consuming its reserve supplies.[5] The deficit in the state

2. I. S. Bliokh, *Finansy Rossii XIX stoletiia*, 2 vols., II., 15.

3. *Ibid.*, II., pp. 37–38.

4. *Ibid.*, II., p. 38.

5. The military budget for 1858 was actually 93,497,086 rubles, although it was officially listed in the state budget as only 76,599,554 rubles, the difference of 16,897,532 rubles representing the consumption by the army of its own reserve stocks. Bliokh, II., p. 42. Miliutin himself noted in a pamphlet circulated to the members of the State Council more than a decade later that the fiscal squeeze of

budget in 1859 was quite small, amounting to about 5,800,000 rubles, but despite the most rigid economies it began again to rise by 1860.[6]

The inability of the Empire to produce more wealth in anything like the quantities necessary for her to maintain her status as a great power demanded more drastic measures. During the year of 1860, another special commission was activated by the Emperor to explore the possibility of further economies in the War Ministry and the military schools.[7] But, short of basic reform, all the fat had already been squeezed out of these bodies by the earlier efforts, and the possibility of further savings was quite limited. The War Minister at this time, N. O. Sukhozanet, while noting that he recognized the urgency of the situation, could trim the 1860 budget by only 1,879,260 rubles.[8] Even this small reduction was not accomplished in fact, for actual expenditures in 1860 exceeded those of the preceding year by more than sixteen million rubles.[9] All the palliatives had by this time been applied, and the army's reserve stocks were reaching dangerously low levels. Further reductions could be effected only after fundamental reforms of the army had helped it to trim its costs by more efficient use of its funds without impairing its capacity to guarantee the security of the Empire.

The need for this reform and the general paralysis which gripped the policy-making elements within the War Ministry brought Dmitrii Miliutin into the post of Minister of War on November 9, 1861. It has been asserted that he was brought into this office on the basis of an intrigue by Field Marshal Bariatinskii, who hoped that a reform of the army along lines resembling the Prussian model would insure for himself a position of great prestige and power.[10] His plan, which apparently gained Alexander's approval, had as its aim the separation of the ad-

---

this critical period forced the army to consume its own reserve supplies as a way of taking pressure off the overburdened state treasury. See Schuyler to Fish, *Despatches from U. S. Ministers to Russia, 1808–1906*, March 6, 1872. Henceforeward referred to as *Despatches*. These documents are deposited in the U.S. Archives in Washington, D.C., and are published on microfilm.

6. Bliokh, II., 47–58.

7. *Ibid.*, II., 60.

8. *Ibid.*, II., 60–61.

9. *Ibid.*, II., *loc. cit.*

10. P. A. Zaionchkovskii, "Voennye reformy D. A. Miliutina," *Voprosy Istorii*, No. 2 (1945), pp. 10–11.

ministrative and logistical functions of the army from the tactical elements. The War Ministry would become a purely bureaucratic support agency charged with feeding, clothing, equipping, and housing the army. The real functions of leadership would rest in the hands of the Chief of Staff, who would be charged with the drafting of all war plans. The Emperor, as the Commander-in-Chief, would maintain liason with the Chief of Staff through a special chancellory, at the head of which Bariatinskii proposed to put Major-General R. A. Fadeev, one of his Caucasus aides and toadies. The post of Chief of Staff, which Bariatinskii reserved for himself, was to allow its holder to play a powerful and independent role in the manner of von Moltke in the affairs of Prussia.[11] Bariatinskii apparently did not realize that the basis of the strength of the Chief of Staff in Prussia lay in the fact that he represented a corporately self-conscious officer caste of a sort that did not exist in Russia and for which the proper social foundation was lacking. In comparing the two states, one finds little similarity between the junkers' concepts of ancient rights to be protected from the crown and the Russian gentry's position as an order which had obtained its privileges through service to the crown. It was unrealistic for Bariatinskii to assume that within Russia he could reduce one of his Majesty's Ministers to the status of a figurehead and transfer all real power to the high command.

Whatever the motives of Bariatinskii, the fact was that in 1860 Miliutin was posted from his position as Chief of Staff for the Caucasus to St. Petersburg where he assumed the office of Deputy Minister of War. The Caucasus had served as a laboratory for experimentation in techniques of military administration. Both Miliutin and Bariatinskii came to the Caucasus with ideas on how to solve the problem of effectively conducting operations in the area, and the fusion of these ideas, together with the experience gained over four years of their practical application, provided the proof of the efficacy of the new approach and gave to Miliutin invaluable insights into the problems that he would face as Minister of War. The commander and his chief of staff enjoyed most cordial relations during their service together—a definite contrast to the personal antagonism that both were to exhibit toward each other in the years to come.

11. Count S. Iu. Witte, *Vospominaniia*, 3 vols., I., 30–31, and *Dnevnik*, I., 19.

The importance of their experiments in the Caucasus was reflected in the close interest maintained within the highest circles of the capital. The Grand Duke Constantine Nikolaevich especially had great hopes for this enterprise. Gravely concerned with the fiscal crisis of the Empire, he felt that administrative efficiency might be a way out of the difficulties in which Russia found herself and that the creation within the Caucasus of order and abundance without great expenditure would make of it "a model of economic achievement."[12] A solid, efficiently managed administration, well grounded upon a good moral base, would serve as a model for the whole Empire, a microcosm of moral regeneration and clinically efficient administration.

The great hopes for the operations in the Caucasus were at least in part justified. The state treasury found some relief in the fact that the more intense activity was actually costing less; the 1858 budget was a half million rubles smaller than in the preceding year.[13] General Sukhozanet is reported to have remarked that all that was really necessary was that the army live off the local economy and not draw upon the state treasury at all.[14] More important was the approval the Emperor gave for the reconstitution of the administration of the Caucasus, which allowed this less expensive army to become a more effective fighting force. When Bariatinskii arrived in the Caucasus, he had divided the entire area into five districts roughly conforming to the natural geographic divisions. The right wing of the Caucasus line was centered in the northwestern part, extending from the Kuban to the Black Sea. The left wing stretched from Terok to the Andiiskii Mountains, with its eastward extension falling in Dagestan. The Lezgin cordon lay to the south of the mountains, while the Black Sea coast and certain of the southern mountain ranges and lowlands formed a fifth region.[15]

In the past, military activities in the Caucasus had suffered from a fragmentation of effort in its operations and from a general inability to co-ordinate the various branches of the armed forces. The commander

12. Zisserman, II., 108–109.

13. *Ibid.*, II., 142–143. This represented the estimate as of October 22, 1857. There did exist at this time some mild optimism, with A. V. Golovnin estimating that the deficit in the state budget for the following year would be only slightly more than half of that for the current year. See *ibid.*, p. 178.

14. *Ibid.*, p. 143.

15. *Ibid.*, II., 84.

of the area had always been too remote from the various theaters of war, a problem compounded by the differences in terrain, type of enemy, and logistical problems within each region. In practice, this meant that the commander could only rarely concern himself with tactical operations and was forced instead to limit his function to general supervision. The consequent need to delegate authority demanded the creation of a regular system of administration which would allow the necessary flexibility without destroying the role of the commander as general supervisor and co-ordinator.

The balance was struck by creating headquarters staffs in each of the five districts and linking them to the central administration. The artillery and engineering branches in particular needed reorientation and had to be brought under the control of the commander within each of the districts. The net effect of these changes was that the over-all task of logistics and general supervision was left to the Caucasus commander, while each of the district commanders had under his control all tactical elements and the necessary independence of action to conduct operations within the limits of his area. This situation granted to the total problem of pacifying the area a flexibility which was a new departure in Russian practice. In addition, it was a recognition of the fact that each natural geographic region had to be dealt with in accordance with its own peculiarities.

The reforms effected in the Caucasus bore their first real fruit when, in 1859, the elusive leader of the mountaineers, Shamil, was finally captured, spelling the beginning of the end of six decades of almost continuous warfare. Miliutin's key position as Chief of Staff in the Caucasus had given him a major role in the drafting and implementation of these innovations, enabling him to reap a large share of the credit for the results. His visits to the capital during the progress of the campaign, particularly that of 1857, helped identify him in government circles with the reforms in the Caucasus. His audiences with the Emperor undoubtedly served to appraise Alexander even further of his high stature as a military administrator.[16] Whatever Bariatinskii's role in bringing Miliutin to the post of War Minister may have been, there is little doubt that Alexander already was convinced of Miliutin's abilities and deliberately appointed him as a reform minister.

---

16. *Ibid.*, II., 89 and 91, and *Sobranie sochinenii R. A. Fadeeva*, 2 vols., I., Part 1, *Shestdesiat' let Kavkazskoi voiny: Pis'ma s Kavkaza*, pp. 43ff.

Miliutin always freely acknowledged the debt he owed to his service under Bariatinskii in the Caucasus. Yet there can be no doubt that the essential elements of his later reforms had taken shape earlier. Even his conception of the military district system, which had its first practical application in the Caucasus, he outlined in a memorandum submitted to the Emperor as early as 1856. Reflecting on this in his memoirs, Miliutin recalled that

> The idea of a territorial system of administration was born in me some years earlier, namely at the beginning of 1856, and was formulated at that time in a memorandum [which] I composed after a discussion with my uncle, Count Pavel Dmitrevich Kiselev, on the subject of the military situation in Russia. This idea was gradually worked out during the course of my work on the structure of the military administration in the Caucasus, and was completely developed at the end of 1861 and during the following years.[17]

This memorandum, entitled, "Thoughts on the Insufficiencies Existing in Russia's Military System and the Means for Their Alleviation," had as its chief recommendation the suggestion that the entire Empire be divided into districts which would assume all responsibility for military administration below the level of the War Ministry. These districts would be of two types: frontier and internal.

It was clear from his recommendation that Miliutin had already been influenced by the experience of the frontier areas of the Empire, where

> there had been a stationary military power for a long while, sufficiently independent not only for managing affairs in time of peace, but also for executing them in wartime, [and] not taking every trifling matter to the central authority in St. Petersburg. . . .[18]

17. Quoted in P. A. Zaionchkovskii, *Voennye reformy 1860–1870 godov v Rossii*, pp. 83–84.

18. *Vsepoddaneishii Doklad Voennogo Ministra: January 15, 1862*, p. 87. This report is published in full together with the Emperor's marginal comments in *Stoletie*, I., and will henceforeward be referred to as *Doklad*, January 15, 1862. See also Miliutin's subsequent appreciation of this matter in [D. A. Miliutin], "Voennyia reformy Imperatora Aleksandra II," *Vestnik Evropy*, No. 1 (1882), p. 26. This article was written by Miliutin soon after leaving the War Ministry and was intended as a defense of the system which he had created during his tenure of office. This article was intended to be the first of a series but the subsequent increments were suppressed by the censor. For Miliutin's own account of this, see *Dnevnik*, IV., 124–125.

Because many of these areas, particularly those in Asia, were engaged in almost perpetual warfare and were too far from the capital to be closely supervised, the greatest possible initiative had to be accorded the local commanders as a practical matter. He therefore proceeded in his 1856 memorandum to draw what he considered the logical conclusions from this experience.

Just as the administrative districts were to be of two types, the tactical elements of the army were to be divided into active and reserve forces. The active forces would be deployed only in the frontier districts and in peacetime would be reduced considerably in strength. But they would retain to the extent possible a large number of units, headquarters staffs, officers, and a large complement from such special branches as artillery or engineers.

The reserve forces would have a large variety of functions. Located in the interior districts, they would induct and train recruits, replace and perform the local duties of the corps of the Domestic Watch, and in wartime would be responsible for providing the personnel to bring the active forces up to strength as well as form new units as a battle reserve. Each district, whether active or reserve, would be under the command of a district general possessing the rights and prerogatives of a corps commander, with all armed forces and military installations within his district subordinate to him.[19]

When Miliutin became the Minister of War he immediately began to draft a comprehensive scheme of reforms to submit to the Emperor for his approval. This was soon completed and placed before Alexander on January 15, 1862. This document was the basic blueprint for the sweeping changes that Miliutin was to implement over the next decade. Circumstances and further reflection at times necessitated changes in detail, but its essential outlines did not change markedly.

At the root of Miliutin's scheme lay the simple fact that the budget had to be reduced without impairing the efficiency of the army as a force capable of guaranteeing the security of the Empire. In this respect, the new War Minister noted that the high cost of maintaining all the various headquarters staffs and the current manner in which administrations were organized were second only to the numbers and com-

19. Zaionchkovskii, p. 84.

position of the armed forces as contributions to excessive military expenditures. These financial savings would carry with them the additional bonus of greater efficiency. The administrative reforms would establish clearer and better defined channels.[20]

Miliutin considered one of the worst ills of the contemporary system to be its over-centralization, which destroyed initiative in subordinate military administrations, thereby sacrificing that resourcefulness and independence so essential in wartime. Nor, as he noted, was this situation confined to the army:

> Your Imperial Majesty has already decided to turn some attention to this present deficiency in our [civil] administration, by directing all possible efforts toward decentralization.[21]

Miliutin's conclusion was that a territorial system of military administration would better serve the needs of the army than the existing method which was based upon the order of battle. He recognized that there were some arguments for this system which centered about the allegation that administrative staffs would serve with their own units in wartime and thus would already be familiar with the personnel with whom they would deal. But such contentions were, as a practical matter, illusory. Rarely in wartime did so large a unit as a corps serve in its normal peacetime composition, and the Crimean War particularly, the War Minister observed, had demonstrated that the corps was too large to be employed within the normally restricted limits of most theaters of war. Most corps in wartime were broken down into detachments, which then necessitated the creation of detachment headquarters staffs. These then suffered because they had to be hastily put together; the personnel had to be drawn from various sources, and of course they had had no experience with the units in which they suddenly found themselves serving.[22]

---

20. The struggle to maintain the army on Russia's limited resources never relaxed during Miliutin's tenure. The War Minister's correspondence with Bariatinskii, for example, almost always contained some reference to the problem. See, Zisserman, III, 317–331. The importance of the matter was further reflected in the close attention paid to it in the *Russkii Invalid*, the official newspaper of the War Ministry. See particularly the article by F. Terner in No. 43 (1863), and the series, O., "Biudzhet voennogo ministerstva i potrebnosti armii," Nos. 81, 91, 107, 124, 125, 126, 133 (1865).

21. *Doklad*, January 15, 1862, p. 88.

22. *Ibid.*, p. 89.

The solution to this practical question was to detach military administration and logistics from the tactical units and to turn these functions over to stationary military districts. Not only would this provide the necessary continuity in both peace and war, it would relieve tactical commanders of this burden, allowing them to devote their full time to the training and deployment of their troops. The territorial system of military administration was based upon the principle that the entire Empire was to be divided into military districts, with the district commander having command over all forces and military installations within the area. He was to be granted as well the supervision of the maintenance of domestic peace within the limits of his command. In effect, the district commanders would assume the functions of the corps commanders, military governor-generals, and chiefs of the Domestic Watch, thereby eliminating these offices and simplifying the entire process of administration.[23]

With the elimination of the corps in favor of the military district, the division would become the highest tactical unit in peacetime. Miliutin pointed out that should these districts coincide with civil governor-generalships, the military commanders could be relieved of all duties in the civil administration.[24]

The delegation of these executive powers to the district commanders would alter the role of the War Ministry. Rather than trying to run the entire army from St. Petersburg, it could assume the more general function of co-ordination and supervision. The power to make decisions at the local level and the regularization of administrative channels would make possible a reduction both of administrative personnel and the volume of correspondence.[25] This would result in substantial savings in the military budget while greatly increasing efficiency.

Alexander was not convinced at first that Miliutin's scheme would accomplish all that he claimed. The more conventionally minded Emperor, commenting on Miliutin's plan, wrote,

I fear that such an organization would not be achieved by the desired decentralization. To me it would seem nearer to the mark to invest military

23. *A. Lavrentiev,* "Mestnaia ili territorial'naia sistema voennogo upravleniia," *Voennyi Sbornik,* No. 7 (1862), especially pp. 132–133.
24. *Doklad,* January 15, 1862, pp. 89–90.
25. Lavrentiev, p. 133.

district commanders with complete power over all subordinate branches or units on the basis of the rights of a corps commander, or, better yet, as supreme army commanders in peacetime.[26]

The Emperor quite clearly was slow to grasp the significance of Miliutin's proposals, particularly the reasons that underlay his desire to separate the tactical organizations from the administration. Alexander at first could only conceive of territorially based corps or armies which would have defeated Miliutin's purpose.

The War Minister reviewed for the Emperor all his arguments for full administrative autonomy for each district, offering sound proofs that by such action both personnel and "red tape" might be significantly reduced. Alexander at length concurred, but added,

> Yes, but only in the event that these staffs will be responsible for all parts of the administration; otherwise, if they are not excluded from direct contacts with the departments of the Ministry, the desired simplification will not be accomplished.[27]

With this final admonition, the Emperor wrote at the top of this section of the report, "Categorically approved."[28]

This document was then read before a meeting of the Council of Ministers on January 25, 1862. The Emperor told the group after the meeting that he would not leave the matter open to discussion but would instead hand it on for further study to those who possessed more expert knowledge in this area.[29] The memorandum was then returned to the War Minister to be drafted into the form of a statute. The General Staff began work without delay on the initial articles, and by May a draft of tentative proposals was ready. This draft was then reproduced and distributed to 211 high military commanders and other experts for debate and criticism.[30]

There began almost simultaneously a discussion in the press of the proposed reform. The first article apparently was written as early as May 11, 1862, by General A. Lavrentiev and was published in the official

26. *Stoletie: Istoricheskii ocherk razvitiia voennogo upravleniia v Rossii*, I., 437.
27. *Ibid.*, p. 438.
28. *Doklad*, January 15, 1862, p. 87.
29. *Dnevnik P.A. Valueva: Ministra Vnutrennykh Del*, 2 vols., I., 141.
30. "R.V.O.: Uchrezhdenie voennykh okrugov i preobrazovaniia v ustroistve mestnykh voisk," *Voennyi Sbornik*, No. 9 (1864), p. 44.

journal of the War Ministry, *Voennyi Sbornik*.[31] There can be little doubt that Lavrentiev's views were those of the War Minister himself and that it was written concurrently with the proposals drafted by the General Staff. One of the most important parts of this article was the consideration of foreign precedents for the contemplated military district system, and the French and Prussian systems were carefully analyzed. Both of these had some system of territorial military administration but were not in any particular respect similar to that proposed for Russia.

Lavrentiev also pointed out that Russia itself had had territorial administrative systems in the past and that vestiges of these former practices still persisted in some parts of the Empire. Before the creation of a standing army, the Russian military forces were made up from a levy which in peacetime lived in their own homes and were responsible for their own maintenance. Peter the Great had created Russia's standing army and had organized it into divisions, each of which in peacetime was quartered in one or another of the provinces charged with its maintenance. But the continuous warfare that characterized the reign of Peter served to divorce gradually the divisions from their respective provinces and the army tended from that time to be quartered in more strategic locations.[32]

When Catherine II came to the throne, the remoteness of the theaters of war together with the personal nature of her rule tended to force the lines of military administration and command to bypass the normal channels. This trend intensified under Paul who took complete personal command over all aspects of the armed forces. Before his accession, all land forces except the Guards had belonged to twelve divisions which he converted into twelve inspectorates. These inspectorates fulfilled in many respects the functions of military districts. In peacetime the army was broken down into smaller units and quartered in permanent installations, and in wartime they were formed into larger bodies, such as corps and armies. These inspectorates were scattered throughout the

31. General Aleksandr Ivanovich Lavrentiev was one of the bright young men in Miliutin's entourage. An 1851 graduate of the Nikolaevskii Academy, he probably came to Miliutin's notice while a student there. He became one of the military members of Miliutin's "party," and with the retirement of Men'kov became the editor of both *Voennyi Sbornik* and *Russkii Invalid*.

32. A. Lavrentiev, "Mestnaia ili territorial'naia sistema voennogo upravleniia," *Voennyi Sbornik*, No. 7 (1862), pp. 150–156.

Empire, but the army was distributed among them quite unequally and concentrated according to economic or strategic considerations. An inspector, who could be any general officer, was appointed for each district. The results of local inspections were forwarded to this inspector who in his turn submitted a report to the Emperor on the first of each month. The duties of the inspectors consisted mainly of maintaining minimum levels of men and horses and closely controlling the number of those who reported sick or who went on leave or into the reserve.[33]

This entire system was abolished during the reign of Alexander I and was replaced by a union of the administration with the tactical organization of the army. The compelling influence of Napoleon in the shaping of military institutions was too great, and the use of the corps as the basis for military administration, in imitation of the Corsican genius, continued to the time that Miliutin became the Minister of War.

The corps system underwent some evolution during its long life. In some cases, several corps were amalgamated into armies which continued to exist even in peacetime and in their turn became the basic units for military administration for those elements of the army over which they had control. Two such armies had been created, but only one, the First Army in the western provinces, still existed in 1862.[34] Deployed in Poland and along the Dvina and the Dniepr, the First Army was composed of three corps and was headed by a supreme commander who was also the Governor-General of Poland. Those corps not included in the First Army were directly subordinated to the Minister of War.

The corps deployed in the frontier areas were handled differently from those in the interior. Here the civil and military administrations were often combined. The commander of the Caucasus forces was also the civil governor of the area. The Orenburg and Siberian corps were composed of only a few rifle battalions, but their commanders also were the civil governors of their respective areas. An almost perpetual state of war existed in the frontier areas, or they were potential theaters of war, and this combination of functions allowed them to remain in a state of constant war readiness. The corps in the interior, on the other hand,

33. *Ibid.*, pp. 146–148.
34. *Ibid.*, pp. 149–150, and [D. A. Miliutin], pp. 22–24.

had no such needs, and there was usually no question of their union with the civil government.[35]

Of greater consequence was the fact that the interior corps suffered from administrative chaos. Each special branch of the army providing support for the corps, the artillery, the engineers, the medical and supply services, were administratively separate from the corps, and each had its own system of territorial administrative districts. The areas of one branch rarely coincided with those of another branch, and a corps commander, depending upon the deployment of his troops, might have to deal with several different districts representing the same branch of arms.[36] Logistics were handled by two separate administrations, each of which maintained its own separate administrative districts. The difficulties inherent in so complex a system are readily apparent, but when one recalls that each of these support organizations had no local autonomy and that every move had to be cleared through St. Petersburg, one wonders how the army was able to function at all. The sheer number of headquarters staffs was staggering. Besides those of the First Army and the several corps, there were the headquarters of the Reserve Infantry and of the Corps of the Domestic Watch and the various administrations of all the special branches of the army and their respective territorial subdivisions.[37]

Even within each of the existing administrations all was not what it should have been. The relationships between different levels were not clearly defined, nor was there any standardization of procedures. Lavrentiev used the First Army as an example of the failure of Russian military administration at the unit level:

The Supreme Headquarters of the First Army with its present peacetime composition [and] maintaining under its authority three army corps deployed over an enormous area, is far from achieving those standards that might be expected from a district administration. Its relationship to the War Ministry

35. *Ibid.*, p. 25.
36. The complexity of this system can perhaps best be understood by consulting the maps delineating the boundaries of the several separate administrations, in *Stoletie: Istoricheskii ocherk razvitiia voennogo upravleniia v Rossii, 1802–1902,* I., 420, 500, 502, and 518.
37. Lavrentiev, pp. 121–122.

does not remotely correspond to those standards of uniform administration [required] of all administrative branches; it is thoroughly dependent in some of its relationships while in others there exists a pernicious independence which violates the harmony of administration. As for its role in wartime, the slight advantage of this headquarters may be demonstrated as fact. This headquarters has become so entrenched that in the event of necessity, its rapid transition to a war footing would hardly be possible. It is more nearly a headquarters for the military affairs of the governor of the Kingdom of Poland than the staff of a supreme commander of our army.[38]

The Crimean War had already demonstrated the likelihood that such a staff as that of the First Army would in the event of war play little or no role in the conduct of operations. This question of rapid and effective conversion to wartime needs was one of the most important elements underlying Miliutin's concept of the reform. Soon after his retirement he wrote,

Our military districts were created expressly in order to overcome the evidences of the severe and long-standing difficulties of the former division into local military administrations. The consolidation was for this reason more necessary than in any of the other European states which were imitating Prussia because armed forces were developing more and more into massive aggregations, and everywhere measures were being taken to facilitate the mobilization of all forces in a short time. . . .[39]

In this connection Miliutin could again assert that no foreign models were necessary, since stationary administrative districts had already long been in existence within the Empire.

The first step in creating order out of the chaos was the simplification and standardization of the entire administrative system. Miliutin advocated that all the corps headquarters staffs, together with the headquarters staff of the First Army, be abolished and that the Empire then be divided into military districts, each with its own headquarters staff. The Headquarters of the Commander of the Reserve Army Infantry could then be liquidated because the reserve forces could be subordinated to their respective military districts. The role of the staff of the Corps of the Domestic Watch would be altered by incorporating its local elements into their local districts.[40] The kaleidoscopic patchwork of the

38. *Ibid.*, p. 123.
39. [D. A. Miliutin], p. 25.
40. Lavrentiev, p. 123.

administrative districts of the several support branches of the army also would be standardized and systematized by their incorporation into the military districts.

The necessary flexibility for an easy transition to wartime would be provided by the use of the *division* as the highest tactical unit in peacetime.[41] As purely tactical units, their number could easily be increased or decreased without disturbing their internal structure or imposing any special administrative handicaps upon the military districts. Perhaps this use of the division as the largest tactical unit in peacetime was the most basic French influence. The French experience showed that divisions could easily be brigaded together in wartime or fused into corps or armies for operations in large theaters of war. The divisions, because of their smaller size and great compactness, were more mobile and could be adapted to a wider variety of situations, yet they were large enough to operate independently.[42] And since they did not exist merely as elements of a corps, no time needed to be taken to dismember the corps and to establish new logistical and administrative systems to conform to the changed circumstances.

The rapid transition of a corps to a war footing was made even more difficult in practice because even in peacetime a corps was not maintained in its full complement. A prime example was the Guards Corps which was really divided into two corps for training, one for infantry and one for cavalry. The various support elements in the Corps, such as engineers and artillery, also were detached to train in their own specialties.[43] The unified existence of the Corps was therefore a fiction; it had to be re-united before it could take the field. Nor was this situation unique. The other corps were in much the same situation, and in peacetime, with their special groups stripped away, they were little more than aggregations of three infantry divisions. But their constituent divisions had no independence and were in fact very tightly controlled by the corps headquarters. This posed no special difficulty if the divisions were physically located in the near vicinity of the corps headquarters, but if they were farther away from the center of control, communications were

41. *Ibid.*, pp. 124–125, and *Doklad*, January 15, 1862, pp. 88–89.
42. *Ibid.*, p. 89.
43. Lavrentiev, p. 126.

more difficult and the disabilities were proportionately greater. There was thus no really valid argument for retaining the corps in peacetime; conversely, there were good arguments for their discontinuation. The subordination of the divisions to a military district would leave many of the executive functions in the hands of the division commanders and would, therefore, allow greater elasticity in the command of tactical units as well as provide administrative continuity.

Within the division itself, the relationship to a military district would have practical advantages. The division commander had the opportunity to gain a personal knowledge of his command, of his officers and his men, to a far greater extent than any corps commander.[44] In the everyday give and take of military administration, such intimate knowledge can be invaluable. Personal acquaintanceship can greatly facilitate the processing of administrative details, and it enables a unit commander to spot defects and bottlenecks that may hamper the efficiency of any future operation.

Of the 211 high military commanders who received copies of the proposals and arguments for the creation of a military district system, 134 forwarded their comments and suggestions to the War Ministry. It was assumed that those who did not reply had approved the project in its entirety. The comments were generally favorable, only ten finding any fundamental fault with the scheme. Of these, only seven were categorically opposed to any change. There were a number of dissenting voices on particular aspects of the reform, with fifty-five proposing minor alterations.[45] These suggestions proved very useful and contributed materially to the final result.

There were also reactions in the public press. The most important of these were a series of three articles written by one Ivan Stanevich appearing in *Sovremennaia Letopis'*, another in the same journal and appearing in tandem with one of Stanevich's articles, signed with the initials N. P., and a commentary in *Severnaia Pchela*. The most significant was that written by Stanevich, who alleged that he was speaking

44. *Ibid.*, p. 129.
45. "R.V.O.: Svod zamechanii na proekt ob ustroistve voennogo upravleniia po okrugam," *Voennyi Sbornik*, No. 3 (1863), p. 222. This will henceforeward be referred to as *Svod*.

for four of those experts who were also responding officially to the proposed reform.

The view expressed in these articles was that the entire Empire should constitute one large military district with the several branches of military administration separate from the War Ministry but subordinate to it. Each would have full control over its own branch of arms with no interruption of its authority by local districts. Stanevich insisted that a military district was a district no matter what its size. He and those whom he claimed to represent maintained that the desired flexibility and initiative would be achieved by allowing each branch of arms to operate independently.[46]

The task of defending the concept of Miliutin's program in the public press was assumed by General V. M. Anichkov, one of the War Minister's close aides and friends. In a series of two articles, also appearing in *Sovremennaia Letopis'*,[47] Anichkov pointed out that the critics of the military districts had misunderstood the nature and goals of the reform. Stanevich had feared decentralization on grounds that this might encourage the bureaucratization of military administration; Anichkov pointed out that the purpose of the reform was quite the opposite. By providing the latitude for greater initiative at the local level, it sought to avoid bureaucratization.

When Stanevich insisted that the French model be followed more closely, Anichkov pointed out that the French army was heavily overadministered and absorbed a disproportionately large number of troops. Moreover, all power and authority in France was heavily concentrated

46. *Sovremennaia Letopis'* was a supplement to *Russkii Vestnik*. Stanevich's articles appeared in numbers 35, 40, and 45 in 1862, under the title "Predpolagaemoe u nas ustroistvo voennogo upravleniia po okrugam."

47. V. Anichkov, "Po povodu tolkov o predpolagaemom vvedenii u nas sistemy mestnogo voennogo upravleniia," *Sovremennaia Letopis'*, Nos. 44 and 45, 1862. Anichkov was especially well qualified to act as a spokesman for the position of the War Minister in this matter as he was a member of the special commission, under Miliutin's personal chairmanship, charged with editing the general regulations governing the new reform. See, "R.V.O.: Obschchii obzor' polozheniia o voenno-okruzhnykh upravleniiakh," *Voennyi Sbornik*, No. 9 (1864), pp. 45–46. Anichkov continued to act as spokesman for the reform until its implementation. See, in this regard, the articles by Anichkov in *Russkii Invalid*, No. 31 (1863), and in Nos. 205, 212, and 253 (1864).

in the person of the War Minister, allowing no latitude whatsoever to any of his subordinates, even the directors of departments within the Ministry itself. Point by point, Anichkov refuted the uninformed, and at times Utopian, views of Stanevich. It was clear that the latter had missed the point of the reform, that the exercise of local initiative allowed the districts to fulfill the general directives of the War Ministry in greater conformity to local conditions.

As is the case in many periods of reform, there were those who opposed the change. Some did not understand the reform's significance; others believed the concept to be in error. Those among the 211 high commanders who opposed the reform categorically did so because they believed that Russia would be exposed to extra danger in the event of war. Their alarm was based upon the belief that in the case of attack there would only be divisions and no army with which to defend the Empire. One of the proponents of this point of view was General of Cavalry Baron Opfenberg, who proposed that Russia model herself on the Prussian system of territorial corps, retaining larger aggregations as an effective battle force.[48] This argument was to be raised again and again in the years to come in an effort to unseat the War Minister and to discredit him with the Emperor.

Other criticism of the proposals were more constructive and at times of real significance. Nowhere were the comments of the experts more helpful than in the territorial delimitation of the districts themselves. The War Ministry proposed division of the Empire into fifteen military districts and a few areas which would be administered separately. Because of the geographic and human diversity of the Empire, these districts necessarily had to vary widely in size, population, and resources. The Grand Duchy of Finland would constitute one district, with headquarters at Helsinki. The St. Petersburg military district would include the provinces of St. Petersburg, Olonets, and Novgorod. A Baltic District, including the provinces of Latvia, Estonia, Kurland, Vitebsk, and Pskov, would be centered on Riga. The Northwestern Military District, based upon Vilno, would include the provinces of Kovno, Vilno, Grodno, Minsk, and Mogilev. Poland would make up another district with headquarters at Warsaw, while Kiev would be the seat for another, embracing the

48. P. A. Zaionchkovskii, *Voennye Reformy 1860–1870 godov v Rossii*, p. 89.

provinces of Kiev, Volynia, and Podolia. The Southern Military District would be administered from Odessa and would incorporate the provinces of Bessarabia, Kherson, Tavris, and Ekaterinoslavl'. The Moscow District would be composed of the provinces of Yaroslavl', Tver, Vladimir, Moscow, Smolensk, Kaluga, Tula, and Riazan.

The Kharkov Military District would be made up of the Poltava, Kharkov, Voronezh, Kursk, Chernigov, and Orel provinces. The Upper Volga District, to be administered from Kazan, would include the provinces of Kazan, Perm, Viatka, Kostroma, and, Nizhnii Novgorod, while the Lower Volga District, centered on Saratov, would incorporate the provinces of Simbirsk, Samara, Saratov, Penza, and Tambov. The Caucasus District would have its headquarters at Tiflis, and the Orenburg and Western and Eastern Siberian Military Districts would be administered from Orenburg, Omsk, and Irkutsk respectively. The region of the Don Cossacks would likely be formed into a special district, while the provinces of Archangel, Vologda, and Astrakhan, because of their remoteness and the small size of their garrisons, would likely be subordinated to provincial military chiefs and not be incorporated into any military district.[49]

This division of the Empire drew a number of comments. Some of the military commanders and experts responding to the proposals of the War Ministry suggested an increase in the size of the districts to reduce their number and thereby cut administrative expenditures even further. On the other hand, there were those who wanted the number of districts increased because of their large size. This latter group, for example, wanted the Caucasus divided into two districts and another district formed by combining Archangel and Vologda provinces. The War Ministry considered and rejected these suggestions, noting that they were not material to the goals of the reform.[50]

Other suggestions on the definition of the reforms had real merit and were worthy of more consideration. One critic argued that Pskov Province, originally included in the proposed Baltic Military District, should instead be incorporated into the St. Petersburg Military District. He pointed out that troops in this area were normally supplied with food-

49. Lavrentiev, pp. 145–146, and *Svod.*, pp. 233–234.
50. *Svod.*, pp. 234–235.

stuffs from the St. Petersburg area via the Narva River and Lake Peipus
and were equipped from the depots in Novgorod Province by way of the
Volkhov and Lopat Rivers. In addition, the railroad pattern favored
Pskov Province's incorporation into the St. Petersburg Military District.[51]

Another respondent felt that Voronezh Province would be better served
if it were transferred into the Saratov Military District, because its most
productive areas were in the south around Rostov and Taganrog. Since
a large part of the Don basin already was to be included in the Saratov
Military District, the further inclusion of Voronezh Province would
create a natural economic unit. By placing the city of Rostov-on-Don in
the Saratov District, it would provide a natural staging area for supplying
the right wing of the Caucasus line. But if Voronezh Province were re-
assigned to the Saratov Military District, adjustments would be necessary within the Kharkov Military District.[52] The city of Kharkov, originally designated as the seat of that district, would be left at the periphery
of the area, while the city of Kursk would then be located more centrally.

A shift of the district headquarters to the city of Kursk seemed to offer
several advantages in addition to its location. First of all, the city was
wealthier than Kharkov in the kind of resources that had military value.
Kursk was an industrial and commercial center, while Kharkov's economy was oriented much more toward agriculture. The population of
Kursk, engaged in trade and manufacturing, provided a more useful
labor force for the needs of a military district headquarters.[53] Other experts suggested on similar grounds that Kostroma Province be included
in the Moscow Military District in order to concentrate all the linen
industry within one district. Still others wanted Astrakhan to become
a part of either the Saratov or Caucasus Military Districts. The War
Ministry looked favorably upon these suggestions and adopted them.[54]

Once some general agreement had been reached on the division of
the Empire into districts, their internal organization and their relationship

51. *Ibid.*, p. 235.
52. *Ibid.*, pp. 235–236.
53. *Ibid.*, p. 236.
54. For descriptions of the districts as they were actually implemented, see
"R.V.O.: Uchrezhdenie voennykh okrugov i preobrazovanie v ustroistve mestnykh
voisk," *Voennyi Sbornik*, No. 9 (1864) and "R.V.O.: Russkaia voenno-administrativnaia sistema," *Voennyi Sbornik*, No. 10 (1864).

to the War Ministry had to be considered. Miliutin wanted the War Ministry to retain only general supervisory and policy-making functions. This would leave to the individual districts the right to make independent decisions on local matters and would give all executive powers to the district and division commanders. This demanded that the closest possible attention be given to the internal structure of the military districts to insure the efficiency and harmony of the system.[55] Since all forces and installations within a district were to be subordinated to the district commander, the rights and mutual relationships of all the elements under his control had to be precisely defined.

Of highest importance was the role of the district commander himself, and the question of his prerogatives, duties, areas of competence, and responsibilities provoked active debate. The first matter was the question of his responsibility: was he to be answerable for his district in the way that a corps commander was responsible for his command, or was he to possess only supervisory powers? The War Ministry in its original project drafted under Miliutin's guidance tried to strike something of a balance between the two. The district commander would have the prerogatives of a corps commander, but the responsibility for the tactical elements would rest with the division commanders, leaving the district chief with a *moral* responsibility.[56]

The exact relationship of the district commander to the forces within his district was a source of much debate. Some of those submitting criticisms of the project felt that the cause of decentralization would be badly served if full powers of control were not given to local commanders. Others thought that strong local commanders would create a general administrative looseness and an atomistic army run by division commanders. A few considered the possibility that the district commanders' supervisory role over the tactical units in peacetime might inhibit their proprietary interests, since they would not lead them in wartime. Those maintaining these views principally wanted the rights of a corps commander to be accorded the district chief in matters relating to personnel and military installations. The first duty of a military commander was the maintenance of strict discipline and control. Such stringent authority, they argued, had to

55. *Doklad*, January 15, 1862, p. 89.
56. *Svod.*, p. 239.

come from some power higher than a division commander if the best interests of the state were to be served. The generals adhering to this attitude felt that the virtues of the military district system would still be preserved if the district chief had full responsibility for his district and all the elements within it.[57] The War Ministry assumed in this regard the position that the suspicion of dissimulation and egotism on the part of division commanders was unwarranted and declared that where independent units already existed there was no evidence of any such disabilities.[58]

Among those who so staunchly defended a hope of retaining the corps or who at a minimum wanted to grant strong powers to the new district commanders were some of highest ranking commanders, for it was such positions and privileges as theirs that were being threatened by the reform. Included was the Commander of the Irregular Cavalry, Baron Opfenberg; the Governor-General of St. Petersburg; Prince A. A. Suvorov; and the Commander of the Domestic Watch, General V. F. von der Launitz.[59] The relatively restricted powers of a district commander, the reduced military and social status of that office, and the greater need for district commanders to restrict their activities to the limits imposed by directives of the War Ministry made many of those threatened by displacement most reluctant to surrender a system wherein they as high commanders had enjoyed so much power and prestige. While Miliutin was victorious over these conservative exponents of a corps system, they never disappeared, and throughout the War Minister's tenure of office they were to raise the question again and again. Eventually, Prince Bariatinskii, who had never submitted an opinion on this reform, was to become their champion and use the question of maintaining corps in peacetime as his weapon in his personal fight with Miliutin.

Miliutin was adamant in his views on the role of the district commander. He insisted that the old titles and concepts could not be retained.

57. *Ibid.*, pp. 240–241.
58. *Ibid.*, pp. 241–242.
59. For a discussion of the views of specific detractors from the proposals of the War Minister, see P. A. Zaionchkovskii, *Voennye reformy 1860–1870 godov v Rossii*, pp. 88–94.

The post was a new one and all such old terms as corps, armies, and governor-generalships were no longer applicable:

> The principles of the rights and powers of the supreme district commander must be created quite independently, upon foundations proper to a new position in our hierarchy.[60]

The post and the concept were to be entirely new; the district commander was to be entirely stationary. His position was not transferable outside his own military district and had meaning only within its boundaries. This fact necessarily governed the relationship between the forces within a district and their commander. If he held the rank of a corps commander, it would inhibit the easy transfer of individual divisions and other tactical units from one district to another in case of need.

Consequently, the War Ministry believed that the powers of the district commander had to be defined in a manner that would make the independence of the divisions real. This was to be accomplished by making his post analogous to that of the War Minister, who never interfered in strategic or tactical operations but who did determine general policy and was responsible for placing the means for the fulfillment of those policies at the disposal of those commanding troops in the field. Also, since the district commander was in charge of a geographic entity, the War Minister considered it essential that he have control over the disposition of the forces within his district. In exercising these rights, the commander was to conform to tactical and strategic considerations as well as to economic, demographic, and topographical conditions.[61] Tactically, however, the divisions would remain entirely independent, with their commanders possessing full executive powers to implement all policies within their respective units.

The relationship of the district commander to the various support elements within the district provoked similar controversies and was solved in much the same way. Some detractors from the policies of the War Ministry again argued for the prerogatives of a corps commander for the district commander, even wanting each district to possess a separate budget from that of the War Ministry and to be entirely responsible for its own supply problems. *All* equipment and foodstuffs, they be-

60. *Svod.*, p. 242.
61. *Ibid.*, p. 243. Cf. Lavrentiev, p. 138.

lieved, could be obtained from local sources.[62] The War Ministry quite predictably rejected this view and adhered to the general principle that the role of the district commander was to be that of a general supervisor.[63] Despite the need for some decentralization, the War Ministry was convinced that all logistical problems had to be co-ordinated at the national level. The power to make policy was vested only in the War Ministry, and only within that body was there the perspective and sense of long-range purpose necessary for the maintenance of a sound logistical system.

This was not intended to deny to the districts a real measure of autonomy in respect to local administrative and logistical activities. The War Ministry hoped to achieve a fine balance between the Ministry and the district commanders, on the one hand, and between the several district administrations and the district commanders on the other. The critical factor lay within the internal structure of the districts themselves, and of particular importance in this respect were the administrations of the several support branches and the powers to be granted to them:

> Such a rational definition of duties constituting the cornerstone of the system demands extraordinary prudence in determining the mutual relationships between the supreme district commander and the district administrations. These relationships can be arranged in such a manner that, in practice, the powers parallel and do not coincide with each other. The district commander, completely embodying the concept of actual control, should in no way engulf the independence of the district administrations; on the other hand, in order that the district administrations, *which reproduce within themselves the executive powers of the Ministry*, may be responsible to it for their actions, they would simultaneously be under the manifold and living control of the supreme district commander as the representative within the area of competence of the War Ministry.[64]

The War Ministry hoped to achieve this fine balance by granting to the district commanders the rights normally accorded to inspectors, which would give them supervisory but not executive control over the district administrations. Their powers to intervene would be limited to cases of mismanagement, extraordinary irregularities, or violations of War Ministry policies and directives.[65]

62. *Svod.*, p. 246.
63. *Ibid.*, pp. 248–249.
64. *Ibid.*, p. 247. Italics in the original.
65. *Ibid.*, p. 249.

The War Ministry was concerned that these carefully defined relationships between the district commanders and their administrations not be upset by the interjection of any intermediate bodies. The district chief, as a high-level administrator, would naturally have a personal staff or chancellory which would include his personal aides and clerical assistants. The War Ministry feared that the strategic position of this staff might allow it to assume an undue influence in the course of day-to-day affairs and therefore ruled out any responsibility to it by the administrations:

the interference of the staff in the relationship between the district chief and the district administrations is categorically pernicious. Neither oral nor written reports of the heads of these administrations need be submitted for review by the chief of staff, who, having neither responsibility for these elements nor a first-hand knowledge of them, may only prejudice matters by his personal influence on the general.[66]

This had the additional virtue of keeping the channels of communications simple, thereby promoting the general efficiency of the system in accord with the general goals of the reform.

Since the district commander's powers were to be those of an inspector, the real key to the district administration was to be found in the district councils. These bodies were to function in two basic ways: on the one hand, they would possess collegial responsibility for the second level affairs of the War Ministry and, on the other, they would act as local departments of the Ministry. Their collegial function would be in many respects similar to those of the War Council within the War Ministry. Just as the Minister of War was chairman of the War Council sessions, the district commander would preside over the district council. The district council was to include as its members the district chief of staff, the district overintendant, the district chiefs of artillery, engineers, and hospitals, a civil deputy for state control, and a personal representative of the War Minister.[67]

The pivotal importance of the districts councils in the War Ministry's scheme provoked endless polemics from the military experts responding to this part of the proposal. As many as fifty-four submitted suggestions

66. *Ibid., loc. cit.*
67. "R.V.O.: Svod zamechanii na proekt ob ustroistve voennogo upravleniia po okrugam," *Voennyi Sbornik*, No. 5 (1863), p. 230. This particular increment will henceforeward be referred to as *Svod*, No. 5.

on this question, and, of these, six categorically dismissed such bodies as not necessary at all. This group believed that the councils would impede the executive function of the district commanders and because of the collegial nature might weaken the individual responsibility of the heads of the several administrations. Those who favored the concept of the district councils saw the duties of the district commander as chiefly the obligation to supervise the proper application of the law. The district councils would ease that burden and at the same time act as a check on the district commander in case of arbitrary impositions.[68] The War Ministry, in reviewing the commentaries, again reminded those disapproving of the district councils of their similarity to the War Council and its relationship to the War Minister. It dismissed the criticisms as unfounded and pointed out that the councils would serve as the link among the several district administrations and insure their harmonious cooperation. In addition, these bodies would aid in the formulation of policies concerning the internal workings of the district. But the councils would themselves be limited in that they would not have the functions of inspectors, and they could exercise no capricious powers over district administration.[69]

The composition of these councils was also a source of some controversy. At least fourteen of the experts wanted a drastic revision of the War Ministry's suggestions in this respect. Most of these dissenters felt that it was awkward to compose these councils from persons who were already the heads of individual district administrations and therefore already subordinate to the district commander. They feared that the independence of such members might be compromised, and because of this they believed that appointments to the district councils should be made from among those who were in no way responsible to the district commanders.[70] The War Ministry rejected this view on the grounds that it would unnecessarily increase the personnel in the district staff and would add to the cost. Aside from this consideration, qualified people simply were not available in sufficient numbers to satisfy the demand that would be created.

68. *Ibid.*, p. 231.
69. *Ibid.*, pp. 231–232.
70. *Ibid.*, p. 232.

In any event, the War Ministry would have its representatives on the district councils. These could maintain a close watch over the conduct of affairs in them and would review all reports to the district commanders by the heads of the several administrations to insure their independence in legislative matters.[71] Within the framework of autocratic Russia, it is interesting to note the close attention paid to "constitutional guarantees," particularly with respect to limitations on the powers of the executive. Nevertheless, one should note further that the district commanders had the power to override on their own responsibility any decisions of the councils if they felt that circumstances warranted.

The independence of the district councils would also be insured in another way. The War Minister wanted to retain all appointments to the district councils in his hands. There were a number of reasons for this. First, all the personnel records of possible candidates were maintained at the War Ministry, allowing the War Minister to review the largest possible number of potential district administrators. The War Minister particularly felt that the removal of the nominations for the district overintendants to the level of the Ministry would serve to free that office from undue influence and, he hoped, the temptations leading to peculation and other corruption. The Ministry, since it was ultimately responsible for the disbursement of funds allotted to it, considered it politic to retain the right of appointing key personnel, thereby insuring for itself the best qualified people to act as its agents in the handling of money. If a district commander objected to a particular appointment, the Ministry, together with the district commander, could work out some compromise.[72] But it was clear that despite its advocacy of the maximum of local autonomy, the War Ministry was not willing to surrender any of its rights to choose those individuals who were going to exercise that autonomy.

One of the most difficult questions of local administration, and the one that held the greatest promise for savings as well as the greatest temptation for corruption, was the entire problem of logistics. It was in this area that the district councils were to play a key role. The War Ministry was most specific in spelling out the rights, obligations, and duties of the council in this respect:

71. *Ibid.*, pp. 232–233.
72. *Ibid.*, p. 235.

1. The determination of price ceilings for bargaining.

2. In the event of the miscarriage of estimates and the impossibility of obtaining stores or transportation by use of the allotted funds, or similarly, in the event of negligence by contractors or of their difficulty in fulfilling their contracts for the stipulated costs, the determination of new estimates for the aforementioned stores and transportation by the use of the functionaries of the intendancy.

3. The determination of stock levels and the affirmation of the methods for their implementation in cases of unexpected demands for such supplies.

4. The investigation of cases of negligence and insolvency in contracts and deliveries, of peculation and the loss of state funds, and the implementation of measures to protect funds from such occurrences.

5. The investigation and resolution of matters concerning the claims of individuals against the intendancy.

6. The authorization for the selling of surplus materials, the value of which are to be appraised to exceed the valuation placed upon them by the intendant himself.

7. The resolution of ambiguities in the execution of the laws, and, in a like manner, the consideration of cases in which there are proposed new regulations, limitations, changes, or amplifications of existing laws.[73]

The powers of the district councils in economic matters were to be extensive and comprehensive, charged with the fundamental supervision over logistics. All this was designed to strike a balance between individual and collegial responsibility in an effort to eliminate Russia's age-old problem of corruption and the misuse of office.

The entire question of the procurement of supplies and foodstuffs lay at the very heart of the reform. One of the most basic motives for the decentralization of military administration was economic, logistics requiring more local control to insure conformity with the particular needs and circumstances of a specific area. The procurement, storage and distribution of equipment and foodstuffs consumed enormous sums of money and had come to amount annually to more than 80 percent of the total military budget. In 1860, for example, from an appropriation of 98,501,892 rubles, 23¾ kopecks, the Proviant Department expended 41,256,072 rubles, 62 kopecks, while the Commissariat Department consumed 39,918,831 rubles, 7¾ kopecks, or a total for the two departments of 81,174,903 rubles, 69¾ kopecks. The budget of the War Min-

73. *Ibid.*, p. 236.

istry for 1861 increased to 108,030,690 rubles, 27 kopecks. The share of the Proviant Department was 45,060,511 rubles, 81½ kopecks, while the Commissariat Department received 42,332,854 rubles, 1 kopeck, totaling 87,393,365 rubles, 82½ kopecks.[74] Miliutin hoped that the improvement of the administration of the Proviant and Commissariat Departments, which were responsible for the expenditure of such a large proportion of the Ministry's budget, would materially reduce costs.

One of the first steps to be taken was the fusion of the two agencies, thereby consolidating the supply functions within one department. The grave administrative flaws suffered by both in the preceding years seemed to find their solution both in decentralization and in the union of their functions. The Proviant Department, which was primarily responsible for the procurement, storage, and disbursement of foodstuffs, was composed of its own headquarters staffs within the War Ministry and five local proviant administrations. The former operated in the thirty-nine interior provinces, while the latter were in frontier areas, including the intendancies of the First and Caucasus Armies, and the Field-Proviant Commissions in Orenburg, Omsk, and Irkutsk.

While highly centralized in the interior, the Department's control over the five frontier administrations was limited to the right to verify their estimates. This led Miliutin to conclude that the War Ministry at least ought to possess the right of general supervision over them. The extreme centralization within the interior provinces was in fact a rather recent circumstance. Local proviant commissions had existed in these areas until a reform in 1858 abolished them. Their elimination had imposed severe hardships upon the War Ministry because of the vastness of the territory involved and the lack of first-hand knowledge of local conditions by anyone in the central authority in St. Petersburg.[75]

74. *Stoletie: Prilozheniia k istoricheskomu ocherku razvitiia voennogo upravleniia v Rossii, 1802–1902*, I., 110, and *Doklad*, January 15, 1862, pp. 122–124. The more specific questions associated with this problem had already been the subject of intensive study by a committee within the War Ministry. This body, made up of thirty experienced members with General von der Launitz as chairman, was charged with the study of the supply problems of all branches of the armed forces. See, "Trudy Komiteta Vysochaishie uchrezhdennogo dlia opredeleniia dovol'stviia armeiskish voisk," *Voennyi Sbornik*, Nos. 9, 10, 11, and 12, 1862.

75. *Doklad*, January 15, 1862, p. 122, and *Stoletie : Istoricheskii ocherk razvitiia voennogo upravleniia v Rossii, 1802–1902* (St. Petersburg, 1902), I., 438–439.

The Commissariat Department, handling finances, equipment, and military hospitals, suffered from almost total centralization, not even having autonomous local administration in the frontier areas. Miliutin not only objected to this feature but also disapproved of the diversity of the duties of the Commissariat Department. The War Minister did not feel that the commissions from this Department could reasonably be expected to procure stocks of equipment and materiel, to be responsible for their storage and distribution, and in addition to maintain the hospitals. In his opinion, the hospitals had to have a separate administration, and the other operations of the Department had to be reorganized according to function.[76]

Recent experience had underscored the need for the reform of the logistical services. In 1861, there were poor harvests because of the poor relations between the landowners and the newly emancipated peasants. Shortages occurred and the procurement of all kinds of grains became a major problem. The problem went beyond the immediate one of finding suppliers to that of insuring that in the future adequate stockpiles would be on hand and easy means for their distribution to the armed forces would be available.

The War Ministry put the matter into the hands of a special committee formed from functionaries of both the Proviant and Commissariat Departments and with the Moscow University Professor of Technology, M. Ia. Kittari, as chairman.[77] The recommendations of this committee served to incorporate the system of logistics into the military district system in accordance with Miliutin's wishes.

Since both the Commissariat and Proviant Departments were engaged in procuring, storing and distributing goods, and providing services, Miliutin wanted the two fused into a single department to be called by a new name, the Intendance. The functions of this new department would be exercised mainly at the district level, ending the awkward and inelastic overcentralization of the past. By making their own arrangements for goods and services in the districts where they would be used, by adhering closely to statutory principles and supervised by the district commanders

76. *Doklad*, January 15, 1862, p. 123.

77. "R.V.O.: Kommisariatskoe i proviantskoe dovol'stviia," *Voennyi Sbornik*, No. 2 (1863), pp. 588–589.

and councils, the new local intendancies could by their more efficient management achieve those fiscal savings that were daily becoming even more necessary. Moreover, the local intendancies could serve the War Ministry in its assessment of the state of the national economy. The War Ministry specifically noted that among their duties would be

the careful collection, verification, and maintenance of exact statistical information concerning local industry, agriculture, manufacturing and trade, bearing on those goods needed for supplying the forces, the prices of those articles, their procurement, etc., etc.[78]

The estimates and requirements sent to the War Ministry could be used as a basis for computing the general budget and in analyzing the material needs of the armed forces. The War Ministry was to retain a general supervisory role over the district intendencies and upon occasion would act as a super agency, directing the acquisition of certain goods that could most advantageously be purchased in the major areas of production, allowing the Ministry to take advantage of better prices or quality.[79]

The task of working out the details of a reform so complicated as this was not simple, and the problem of reshaping the functions of the Commissariat Department was considerably more complicated than that of the Proviant Department. First, the Commissariat had to be decentralized and some of its functions detached. The speed at which this was done was aided considerably by the force of circumstances.

Because of current pressures in the Caucasus and in Siberia, Miliutin considered it wise to unite the local Commissariat commissions in those areas as soon as possible with the local organs of the Proviant Department. Since these regions were physically very large, a division of functions seemed to be in order. Accordingly, Miliutin thought it advisable to separate the management of warehouses from the Commissariat Department by turning this service, together with the distribution of goods, over to special inspectors.

On the other hand, he wanted the procurement of equipment to be in the hands of officers and supply experts who were serving with the active forces. This separation of storage and distribution from the acquisition

---

78. Lavrentiev, p. 139. Cf. *Doklad*, January 15, 1862, 124, and "Obzor' deiatel' nosti voennogo ministerstva," *Voennyi Sbornik*, No. 10 (1865), p. 227.

79. *Svod.*, No. 5, p. 237.

of supplies and the detachment of both from the Commissariat Department left it as a purely administrative body except for its maintenance of the military hospitals.[80]

The contemporary difficulties in hospital administration were keenly appreciated by Miliutin. The hospitals as noted above were under the administrative control of the Commissariat Department—a fact that made efficient management most difficult. Not only were they the stepchildren of the Commissariat, they were also dependent in one way or another upon the Proviant Department, the Inspectorate of Engineers, and the Inspectorate of Medicine.[81] The hospitals were serving so many masters that no unity of policy or of administrative responsibility was possible. Miliutin wanted the hospitals to have a separate administration and to depend upon the other departments only for those support services which they normally rendered. The removal of the hospitals from the Commissariat Department would then remove the last barrier to its union with the Proviant Department. This process began early in the Caucasus and in Siberia where local Intendance Administrations came into existence during 1862.[82]

The proposals of the War Ministry concerning purely economic matters drew fewer comments from the military experts, partly at least because of general approval. The Ministry's program prescribed that the district intendancies would accumulate stocks of supplies, make purchases, conclude contracts, supervise deliveries, and take appropriate action in cases of nonfulfillment of contracts. While sharing some of these functions with the War Ministry, the local organs would have the sole responsibility for purchasing foodstuffs. In addition, they would be obliged to determine the fiscal and material needs of the forces, to distribute all stores, to act as paymaster, to perform audits, to supervise transportation, to maintain supply records, to establish strategic and rotating caches of goods, to inspect warehouses and magazines, to keep

80. "R.V.O.: Kommissariatskoe i proviantskoe dovol'stviia," *Voennyi Sbornik*, No. 2 (1863), p. 590; *Stoletie: Istoricheskii ocherk razvitiia voennogo upravleniia v Rossii, 1802–1902*, I., 440–441; and *Stoletie: Prilozheniia k istoricheskomu ocherku razvitiia voennogo upravleniia v Rossii, 1802–1902*, I., 124.

81. *Doklad*, January 15, 1862, pp. 125, 131–132.

82. *Stoletie: Istoricheskii ocherk razvitiia voennogo upravleniia v Rossii, 1802–1902*, I., 440–441.

supply buildings in good repair, to render accounts to the War Ministry, and to be responsible for their own personnel. The district intendancies also would assume a responsibility previously discharged by the engineers, that of providing heat and light for troops' quarters.[83]

Nevertheless, a number of the generals felt that clarification was necessary. Their most common response was to question precisely where the responsibility for maintaining the stock levels would lie. Would the plans for such accumulation be drafted in the War Ministry or within the district administrations? Where, and precisely by whom, would the various transactions be approved? What expressly would be the significance of those estimates sent on to the War Ministry as plans for partial stockpiling; and, who would determine the limits of supply estimates for bids?

Besides these questions, nine generals wanted to maximize the decentralization and opposed the proposition that any comprehensive plan be drawn in the War Ministry. They wanted instead partial programs that would originate in the district administrations. Their argument was that the War Ministry was too remote from the scene to make valid and realistic appraisals. After all, they said,

> It would seem to be more in conformity with the purpose if each [district] overintendant would submit to the War Ministry his own plan for stockpiling, and the responsibility would lie with the War Ministry to fuse all these plans into one whole, altering the proposals of the overintendants only in cases of extreme need.[84]

According to this view, the local overintendants would assume almost full responsibility and would not be supervised by any special organ of the War Ministry. The participation of the Ministry in the procurement of supplies would be limited to those commodities that could not be produced or readily obtained locally. This concept of extreme decentralization found some support in other ways from the critics of the War Ministry's program. For example, one group of military leaders wanted to allow entirely autonomous district intendancies to make arrangements with one another for those items more readily available in other districts. The War Ministry would act in these negotiations only in the capacity of a general supervisor.

83. Lavrentiev, p. 141.
84. *Svod.*, No. 5, p. 239.

These views obviously did not find great favor in the War Ministry. In response, the Ministry reaffirmed that it alone could direct the national policies of the administration of the armed forces. Any other arrangement, it argued would be detrimental to the coherence and cogency of the military administration's adherence to imperial goals and, moreover, would necessitate such a large volume of correspondence that the entire purpose of the reform would be lost.[85]

Another question that exercised the minds of the generals was exactly where within the military district intendance the negotiations for the purchase of commodities would take place and who should conduct them. Some felt that the determination of these matters was the natural province of the district councils, which, as we have seen, were to have broad powers in economic affairs. Others thought of the councils in these matters acting only as courts of the second instance. They reasoned that the purchasing commissions would include the appointees of the overintendants, the members for Civil Control, and the representatives from the War Ministry, all of whom sat on the district councils. Therefore, they proposed that the actual purchases be made under the chairmanship of the provincial military chiefs. The bargaining in this manner would take place only within the intendancies and would be referred to the councils only in the event of failure. The War Ministry saw considerable merit in this last proposal and moved to its adoption.[86]

The exact balance to be struck between the latitude granted to the local intendancies and the limits of general control retained by the War Ministry was not easily defined. The great question was how the War Ministry could direct over-all policies without at the same time inhibiting local initiative. Practical necessity dictated that for ease of distribution, uniformly good quality, the standardization of goods, and the predictability of costs, the power to deal with the manufacturing enterprises should remain with the War Ministry. Decentralization in this area may have led to a situation wherein several different agencies of the War Ministry would be bidding against one another for the same goods and services and would thereby raise the price levels. The local organs would possess full executive powers to procure the quantities

85. *Ibid.*, p. 241.
86. *Ibid.*, pp. 241–242.

needed, both for immediate use and for stock piles. The responsibilities for stock levels were left entirely in the hands of the district intendancies, while the warehouse supervisors were to be included in the purchasing commissions.[87]

The ultimate purpose of procuring and storing supplies was of course to support the active field forces. The division was to be a self-contained and autonomous entity, capable of easy transfer from one military district to another. For purposes of distributing materiel and providing services for the divisions, each would have its own intendance directly responsible to the overintendant of the military district in which it happened to be deployed.[88] This organ acted very much like an umbilical cord, allowing a division to sustain itself simply by attaching itself to the intendance of any military district. The division intendant had within his competence the following duties:

1. the verification of personnel musters roles, and the number of horses in the military units, making note of the number of effectives;
2. the verification of the numbers of sick in the hospitals against the reports and claims;
3. the on-the-spot auditing of a running bookkeeping and accounting administration within the tactical units;
4. the review of materiel in regimental supply dumps, armories, etc., and the assurance that all the regimental equipment is in good working order;
5. verification of a proper assemblage of horsecarts by the forces for a campaign; and
6. the guarantee of the actual prices paid by the forces in the matter of the proper maintenance of the horses by the regiments.[89]

The division intendant, as a member of the active army, would go into combat with his unit. By so doing, he would preserve the experience and personal knowledge of peacetime supply operations and would materially aid the continuity of an effective logistical program. This would facilitate a rapid transition from peace to war, allowing a division to perform whatever tasks that should be assigned to it (even if those assignments took it beyond the limits of its own military district) without any necessity to alter its internal administration. When transferred, the

87. *Ibid.*, p. 243, and Lavrentiev, pp. 141–142.
88. *Svod.*, No. 5, pp. 249–250.
89. *Ibid.*, p. 250, and Lavrentiev, p. 142.

division could draw upon the supply dumps of the area to which it was sent without any particular inconvenience.

Perhaps less complicated, but reflecting some of the same difficulties, was the problem of integrating the engineers and artillery into the system. The plan was relatively simple: the hitherto scattered elements of the artillery administration were to be fused into a single unified body and then decentralized by placing all executive powers in the hands of the military district chiefs of artillery. The reform of the administration of the engineers was to parallel this closely.[90]

A rather touchy question arose quite early over the possibility that the district commanders might usurp control over these two branches of the army. These elements had always jealously maintained their administrative independence from the tactical commands and feared the loss of their freedom. This was complicated by the fact that these branches had often in the past been accorded the special prestige of being headed by a member of the Imperial Family. It was clear that the problem of insuring the independence of the artillery and engineers within the framework of the district system was critical; any disharmony over policy or control could wreck the whole purpose of the reform.

The War Ministry considered this aspect of the problem and commented that the creation of district artillery engineering administrations would not remove these branches of service from the jurisdiction of the heads of their respective branches. The local and central administrations would simply be operating in different spheres. In the case of the artillery, all the active and reserve forces would be subordinated to the district commanders through the chiefs of the district artillery administrations who would have their commissions in that branch of arms. To insure the status of the district artillery chiefs, they would have the prerogatives of the former commanders of the artillery brigades and divisions.[91]

This plan was sharply questioned by some of the generals who wanted to reduce the artillery commands to purely administrative bodies having supervision over artillery support installations and stationary troops.[92]

90. *Doklad*, January 15, 1862, pp. 146–147, and Lavrentiev, pp. 143–144.
91. See, for example, *Svod.*, pp. 238–239, and *Doklad*, January 15, 1862, pp. 146–166. Cf. *Russkii Invalid*, No. 72, 1863.
92. *Svod.*, No. 5, pp. 258–261.

The opposition in this matter was motivated by causes similar to those held by the opponents of the destruction of the corps. By the placing of all artillery commands within a district under the district artillery chief, the War Ministry was ending the virtual autonomy that had been the source of prestige and power for tactical commanders in the past. From the point of view of the War Ministry, the test of the validity of any administrative or command arrangement had to be found in utility or logic. For example, the Ministry proposed the abolition of the artillery division headquarters staffs:

> In peacetime it is necessary to retain within the forces only those staffs which are actually useful in war. Division artillery staffs are useless in war-time, since when they go into combat, they rarely have under their direction any batteries belonging to the division because they are distributed about in various detachments. . . .[93]

From among the military experts commenting on this part of the War Ministry's proposal, thirty-three favored dropping the artillery division staff while eighteen categorically opposed it. Of the thirty-three, only twenty-three (including nine generals of artillery) voted for the abolition of the artillery division without any comment, signifying their complete approval of the War Ministry's proposal.[94]

The proposals and problems for reforming the engineering administrations closly resembled those for the artillery branch. The most critical question here was whether to subordinate the engineering units to the heads of the district engineering administrations or to place them under sapper brigade commanders possessing the rights of division commanders. The concensus of the experts in this branch of arms was that the sappers needed an independence of function because their function differed from that of the engineers. They believed that the heads of the district engineering administrations would have enough to do concerning the construction and maintenance of fortresses and barracks without becoming intimately involved with the sapper units.

The War Ministry emphasized the contradictions in this argument by pointing out the situation in the Caucasus and the First Armies. In both these organizations, the construction battalions and sapper units

93. *Ibid.*, p. 258.
94. *Ibid.*, p. 257.

were united under one head, with neither suffering any particular disability. Some experts felt that the matter could easily be resolved by appointing deputies to the chiefs of the district engineers whose duties would be concerned with the tactical and technical training of the sappers.[95]

On the question of abolishing the sapper brigades in the same manner as that already proposed for the artillery divisions, the generals presented a wide variety of opinions. A slight majority favored their dissolution, but the same number of engineering officers wanted to retain the brigades as wanted to dissolve them. Those who favored their dissolution saw the sappers and engineers as forming a single branch of the army and noted that in wartime both conducted siege operations and the defense of fortresses. These co-ordinated efforts demanded that each element be familiar with the other's capacities and techniques. This required joint training and the kind of mutual understanding that could only be gained by long association in peacetime. The War Ministry in its turn pointed out that only nine of the military districts would contain engineering administrations, and of these only two or three would have sapper units attached to them. As a practical matter, the high degree of specialization of the sappers meant that there were too few generals sufficiently qualified to command sapper brigades.[96]

The installations maintained by the engineers posed yet another problem—that of whether they were to be subordinated to their respective district administrations. The generals replying to this part of the War Ministry's program were much divided, there being nearly as many different views as there were respondents. Two, for example, wanted the engineering arsenals to be subordinated directly to the Inspector-General of Engineers, while another wanted to place them, together with the parks containing pontoons and siege equipment, under the district administrations. Others simply wanted the War Ministry to retain direct control.[97]

The War Ministry was particularly eager to reform effectively the engineering administration. Not only was this critical for the engineers'

95. *Ibid.*, p. 262.
96. *Ibid.*, p. 263.
97. *Ibid.*, p. 265.

role in support of the other branches of service, but it was reasonable to assume that such reform would substantially assist in reducing costs. The complications inherent in the rendering of those support services interfered with effective supervision. Before this reform, it had never been possible to determine whether money allotted for this purpose had been spent properly. The new administrative norms established by the War Ministry were designed to facilitate the rational appropriation of funds and the maintenance of proper accounts.

Miliutin also hoped that some continuity, the lack of which constituted a chronic problem, would be attained by encouraging experienced personnel to remain in this branch of arms. Particularly, the War Minister believed that a simplification of the criteria for establishing the responsibility for the fulfillment of work and the granting of more time for the completion of contracts would insure a better return in the long run.[98] These matters, along with an improved system for compiling and considering work estimates, could be decentralized by allocating them to the district administrations.

The War Ministry's plans for creating new district administrations for the military hospitals were more tentative. The separation of the hospitals from the Commissariat Department had not yet been effected, and the shape that this new branch was to take awaited definition:

> The spheres of activity for those establishments and their composition may not be defined at the present time, until the question of the organization of the military hospitals themselves is resolved. If in the latter, the priority in administration is granted to the head doctor, then the district inspector of hospitals may be the over-staff-doctor of the district, uniting in his person the control of the personnel of the medical corps with inspectorate duties in respect to the administration of the hospitals. If this is permitted, it will be necessary to retain the independence of the administrative element; that is, in the district administrations, the medical administrations may not be united with the hospital inspectorates.[99]

It was clear that despite the fact that little had been done about the hospitals other than the taking of the decision to remove them from the Commissariat Department, the War Ministry foresaw their integra-

98. *Stoletie: Istoricheskii ocherk razvitiia voennogo upravleniia v Rossii, 1802–1902*, I., 444–445.
99. *Svod.*, No. 5, p. 266.

tion into the military districts in much the same manner as the artillery and engineers with the hospitals in a role analogous to the tactical units within those two branches.

The military district system was born fundamentally from native Russian roots. Although district systems of one sort or another existed elsewhere in Europe, particularly in France and Prussia, it must be concluded that the system as it was conceived by Miliutin was based upon the experience of administering the Empire's frontier areas, and most particularly upon his own practical experience as Chief of Staff in the Caucasus. While he was already thinking along some of the lines which later underlay his reform, his service in the Caucasus was essential to give his ideas form and to provide a practical testing ground. He made this quite clear when in 1873 he was defending himself from the bitter attacks upon himself and his accomplishments:

> The basic ideas for the establishment of military district administrations were born out of the structure of those stationary administrations which have been with us for a long time in the Caucasus and in other frontier regions in the Empire.[100]

The lessons learned from the experience of the frontiers and the organizational and logistical failures of the Crimean War caused Miliutin to seek a formula which allowed the maximum of flexibility without surrendering all control. The proposals which he presented to the best military minds of the Empire largely met with their approval and a great many of them made positive contributions complementing Miliutin's basic plan.

However reasonable Miliutin's program was as a system and however necessary the reform of the system of military administration, it is highly doubtful that so basic a reconstruction would have been possible without the catalyst of near bankruptcy. Alexander's accession to so sweeping a reform was at least as much based upon a desire to balance the state budget as it was to increase the efficiency of the armed forces. Miliutin's very appointment as War Minister was likely a consequence of his having reduced costs while achieving victory in the Caucasus and the hope that his formula would help the state reduce expenditures without sacrificing the national security.

100. Zisserman, III., 235.

3

The Implementation of the Reform

THE INITIAL program of reform proposed by Miliutin, that of creating a military district system, received an unexpected boost from the disturbances then taking place in Poland. These difficulties, a product of intense Polish nationalism, the revolutionary fervor particularly of the youth, the need for basic social reform against the background of the Russian emancipation of the serfs, and the willingness of the Russian government to relax some of the more stringent controls in the Kingdom of Poland, grew in intensity until 1863, when they became an insurrection which disturbed not only the peace of the Russian Empire but threatened to embroil all Europe.[1] Russia simply was not ready for war; her army was essentially as it had been during the Crimean War and the resources of the state had already been taxed to the limit.[2]

It was within this framework that Miliutin's plans for the creation of a military district system began to be realized. In a letter to Bariatinskii, dated May 30, 1862, Miliutin informed his former commander in the Caucasus of the rapid pace of events:

1. Two of the more recent and useful works on this subject are R. F. Leslie, *Reform and Insurrection in Russian Poland, 1856–1865,* and V. G. Revunenkov, *Pol'skoe vosstanie 1863 g. i evropeiskaia diplomatiia.* Also of interest is, M. V. Misko, *Pol'skoe vosstanie 1863 goda.*
2. A. F. Fedorov, *Russkaia armiia v 50-kh - 70-kh gg. XIX v.,* pp. 27–28, and Revunenkov, pp. 257–258.

In the Polish matter a new era is beginning with the naming of the Grand Duke Constantine Nikolaevich as Governor and Wielopolsky as his Deputy for Civil Affairs. May God grant that this combination achieves happier results than has been the case up to now. With the arrival of the Grand Duke in Warsaw, the First Army and its headquarters are being liquidated and in their place are being formed new separate military administrations in Warsaw, Vilno, and Kiev, [which] are structured approximately on the principles of those ideas which were detailed in my project for a general reform of our military administration. A copy of this proposal is enclosed. The administration by troop commanders (*komanduiushchii voiskami*) established by Your Highness in the Caucasus served as the prototype for the new district administrations.[3]

The military districts, a product of circumstances, were being created even while the military experts were discussing the War Minister's proposals.

It is clear from this that the Emperor had accepted the fact as well as the principle of the proposed reform and was willing to proceed even before the formulation of the regulations was completed. Alexander followed up the first steps by issuing a directive on July 6, 1862, formally authorizing the dismemberment of the First Army and the creation on the territory it occupied of three military districts. The headquarters staff of the First Army reconstituted itself as the staff of the Warsaw Military District, and the staff of the First Corps, a part of the First Army, was integrated into the headquarters of the Vilno Military District. In a like manner, the Third Corps headquarters was absorbed by the Kiev Military District. The Second Corps disbanded and shared its elements among the three new military districts. These three were soon joined by a fourth, the Odessa Military District, which was added in December of the same year.[4]

But the Polish difficulties by January 1863 became a Polish War and the War Ministry had to turn its attention to the prosecution of

3. Zisserman, III., 328. The critical influence of the Polish insurrection accelerating the implementation of the district system is also noted in a memorandum composed by the War Minister: "Obshchii obzor' polozheniia o voenno-okruzhnykh upravlenii," *Voennyi Sbornik*, No. 9 (1864), p. 45.

4. General M. Bogdanovich, *Istoricheskii ocherk deiatel'nosti voennogo upravleniia v Rossii v pervoe dvadtsati-piatiletie blagopoluchnogo Gosudaria Imperator Aleksandra Nikolaevicha (1855–1881 gg.)*, 6 vols., IV., 31–33, and [D. A. Miliutin], pp. 28–29.

that conflict and as a consequence had to set aside further reform until the end of hostilities. Nevertheless, the struggle gave the War Ministry the opportunity to test the worth of the new administrative and logistical system. In a report for the year 1863, Miliutin wrote,

The suppression of the armed rebellion demanded special activities on the part of the local military authorities and their co-ordinated utilization of all the military means within the area. Communications were made difficult by bands of insurgents wandering about the countryside, while orders from Warsaw or St. Petersburg would not arrive on time nor would they be in conformity with the situations as would the instructions of the local commanders. The former corps commanders could not replace [the district commanders] in any way because they had under their command only regular field forces, while the district commanders could act with a greater range of powers since they controlled all the forces of a district, regular and irregular, field and stationary. . . .[5]

Miliutin gave a great deal of credit to the new system for helping to contain the Polish problem before it could become even more serious. Without doubt, he convinced the Emperor of this as well and won his full support for the further implementation of the reform.

On August 6, 1864, the Emperor issued a directive extending the military district system throughout the Empire and instructing the War Minister to proceed with its implementation.[6] Four days later, on August 10, Miliutin issued the *prikaz* which defined the military districts within the European part of the Empire. Ten districts, including the four created two years earlier, came into existence: Petersburg, Finland, Riga, Vilno, Warsaw, Kiev, Odessa, Kharkov, Moscow, and Kazan. The War Minister directed that as each new district opened the older organs of military administration were to be abolished. With this order, Miliutin abolished the headquarters staffs of the corps which had not yet been reformed: the Headquarters of the Corps of the Domestic Watch; the Administration of the Chief of Reserve Artillery; the headquarters of the artillery districts of St. Petersburg, Moscow, Duneburg, Brest-Litovsk, Kiev, Kremenchug, Voronezh, Kazan, Tambov and Simbirsk; all the

5. *Ibid.,* p. 29.

6. *Journal de St. Peterbourg,* August 12, 1864. For an account of the legislative process by which the Regulation became law, see the memorandum by Miliutin, "Obshchii obzor' polozheniia o voenno-okruzhnykh upravleniiakh," *Voennyi Sbornik,* No. 9 (1864), pp. 45–47.

administrations of the Over-Proviant Master except in the Caucasus; and
the duty administrations (*dezhurstva*) in the Lithuanian, Estonian,
and Kurland Provinces and in the Military Provinces of Kazan and
Astrakhan.[7]

In addition to the elimination of these administrative bodies, the
already existing military districts of Warsaw, Vilno, and Kiev together
with the new district of Finland, were to be brought quickly into conformity with the standard table of organization prescribed for the military district system. The other new districts were to change more slowly,
and because of their special characteristics, the Caucasus, Orenburg, and
Siberian regions were to remain temporarily just as they were. The
Guards, normally stationed in and around the capital, retained their
designation as a corps but were to be commanded by the Chief of the
St. Petersburg Military District.[8] The title of corps was to be dropped in
all other cases, except in time of war or national emergency when corps
would be formed if the occasion demanded it.

Three days after issuing this order, Miliutin liquidated the Corps of
the Domestic Watch and transferred its functions to the new stationary
forces. Included in these were the fortress regiments and battalions performing garrison and guard duty, the stage detachments manning the
relay stations, and the provincial battalions and district detachments.
These latter units inherited the tasks of inducting, equipping and training recruits, then posting them to the field forces as reserves. Most of
these forces simply remained in their former duty stations, but the
administrative responsibility for them was now shifted to the military
district commanders of stationary troops and to the provincial military
chiefs.[9]

In the following year, sufficient progress had been made for the Emperor to give the order to incorporate the non-European parts of the
Empire into the military district system. This was quickly accomplished

7. The *prikaz* (No. 228 of the War Minister) creating the new districts is published in the official section of *Russkii Invalid*, No. 177 (1864). For a systematic
table precisely defining the limits of each district, "Otchet glavnogo upravleniia
general'nogo shtaba za 1865 god," *Vsepoddaneishii otchet za 1865 god* (St. Petersburg, 1867), pp. 66–67.
8. "Ofitsial'nyi otdel'," *Voennyi Sbornik*, No. 9 (1864), pp. 49–50, and *Public
Records Office*, FO 65/662, September 28, 1864.
9. "Ofitsial'nyi otdel'," *Voennyi Sbornik*, No. 9, 1864, pp. 50–51.

by the creation of four new districts: the Caucasus, Orenburg, Western Siberia, and Eastern Siberia.[10] In the following decade, after the conquest of Turkestan, that great expanse of newly won territory was constituted as the fifteenth military district.[11]

Miliutin kept the process of drafting the final legislation and the working out of final details under his personal supervision. He set up a special commission under his personal chairmanship which had as its members Privy Councillor Ustrialov, Lieutenant General Polivanov, Privy Councillor Piktorov, and Colonel V. Anichkov. This body was particularly interested in the organization of the logistical systems of the military districts, and, working through the Inspectorate Department of the War Ministry, it assigned the personnel to all the newly established administrations.

So that the workings of the War Ministry and this commission would not depart from the real needs of the future districts, Colonel Anichkov acted as liaison with the headquarters staffs of the districts. In addition to this, Colonel Anichkov was the public relations representative for the military district system and continued in this role to write articles explaining and defending the reform.[12]

So well did the process of the reform go that the creation of each district was quickly followed by the completion of its internal structure. Even during the course of the Polish Insurrection the War Ministry was able to proceed with the creation of the several administrations in the Warsaw, Vilno, Kiev, and Odessa districts, and with the restoration of peace and the foundation of new districts the process went swiftly. The completed districts closely followed the pattern of organization which Miliutin had proposed. Each district had a council composed of the heads of the several administrations plus a nominee of the War Ministry. There was a headquarters staff, an intendance, an artillery administration, an engineering administration, a military medical administration and an inspectorate of military hospitals. These latter two were soon to be merged to form a single unified district medical administration.

10. "R.V.O.: Primenenie voenno-okruzhnoi sistemy k kavkazu, Orenburgskomu kraiu i k Sibiri," *Voennyi Sbornik*, No. 9 (1865).

11. [D. A. Miliutin], p. 33.

12. "Obshchii obzor' polozheniia o voenno-okruzhnykh upravleniiakh," *Voennyi Sbornik*, No. 9 (1864), pp. 45–47.

An Imperial order subordinated to each of these administrations all appropriate military installations within the district. For example, all artillery parks, depots and other installations associated with the artillery branch were placed under the chief of the district artillery administration.[13] The balance that Miliutin had desired was finally substantially achieved.

So rapidly did this progress that by early 1865 the War Ministry could say with justifiable pride,

> As we know, the system of military district administration, despite its recent implementation, is already solidly grounded. The administrative structures in which are embodied the district administrations, are in existence in almost all the military districts and [are] maintaining among themselves that necessary communication upon which depends the reasonableness of the execution of administrative and logistical tasks.[14]

The War Ministry considered the entire system to be working well enough that there was every reason to have confidence in the future. The Ministry was able to retain full control over policy as well as ultimate responsibility for all administrative organs. The actual administrative control rested in the new administrative bodies and in the persons of the district commanders, while all the executive powers lay in the hands of the individual heads of the district administrations and of the division commanders.

In addition to Miliutin's conviction that the new military districts had contributed materially to the successful suppression of the Polish rebellion,[15] the new system began to demonstrate its worth in other ways. One of the most important motives for instituting the reform has been to effect substantial savings in the military budget. Even very early in the reform it proved possible to reduce the complement of administrative personnel. By September 1864 the creation of the four western military

13. "Uchrezhedenie voennykh okrugov i preobrazovaniia v ustroistve mestnykh voisk," *Voennyi Sbornik*, No. 9 (1864), p. 50; Bogdanovich, IV., 40–42; and P. A. Zaionchkovskii, *Voennye reformy 1860–1870 godov v Rossii*, pp. 94–95.

14. "R.V.O.: O voenno-okruzhnom upravlenii," *Voennyi Sbornik*, No. 1 (1865), p. 28.

15. "Uchrezhdenie voennykh okrugov i preobrazovaniia v ustroistve mestnykh voisk," *Voennyi Sbornik*, No. 9 (1864), p. 66.

districts alone had resulted in a net reduction of 439 officer ranks and 1,301 enlisted men. Writing shortly after his retirement, Miliutin pointed out that before the reform military administration had required 2,525 officers or civilians with equivalent ranks, while the district system demanded only a total of 1,797. This amounted to a net reduction of 728 officers or 28 percent. Even with the subsequent expansion of the base of the Empire, and particularly with the incorporation of the huge Turkestan Military District, the total figure never exceeded 1,972.[16] Some of the funds saved by this reduction were used to augment the salaries of those who remained in an effort to improve the quality of the administrative corps and to provide incentives for efficient officers to remain at their posts, thus assuring greater continuity.[17] These savings also were available to be applied to meet the rising costs of the War Ministry in other areas.

The successful implementation of the military district system was important for another of Miliutin's reforms. When he recast the system of military administration, he put a new face on military justice. The problem was not one for the army alone but was basic to the whole of society. The question can most easily be divided into two parts, moral and legal. The moral side of the problem was concerned with Russia's position among the civilized nations and the effects of corporal punishment upon the individual Russian subject. Russia's image in Europe, particularly since the visit of the Marquis de Custine,[18] was the knout, the symbol of corporal punishment in Russia. This had the effect of placing Russia alongside the half-civilized and barbaric peoples of Asia, and therefore the end of corporal punishment was seen as a great step in the life of the nation. The system in Russia, moreover, had the effect of dividing society into two parts: those liable to corporal punishment and those who were not. This interrupted the organic unity of society by

16. [D. A. Miliutin], p. 33.
17. *Ibid., loc. cit.*
18. Marquis de Custine was a French nobleman who visited Russia in 1839 and upon returning home published an account of his travels and impressions. His observations profoundly shocked Russian sensibilities while presenting Russia to Europe as a barbaric despotism. The truly shocking element of his views was the fact that they reflected much truth.

creating a legal difference between the classes, a circumstance which Miliutin ideologically opposed.[19] Within the army, corporal punishment had the effect of degrading not only the individual punished but had in addition a pernicious effect upon all soldiers.[20]

The legal question was that of recasting the machinery of justice to provide procedural and other guarantees, improving the moral qualities of the application of the law. The military court system at the time Miliutin became War Minister was basically the creation of Peter the Great, having been amended or added to piecemeal, without proper co-ordination, whenever the occasion demanded. Contradictions both in the laws and in the legal procedures had arisen, making chaos of the entire system of administering justice. In the light of the evolution of western European jurisprudence and legal systems, the Russian system was hopelessly out of date.

The independence of the military courts was abridged by the right of military commanders or auditors-general to set aside court decisions and to capriciously revise sentences either up or down. On the other hand, neither the military commanders nor the auditors had the right to cross-examine either the defendants or the witnesses and instead had to rely solely upon written depositions. Miliutin believed one of the worst difficulties lay in the critical shortage of officers with the necessary qualifications and training for efficiency and the just execution of court functions.[21] All efforts had to be made to assure a supply of properly trained legal officers.

Preparatory studies were already under way when Miliutin came to office. As early as 1846, the Emperor Nicholas had appointed a special commission under the chairmanship of General-Adjutant N. N. Annenkov to compose a new regulation on criminal justice within the armed forces.[22] Subsequently, Senator I. Kh. Kapger was named to this com-

19. Miliutin's social views will be dealt with in a subsequent chapter. For a review of the broader aspects of the reform of the court system and the significance of the contemporary penal practices, see A. Lokhvitskii, "Unichtozhenie telesnykh nakazanii," *Russkii Invalid*, No. 87 (1863).

20. *Russkii Invalid*, No. 90 (1863).

21. *Doklad*, January 15, 1862, pp. 104–105.

22. *Russkii Invalid*, No. 130 (1868). Apparently the question had already been under active consideration since at least as early as 1837. See Bogdanovich, IV., 450–451.

mission and in the course of events and with Imperial sanction he assumed the task himself. Beginning in 1856, Senator Kapger, together with the Auditor-General and other individuals from the War Ministry and in co-operation with the representatives from other interested agencies, made plans for reform. This work, almost finished by early 1862, had as its basic goals the elimination of such cruel forms of punishment as the gauntlet (*spiessrute*), the limitation of corporal punishment, and a reduction in the severity of the punishments for certain major crimes.[23] Along with the goals of Kapger's committee, Miliutin proposed to reform the penal battalions of the army by basing them upon the principle of rehabilitation rather than vengeance.[24]

Miliutin also reviewed the system for the administration of justice. After study, he recommended that a new regular military court system be created with regularly appointed court officials with a guaranteed independence from tactical commanders. The defendants were to be granted specific rights. Charges against them were to be read in their presence, and they were to be guaranteed the right to retain competent defense counsel. Trials were to be open and would be conducted orally. Aside from this, Miliutin felt that as a matter of course competent legal officers ought to be available in each regiment to give advice and to aid in minor legal matters. Since one of the more pressing needs was for more qualified legal personnel, the Auditor School was to be reformed so that it might train specialists as well as give legal training to non-specialists.[25]

Since many of the preliminary studies had already been made and because the new court structure was to be a part of the military district system, the War Minister made rapid progress. In 1862, he created two committees from among individuals drawn from both the War and Naval Ministries. Chairmen of these two groups were respectively General-Adjutants Sukhozanet and N. A. Kryzhanovskii. Both bodies completed their work in 1863, and Miliutin submitted their findings to the Emperor. One committee, which dealt with the question of punishments,

23. *Doklad*, January 15, 1862, p. 106.

24. *Ibid.*, pp. 106–107, and A. Lokhvitskii, "Unichtozhenie telesnykh nakazanii," *Russkii Invalid*, No. 87 (1863).

25. *Doklad*, January 15, 1862, pp. 107–109.

drafted a new Regulation on military discipline, prescribing penalties which might be imposed for breaches of discipline. The Emperor promulgated this Regulation as early as July 6, 1863, since it was largely based upon the thorough studies of Senator Kapger.[26]

The work of the second committee, that on court structure and procedure, took much longer. The findings and recommendations of this body needed more study, and, accordingly, Miliutin distributed them to a number of high military commanders for their comments and discussion. After their remarks were returned to the War Ministry, the project was given over early in 1864 into the hands of the Auditors-General of the Army and the Navy. These experts added the final touches and the results were approved by Alexander on October 25, 1865. This study formed the basis for the reform of the court system in both the army and the navy. Under Miliutin's personal supervision, as well as that of the Auditor-General, the project was codified and issued in final form in 1867. A special commission, including the War Minister, gave the program a final review on September 1, 1867, and the implementation of the new system began in the St. Petersburg and Moscow Military Districts.[27]

The reform was a basic transformation of the courts created by Peter I. The judges in the old courts had not only established the innocence or guilt of the defendants and determined their sentences, but their powers extended to conducting the investigations and acting as public prosecutors. The defendant had no rights and was at the mercy of the court. The new system greatly narrowed the competence of the judges. Prosecutors and defense attorneys became separate court officers and decisions of innocence or guilt had to be based upon evidence produced in open court and upon the trial proceedings. Public trials became manda-

---

26. *Russkii Invalid*, No. 255 (1865), and "R.V.O.: Osnovnyia polozheniia preobrazovaniia voenno-sudnoi chasti," *Voennyi Sbornik*, No. 12 (1865), pp. 167–168.

27. "Izmeneniia i uluchsheniia po voenno-sudnoi chasti," *Vsepoddaneishii otchet voennogo ministerstva za 1863* god, p. 33; "R.V.O.: Kratkii obzor' deiatel'nosti voennogo ministerstva v 1863 godu: V. Voenno-sudnaia chast'," *Voennyi Sbornik*, No. 5 (1864), pp. 26–27; "Sostavlenie novogo ustava o voinskikh prestupleniiakh i nakazaniiakh," *Voennyi Sbornik*, No. 2 (1863), pp. 481–582; "R.V.O.: Russkaia armiia v 1867 godu," *Voennyi Sbornik*, No. 12 (1869), pp. 135–136; and, "Obshchii obzor' deiatel'nosti voennogo ministerstva za 1866 god," *Vsepoddaneishii otchet voennogo ministerstva za 1866 god* (St. Petersburg, 1868), p. 93.

tory and the procedure allowed both the prosecution and the defense to cross-examine witnesses.[28] The reform of the civil courts in 1864 served in these respects as the living model for the procedural guarantees which were granted to the ordinary Russian soldier for the first time.

Especially important in the new system was the role of the defense lawyers who reflected the influence of their English and French counterparts. Every legal and procedural right was accorded to the defense. It could call witnesses, produce evidence, or appeal court decisions. The defense lawyers, who were called advocates (*prisiazhnye povereniia*), had to complete a recognized law school, be at least twenty-five years of age, and have at least five years of practical court experience. If the defendant did not otherwise provide himself with one, the court was obligated to appoint competent counsel on his behalf.[29]

The structure of the courts themselves was closely integrated into the military district system. They existed at three levels: the Regimental, the Military, and the Supreme Military Court. The Regimental Courts tried only those enlisted men who did not avail themselves of their special rights to be tried in a higher court or whose crimes were not serious enough to warrant either their impressment into a penal battalion or some more serious punishment. The Military Courts, each of which consisted of a Court President and at least two associate judges appointed by the Emperor, could try enlisted men who fell outside the competence of the regimental courts as well as all officers, generals, and civil officials of the War and Navy Ministries. Each Military Court was located within a military district and took its name from that district.[30]

The Supreme Military and Naval Courts were seated in St. Petersburg, although they established branches in far-flung parts of the Empire, such as the Caucasus and Siberia. The Presidents and associate judges of these Courts were appointed by Imperial *ukaz* from among candidates having

28. N. Maksimov, "Ocherk osnovnykh polozhenii predstoiashchogo preobrazovaniia voenno-sudnoi chasti v Rossii," *Voennyi Sbornik*, No. 6 (1865), pp. 245–247.

29. *Ibid.*, pp. 258–259 and 262.

30. For a brief description of the court structure and procedures, see, "R.V.O.: Voenno-ugolovnoe sudo-ustroistvo," *Voennyi Sbornik,* No. 12 (1865), pp. 168–169. Cf. "R.V.O.: Osnovnyia polozheniia voenno-sudnoi chasti," *Voennyi Sbornik,* No. 7 (1863), pp. 181–182.

the rank of general or its equivalent. The Supreme Courts acted as appellate courts and, in addition, debated all proposed legislation in the War Ministry which touched upon the question of punishments. The opinions rendered by these Courts were reported to the War Minister who in turn introduced them into the State Council.[31]

Besides the regularization of the court structure and the provision for the first time of procedural guarantees for the defendants, the punishments meted out by the new courts were more humane. To be a good soldier, a man had to have self-respect and a sense of the justice of the system he served. The revised scale of punishments followed the new civilian code closely. In 1864, Miliutin issued an order in the War Ministry eliminating some of the more brutal forms of punishment, particularly that of running the gauntlet. Corporal punishment was limited; a soldier could be beaten only after having been properly convicted, and enlisted ranks with more than six years' active service were immune from the knout even if convicted. Individuals serving sentences in penal battalions, however, were subject to *summary* punishment, including whipping. Various lighter punishments were prescribed in the hope that the spiritual and moral development of the individual soldier would progress and that his confidence in the justice of the system could not be shaken.[32]

The qualified legal personnel necessary to make the new court system work were trained in the Auditor's School which was directly subordinated to the Auditor-General. The school, which had formerly given some legal training to officers already in service and for whom legal matters were only a sideline, was directed by Miliutin on November 11, 1864, to reform itself. It expanded to accommodate about 170 students from both the army and the navy. The curriculum was graduated into five classes, the first two being composed of general subjects to make up for the inadequacies of the Empire's poorly developed educational system, and the latter three were made up from specialized law courses. Many students were admitted without charge, others with the payment

31. *Ibid.*, pp. 183–184.
32. "R.V.O.: Uluchshenie v sisteme ugolovnykh i ispravitel'nykh nakazanii," *Voennyi Sbornik*, No. 5 (1863), pp. 225–228, and, "Prikaz voennogo ministra, Aprel' 17, No. 120," *Ruskii Invalid*, No. 85 (1863).

of only partial fees, and the general tuition itself was subsidized.[33] The War Ministry was willing to make every effort to attract capable young men to prepare themselves for careers in military law.

The implementation of the military district system and the reform of the military court system were not the only reforms of military administration that Miliutin effected. All the changes at the lower levels demanded compensating changes within the War Ministry itself. The rate at which the Ministry was reformed was somewhat slower than was the case of the districts and the courts, but the changes were no less important. Miliutin's motives in reshaping the Ministry were much the same as those which led him to create the district system—to reduce expenditures and to promote administrative efficiency by "simplifying the mechanism." The logic of the military district system extended also to the central administration:

> With the establishment of these districts, the duties of the War Ministry would be significantly eased by concentrating the broader aspects of power and obligations in the hands of the military district chiefs; the administration of logistics would take on a more regular organization, while an immediate consequence of the proposed measure would be the reinforcement of the closest actual supervision over the activities of the several local establishments.[34]

The transfer of most executive functions to the local administrations necessitated changes within the Ministry, but Miliutin believed that the overcentralization had been only one barrier to efficiency.

Such features as divided responsibility and the overlapping of functions were equally at fault. They not only promoted inefficiency but they also demanded unnecessary personnel, which added to the costs. Miliutin had not only to reform the War Ministry to compensate for the loss of most of its executive functions; he also had to consolidate and regularize offices dealing with similar functions.[35]

When Miliutin came to the War Ministry its internal order was chaotic. It had been established at the very beginning of the reign of Alexander I and new offices and bureaus had from time to time been

33. "Auditorskoe uchilishche," *Voennyi Sbornik*, No. 1 (1865), pp. 26–27.
34. *Doklad*, January 15, 1862, p. 89.
35. *Ibid.*, pp. 122, 146, and 166.

incorporated into it whenever they were thought necessary. The Emperor Nicholas I had made some attempts to regularize and reform the central administration by means of his Regulation of March 29, 1836, and again Prince Dolgorukov and his successor, N. O. Sukhozanet, had made some minor attempts after the Peace of Paris. These latter changes were aimed chiefly at bureaucratic inefficiency of the sort Miliutin still had to deal with. Sukhozanet attempted to simplify the forms and orders for internal correspondence, to eliminate parts and sometimes even whole offices by uniting related functions, and to increase the powers of the lower levels of administration.[36] His success in these endeavors was slight because he lacked the boldness to apply anything more than palliatives.

Miliutin's policy was to streamline and to regularize the functions of the Ministry and to take into account its new relationship with the military districts:

The general idea of the reform was to bring the entire edifice into harmony and to simplify all the intricacies of its mechanism; therefore it was agreed for utility above all, to merge units similar in their spheres of activity and to eliminate superfluous outgrowths, which in the course of time were formed more or less casually without any general plan.[37]

This redefinition of administrative lines made possible a reduction in personnel:

in anticipation of the radical measures to reduce the present complement of the Ministry, it is proposed as absolutely necessary to review its organization and materially to assess the rights, duties, and relationships of all personnel and institutions incorporated into it.[38]

The reform was nevertheless not to be one merely of merger and the elimination of offices. The War Ministry was also to incorporate such new elements as the Institutions of Military Instruction, which had previously existed separately.

One of the problems emanating from the reform of the War Ministry was the charge by Miliutin's critics that he had made his post very powerful in the process. Miliutin was at great pains to reply that his powers were checked by a number of limitations, although the simple fact of a

36. [D. A. Miliutin], p. 9, and Bogdanovich, IV., 13.
37. [D. A. Miliutin], p. 13.
38. *Doklad*, January 15, 1862, p. 172.

more regularized and functionally consolidated administration made it easier for the Minister to exercise control.[39] Moreover, the military district system, eliminating as it did the almost independent army and corps commanders and replacing them by district commanders who were functionaries of the War Ministry, did give Miliutin greater control over the armed forces than any other Minister of War had ever possessed.

When Miliutin assumed the post of War Minister, he wanted to relieve that office of much of the administrative *minutiae* which had plagued his predecessors and which had made it so difficult for them to perceive and deal with the larger picture. The transfer of many of the War Minister's executive functions to the military districts had already accomplished this in part, but much still remained. Miliutin's desire that the War Minister alone have the right to speak for the several departments of the War Ministry arose from the fact that the intentions of the Regulation of 1836 had not been reflected in actual practice. Some offices such as those of the General-Feldzeugmeister or the Inspector of Engineers were often occupied by members of the Imperial family who had direct access to the ear of the Emperor, making their relationship with the War Minister somewhat ambiguous. In addition, the Institutions of Military Education existed as a separate agency and its Chief, also often a member of the Imperial family, had many of the prerogatives of a minister, including that of reporting directly to the Emperor.[40]

One other ambiguity in the position of the War Minister within his own Ministry was the position of the General Staff. Miliutin wanted the role of this body to be re-evaluated and then reformed along the lines of the French model. This markedly contradicted the desires of some, including Field-Marshal Bariatinskii, who favored the adoption of the Prussian system whereby the General Staff would be the real head of the army while the War Ministry served as an administrative figurehead. Besides the somewhat autonomous position of the Russian General Staff, Miliutin complained of the overly technical and specialized role played by its members, separating them from the practical needs of the general service. This had to be corrected by reintegrating them into the armed forces to establish a closer harmony.[41]

39. [D. A. Miliutin], p. 11.
40. *Doklad*, January 15, 1862, p. 173.
41. *Ibid.*, p. 90.

The Emperor generally agreed with Miliutin's observations and allowed him to proceed. Although Miliutin's conception of what he wanted was well worked out from the beginning, the actual process of reform spanned the years 1862 to 1869, when the work was capped off by the issuance of a new General Regulation giving precise definition to the role and structure of the Ministry.[42] The earliest reforms were largely those of consolidating offices. For example, the Department of Engineers was merged with the Inspectorate of Engineers to form a single Supreme Engineering Administration, and in a like manner the Department of Artillery was fused with the staff of the General-Feldzeugmeister to form the Supreme Artillery Administration. Each of these had a single head who was directly responsible to the War Minister, and each Supreme Administration assumed the sole responsibility for the higher administration of its respective branch of arms.[43] Early in 1863, a third Supreme Administration came into existence with the incorporation into the War Ministry of the Institutions of Military Instruction.[44] In the following year, the Proviant and Commissariat Departments reflecting the union that had already taken place in the military districts united into the Supreme Intendance Administration and brought under one single head the entire system of logistics.[45]

One of the most significant reforms, that of the General Staff, continued over a period of years. Miliutin on the one hand improved the Staff's technical competence, but on the other he reconstituted it as but another of the Supreme Administrations forming the War Ministry and thereby effectively eliminated it as a base for any competition with the prerogatives of the War Minister. He strengthened the General Staff by incorporating into it the Military Topographical Depot and the Nikolaevskii Academy. The new General Staff emerging from this union was

42. Bogdanovich, IV., 10–11.

43. *Russkii Invalid*, No. 57 (1863) and "Obzor deiatel'nosti voennogo ministerstva v poslem piatiletie," *Voennyi Sbornik*, No. 10 (1865), p. 233. Cf. P. A. Zaionchkovskii, *Voennye reformy 1860–1870 godov v Rossii*, p. 100.

44. This will be treated in greater detail in a subsequent chapter.

45. "Obshchii obzor deiatel'nosti voennogo ministerstva za 1864 god: Ustroistvo intendantskogo upravleniia," *Vsepoddaneishii otchet voennogo ministerstva za 1864 god*, p. 17. Cf. "R.V.O.: Kommissariatskoe i proviantskoe dovol'stviia," *Voennyi Sbornik*, No. 2 (1863), pp. 586–590.

headed by the Quartermaster-General and was subdivided into several sections along functional lines.[46]

One of the most important of these sections was a special Consultative Committee which had very broad powers. This Committee, for example, directed military studies in all branches of the service as well as within the General Staff and the Corps of Topographers. In addition, this body made any special investigations or studies which the Quartermaster-General or the War Minister might direct. It is worthy of note that Miliutin himself in a much more informal way had personally played such a role during the Crimean War and this may have been in part an institutionalization of his own experience. The Consultative Committee also looked into questions of the administration of the schools, investigated any proposals for changes and improvements in the General Staff and Corps of Topographers, considered the various instructions issued by the several Supreme Administrations, and served as the agency for disseminating information to the officer corps of the army.[47] One can assume that it in part was a watchdog over the whole of military administration.

Another section of the new Supreme Administration of the General Staff performed such special services as co-ordinating transportation facilities and making surveys of potential theaters of war. The Chancellory performed all internal administrative and clerical duties. The General Staff itself, as a Department of the Supreme Administration, performed the duties of an inspectorate, managed the deployment of the armed forces, and gathered intelligence. The Military Corps of Topographers conducted surveys and made charts and maps. The Nikolaevskii Academy of the General Staff trained all officers who entered the General Staff, and to insure its independence it was subordinated directly to the Quartermaster-General.[48]

Three years after these changes, in 1866, the General Staff was merged

46. "Kratkii obzor deiatel'nosti voennogo ministerstva v 1863 godu," *Voennyi Sbornik*, No. 7 (1864), p. 40.

47. "R.V.O.: Polozhenie o glavnom upravlenii general'nogo shtaba," *Voennyi Sbornik*, No. 12 (1863), pp. 517–518.

48. *Ibid.*, pp. 520–521; Bogdanovich, IV., 10; and, N. Glinoetskii, *Istoricheskii ocherk Nikolaevskoi akademii general'nogo shtaba, passim.* In the last work cited, see particularly the introductory chapter.

with the Inspectorate to form the Supreme (*Glavnyi*) Staff. The Inspectorate Department of the War Ministry had been concerned with the order-of-battle of the armed forces, their employment, and with personnel. The close relationship of these duties to the functions of the Supreme Administration of the General Staff made their administrative union quite natural, but Miliutin had other motives. His basic desire was to bridge the gulf between the general service officers and those of the General Staff to make the latter more sensitive to the actual needs of the service.[49] This union coincided with the final dissolution of the vestigial Supreme Headquarters of His Imperial Majesty, and the Supreme Staff also assumed its functions.

Miliutin was very sensitive to the nature of this reform, especially the fusion of the Department of Inspectorate with the General Staff, since it proved to be one of the chief targets of his critics. While they were undoubtedly disturbed by the reduction of their prerogatives, Miliutin was concerned with administrative soundness and practical necessity:

The Department of the General Staff, restricted by its own specialties to such narrow limits, did not have any independence in peacetime; within it were drafted troop itineraries, disposition charts, etc. Therefore, since all general arrangements, especially any recommendations for changes, were concentrated within the Inspectorate Department, it was in effect the center for all the activity of the War Ministry. Besides this, there was another consideration. For a long time we had been hearing complaints about the one-sidedness of General Staff service, and we therefore sought the means to remove those deficiencies which were the consequence of over-concentration.[50]

Miliutin's practical nature operated on the principle that no organization can be efficient in which the pedantic specialist is not closely acquainted with actual practice. His reform in this respect served to bring the officers of the General Staff into close contact with the kinds of practical problems they would have to face while serving as the chiefs of staff in tactical units. Miliutin made of the General Staff both a more competent technical organization and a body more responsive to the real needs of the

49. P. B., "Neskol'ko slov o general'nom shtabe," *Voennyi Sbornik*, No. 5 (1871), pp. 140–144, and, M. G., "Ustroistvo i sluzhba general'nogo shtaba," *Voennyi Sbornik*, No. 7 (1873), pp. 88–89.
50. [D. A. Miliutin], p. 13.

armed forces, but in accomplishing this he turned it away from playing any critical role in the formation of general policy.

The bulk of the reform of the War Ministry was complete by 1867, and Miliutin issued the Regulation defining the organs of the Ministry and their relationship to each other at the beginning of 1869. According to this new Regulation, the Minister of War stood at the head of his Ministry, and he alone was able to speak for the several departments and other agencies within it. While a strong figure such as Miliutin appeared to dominate the Ministry totally and to control all policy within it, the legal prerogatives of the War Minister were not so great as they appeared. The War Minister functioned as the Chairman of the War Council, on the basis of *primus inter pares*, which in theory possessed the right to resolve all administrative and policy matters. This was a rather large body, having as many as twenty-seven members and including within it the key administrators and specialists from the Ministry. The Council had within it a number of subcommittees, such as the Military Codification Committee and the Military Hospitals Committee.[51]

Besides the War Minister and the Military Council, eight Supreme Administrations represented the several branches of the army: the Supreme or General Staff, the Supreme Intendance Administration, the Supreme Artillery Administration, the Supreme Engineering Administration, the Supreme Military Medical Administration which included the Medical-Surgical Academy, the Supreme Administration of Irregular Forces, and the Supreme Military Court Administration. Two other offices were independent and responsible only to the War Minister: the Supreme Military Court and the Committee for the Wounded. In addition, there were a variety of minor committees and chancellories.[52]

With the completion of his reform of the War Ministry, Miliutin completed the process of reconstructing Russian military administration, giving it a form which in its broad outlines it retains to the present time. He had achieved by this substantially what he had set out to do. By retaining for the War Ministry only policy-making powers and turning

---

51. *Ibid.*, p. 11; *Russkii Invalid*, No. 89 (1867), and Bogdanovich, IV., 11.

52. See the schematic chart in *Stoletie : Istoricheskii ocherk razvitiia voennogo upravleniia v Rossii*, p. 482.

over executive functions to local authorities, he substantially reduced the amount of correspondence needed in the administration of the armed forces. In his official reports to the Emperor on January 1, 1870, and January 1, 1871, Miliutin demonstrated what this reduction meant in concrete terms. The volume of correspondence between the years 1863 and 1869, a period of transition, declined by 40 percent for items coming into the Ministry and by 35 percent for outgoing matter.[53] Ten years later, after leaving the War Ministry, Miliutin published the figures taking in the period down to 1875, which included the addition of the new Turkestan Military District:

	Incoming Correspondence	Outgoing Correspondence
In 1863 (before the reform)	446,044	332,796
In 1866 (after the reform)	332,796	228,796
In 1869	273,048	212,956
In 1872	260,179	203,034
In 1875	244,291	185,882[54]

Miliutin declared that for the twelve-year period this represented a net reduction of about 45 percent in both incoming and outgoing correspondence. The relief thus accorded to the War Ministry allowed the Ministry to reduce its officer personnel by 846, including the expansion of the administration to incorporate into it the Turkestan District.[55]

Not all of Miliutin's efforts endured, but, on balance, his reforms fared better during the reaction in the reign of Alexander III than did many of the other features of the Great Reforms. To be sure, a commission assembled to review the system of military administration which Miliutin had created and the malevolent charges of Bariatinskii were revived in the press, but it was clear that the responsible administrators wanted the system to endure. Even the popular hero General Skoboliev struck a

53. The figures given in the several sources vary slightly. For example, the official report for 1871 gives the figure for the incoming correspondence in the year 1863 as 446,046 items, rather than 444,044 as it appears in the 1870 report. The 1871 report gives the incoming material for 1865 as 303,906 items, as opposed to 333,906 in the 1870 report, etc. These are quite likely copyist errors. See, *Vsepoddaneishii Doklad Voennogo Ministra: January 1, 1870*, p. 169, and *Vsepoddaneishii Doklad Voennogo Ministra: January 1, 1871*, p. 134.

54. [D. A. Miliutin], p. 18.

55. Zisserman, III., 256, and *Dnevnik*, IV., 129.

blow on behalf of the former Minister of War, suggesting that the commission reviewing the system of military administration invite Miliutin to come to St. Petersburg and assume the leadership in its further work.[56] The commission in the end changed nothing substantial, altering only those particular features which were most odious to the conservatives. Among these, the commission again separated the Inspectorate from the General Staff, a move which Miliutin thought to be "stupid and absurd."[57] Nevertheless, the basic structure survived and did in fact prove its worth in the years to come.

56. *Ibid.*, IV., 108–115.
57. *Ibid.*, IV., 140.

4

The Reform of the Military Schools

No system, however nearly perfect, is by itself sufficient to insure even minimum efficiency or the achievement of any desired goals. Tables of organization and clear channels of communication alone cannot assure smooth operation. Institutions are made up of men and are subject to the limitations or greatness of the men who constitute them, and in the performance of their duties they must rely not only upon their own natural capacities and instincts but also upon their education and training. One of Russia's greatest weaknesses lay in her failure to develop her human resources. The late survival of serfdom and the failure to develop a truly comprehensive system of popular education was as important a source of her national weakness as her economic and fiscal failures and indeed was closely related to them.

A few in Russia were educated very well indeed, but the overwhelming majority received little or no education. Perhaps one of the best indicators of the low literacy level of the general population of the Empire during the 1860s was the literacy rate among the recruits being inducted into the army. In 1866, 7.3 percent of the levy was literate, in 1867 this figure rose to 8.5 percent, in 1868 it was 9.7 percent, and in 1869 was 10 percent.[1] Not all of even this modest proportion possessed the same

---

1. The several sets of figures given for these years vary slightly. Miliutin, for example, in his circular submitted to the State Council (*Despatches*, March 6,

level of competence, there being a wide variation in the level of their achievement, with the line between literacy and illiteracy being rather thin.[2]

Perhaps nothing else illustrates as well the failure of Russian society to adapt to the rapid changes taking place in western European society. It posed a special handicap for the armed forces because the uneducated recruits were harder to train and were less adaptable to the more modern techniques of warfare. The magnitude of the contrast to the western powers is best understood when one considers that the literacy rate in Prussia was over 96 percent, that in France was 75 percent, and in England 85 percent.[3] This picture becomes even more grim when one views the educational trends in Russia. Even with the positive achievements of Minister of Public Instruction A. V. Golovnin during the early years of Miliutin's administration there did not appear on the horizon any immediate hope that civil education, even at the primary level, would become either general or universal.

The question of educating the ordinary soldier became a matter of great importance after the humiliating defeat in the Crimean War, and the decade which followed saw much concrete progress in this respect. As early as 1857 the War Ministry created schools within many of the tactical units where soldiers were taught to read. Operating largely during the inactive winter months, the schools were of two basic types. The first, sometimes called "literacy teams," existed at the company, squad-

1872) gave these figures: 1867, 8.6 percent; 1868, 9.7 percent; 1869, 10 percent. In P. Bobrovskii, "Vzgliad' na gramotnost' i uchebnyia komandy v nashei armii," *Voennyi Sbornik*, No. 12 (1870), pp. 281 and 281n., the figures are: 1867, 9.1 percent; 1868, 9.5 percent; and 1869, 9.8 percent. The literacy rate of those entering the Guards ran considerably higher, averaging about 60 percent. This figure is quite misleading, however, since it included virtually anyone knowing the alphabet, and, in addition, the Guards were drawn exclusively from among the gentry class. It is most difficult to find any other sources which would shed any further light upon the literacy rate in the country as a whole at this time. See I. M. Bogdanov, *Gramotnost' i obrazovanie v dorevoliutsionnoi Rossii i v SSSR*, pp. 20–23.

2. Ia. Barabash, "Neskol'ko myslei o gramotnosti v voiskakh," *Voennyi Sbornik*, No. 2 (1866); A. Pogoskii, "O gramotnosti v voiskakh," *Voennyi Sbornik*, No. 6 (1866); and Lt. General Krenke, "Gramotnosti v armii," *Voennyi Sbornik*, No. 12 (1868).

3. P. Bobrovskii, "Vzgliad' na gramotnost' i uchebnyia komandy v nashei armii," *Voennyi Sbornik*, No. 12 (1870), p. 281.

ron, or battery level, with a curriculum devoted basically to teaching the rudiments of reading and writing and sometimes elementary arithmetic. The second type were those schools at the regimental level which had the purpose of educating noncommissioned officers and clerks, providing them with both general and specialized subjects. The budget for these schools was modest in the extreme. The more sophisticated regimental schools, for example, operated on budgets of from twenty-five to fifty rubles per year, although one school working on the basis of one ruble per student per year reached a level of sixty-four rubles per year. Officers sometimes taught these courses voluntarily and when the expenses exceeded the budget as they often did, they would sometimes make up the difference out of the unit commander's own resources.[4]

For all the modesty of outlay, the program did accomplish a great deal. During the 1860s, when the literacy rate of recruits being inducted into the army was running about 8 percent, the literacy rate within the army was significantly higher. By the year 1866, as much as 24 percent of the army could read and write. This grew year by year to 25 percent in 1867 and 28 percent in 1868. Added to this were those who only knew how to read. By the end of the sixties, this latter category reached a level of about 22 percent, so that this group taken together with those who could both read and write meant that about half the enlisted ranks in the army possessed some degree of literacy.[5] Truly, the army had become even at this early date the school of the nation and was proving more effective at the dissemination of primary education than was the Ministry of Public Instruction.

This literacy rate was not, however, evenly distributed throughout the army. The highest rates were in the sharpshooter battalions, where the

4. For a systematic contemporary summary of those accomplishments, see *Obzor Deiatel'nosti Ministerstva Narodnogo Prosveshcheniia i Podvedomstvennykh emu Uchrezhdenii v 1862, 63, i 64 godakh.* The Imperial order creating these schools in 1857 seems to have grown out of an order given two years earlier, arising from the loss of the Crimean War, and directing that soldiers ought to be required to have target practice!!! The schools got off to a slow start but began to grow quickly with the beginning of Miliutin's administration. P. Bobrovskii, "Vzgliad' na gramotnost' . . . ," *Voennyi Sbornik,* No. 12 (1870), pp. 283–294. Cf. V. Patrakov, "O gramotnosti nizhnikh chinov i o vedenii otchetnosti po etomu predmetu," *Voennyi Sbornik,* No. 5 (1870), pp. 53–58.

5. P. Bobrovskii, "Vzgliad' na gramotnost' . . . ," *Voennyi Sbornik,* No. 12 (1870), p. 282, and *Despatches,* March 6, 1872.

over-all average was as high as 72 percent, and at least one battalion, the Finnish Light Guards Sharpshooter Battalion, was 100 percent literate. As a group, the stationary troops came next, followed by the ten cavalry divisions. The lowest rate was to be found in the forty-seven infantry divisions and in the reserve battalions where the raw recruits were trained.[6]

While some progress was made at this level, the most pressing problem was that of developing general education at the higher levels, particularly that of insuring an adequate preparation for leaders and specialists in the army. The Crimean War clearly demonstrated that the army's leadership at all levels had been inadequately prepared. The deficiencies in education, morale, and initiative had been noted by a number of observers, but none was more explicit in his criticisms or his suggestions than the Commander of the Guards and Grenadier Corps, Count F. V. Rüdiger. During the spring and summer of 1855 he composed a number of memoranda in the form of letters which he sent to the War Minister, Prince V. A. Dolgorukov, and which the latter then forwarded to the Emperor.

In one of these memoranda, Rüdiger wrote that the ineffectiveness of Russia's defenses was the result of basic flaws within the military system and particularly with that aspect involving leadership. He boldly stated that many incompetents were occupying high positions in the Russian army[7] and that this was obvious to the whole army and adversely affected its morale. This incompetence, he felt, was at least in part a consequence of the officers' lack of proper preparation to bear the responsibilities imposed upon them. This deficiency in its turn was the result of either insufficient training and education or a lack of experience in active military service. The overcentralization of the Russian military system stemming from the desire of Nicholas I to supervise every detail bred mediocrity and inertia.[8] This molded leaders who were prepared neither for warfare nor for normal field commands.

This problem, according to Rüdiger, was augmented by another serious

---

6. *Russkii Invalid* (No. 11), 1869, and, P. Bobrovskii, "Vzgliad' na gramotnost' . . . ," *Voennyi Sbornik*, No. 12 (1870), pp. 303–304.

7. *Ruskii Invalid*, No. 11 (1869), and P. Bobrovskii, "Vzgliad' na gramotnost' . . . ," *Voennyi Sbornik*, No. 12 (1870), pp. 303–304.

8. *Stoletie: Prilozheniia k istoricheskomu ocherku razvitiia voennogo upravleniia v Rossii, 1802–1902*, I., 20.

flaw. It seemed clear to him that there had been a serious degeneration of the military spirit. He granted that individual officers were brave enough when leading their men under fire, but he claimed their general abilities to conduct operations and to seize the initiative when possible had been lost. The loss of these qualities were, in his opinion, the direct consequence of their slavish dependence upon the prescribed regulations and manuals, and of parade-ground formalism.[9] While noting some of the virtues of these practices, he concluded that greater flexibility was necessary. The parade-ground, while a useful place to teach discipline, simply did not duplicate the battlefield. The purpose of the army was to fight and troops had to be trained under conditions as closely resembling battle conditions as possible.

Rüdiger also urged the need for a good general education for the officers to provide them with that breadth of background so vital for field commanders. Education, he argued, should not end at maturity, but, quite on the contrary, officers should be encouraged to pursue their studies, both general and professional.[10] Physical training and gymnastics also needed to be fostered to keep officers and troops in garrison in peak condition.[11]

Further, Rüdiger believed that the interests of both competence and morale might best be served if merit alone became the criterion for promotion, rather than seniority or family connections. One way of determining merit for promotion was the greater use of competitive examinations; another was to place greater emphasis upon practical service with greater attention being paid to promotion recommendations forwarded by the candidates' field commanders.[12] Rüdiger's criticisms might best be summed up by saying that the fault with the Russian army lay in the fact that it had come to exist independently of the practical needs of warfare and that its leadership was dominated by mediocrities bred by poor education and training coupled with bureaucratic inertia.

In a subsequent letter,[13] Rüdiger enjoined the Emperor to take some

9. John Shelton Curtiss, "The Army of Nicholas I: Its Role and Character," *The American Historical Review*, LXIII, No. 4 (July 1958), 884–885.
10. *Ibid.*, pp. 885ff., and *Stoletie: Prilozheniia* . . . , I., 20–22.
11. *Ibid.*, p. 23.
12. *Ibid.*, p. 27.
13. *Ibid.*, p. 28.

concrete steps to effect some improvements. For example, he wanted greater care in the selection of officer material, and those who qualified he wanted given every encouragement to become officers. He also considered the paucity of military literature to be a grave fault, and he therefore wanted the high command to foster writing on military subjects to provide the means for officers to keep abreast of the new developments within their profession.[14] He wanted libraries established within each regiment, and in accord with this he favored the writing of regimental histories especially detailing recent actions in which the unit had participated. The inactive winter months could be given over to officers' seminars in subjects appropriate to their individual ranks and specialties.[15]

Rüdiger was one of many critics of the quality of the officer corps in those first years after the Crimean War. In the very first issue of the *Voennyi Sbornik* there appeared an article analyzing the educational backgrounds of the officers then on active duty. On the basis of this analysis the article offered a number of concrete suggestions. The study generally concluded that Russian officers almost universally lacked sufficient education and training, and the author of the article went so far as to say, "Actually with us in the army, one rarely meets an officer who would be able to fulfill any task demanding a knowledge of military science."[16] This gloomy outlook was nothing less than a sweeping indictment of the professional capacities of the entire officer corps leading to the conclusion that incompetence was the norm.

Behind this failure, the author saw the deficiency of officers' education. At first glance, the system of educating and training young men to become officers seemed quite sound. Twenty-one cadet corps were deployed throughout the Empire, enrolling 7,088 students. Since the Russian army had an officer corps of about 30,000, this seemed sufficient to supply the needs of the army, but the author quickly destroyed this illusion. Those finally completing their studies were too few, and, moreover, the quality of their training was not commensurate with military requirements. Even so, most of the graduates of the cadet corps were

14. Dated August 19, 1855.

15. *Ibid.*, p. 44.

16. L. K., "Vzgliad' na stepen' obrazovaniia Russkikh ofitserov v armii," *Voennyi Sbornik*, No. 1 (1858), pp. 145*n* and 147.

posted to the Guards, the artillery, or other elite units, with only a very few finding their way into the regular army.[17]

To demonstrate what this meant in practical terms, the author analyzed a typical army division. Within this division were 481 officers; of these only sixty-five had been enrolled in the cadet corps and these had not completed the course. Only five had earned degrees at institutions of higher learning, while thirteen had successfully completed the course in a *gymnazium*. On the other hand, 329 of the officers possessed a level of education either lower than the secondary level or of the uncertain quality of home instruction. The remaining fifty-one officers in the division had been commissioned from the ranks, and the odds were that their education was almost rudimentary, if they had any at all.[18]

In later issues of the *Voennyi Sbornik* this question was challenged and debated.[19] One detractor felt that the sample was too small for any valid conclusions and that the author had not given proper weight to those who had enrolled in a *gymnazium* course without completing it. Moreover, the conditions were abnormal since the Crimean War had demanded a rapid expansion of the armed forces and there had been a general lowering of standards. Another writer, one N. Maslov, upheld the essence of the original thesis. Reviewing the various arguments, he affirmed that the educational level of the officer corps was indeed very low and that the dilution of standards by the war emergency was offset by the fact the war had also brought into the officer ranks many individuals who had completed higher institutions of learning in roughly the same proportion as in peacetime.[20]

17. *Ibid.*, p. 148.
18. *Ibid.*, p. 149. Those officers who were commissioned from the ranks were often referred to as being "from the Bourbons." Possibly this was reference back to the French emigre officers who served in the Russian army during the French Revolution and who represented an alien element in the officer corps.
19. There were several opposing views, including: S.V-skii, "Ob ofitserov armeiskikh pekhotnykh polkov, po povodu stat'i pomeshchenoi v 'Voennom Sbornike' za 1858 god: 'Stepen' obrazovaniia ofitserov v armii,' L.K.," *Voennyi Sbornik*, No. 10 (1859); M. Apolev, "Neskol'ko myslei po povodu stat'i pomesh-chennoi v No. 10 'Voennogo Sbornika' za 1859 god, pod zaglaviem: 'Ob armeiskish pekhotnykh ofitserakh'," *Voennyi Sbornik*, No. 5 (1860); and, P.Ch-ov, "Neskol'ko slov na stat'iu g. M.Apoleva," *Voennyi Sbornik*, No. 8 (1861).
20. N. Maslov, "Iunkerskie shkoly v armii," *Voennyi Sbornik*, No. 6 (1861), especially p. 379.

A later investigation, taking a larger sample, generally confirmed these findings. This study used statistics drawn from the Guards and Grenadiers Corps along with several army corps and special units, constituting a sample that would tend to have a larger proportion of better educated officers than the armed forces as a whole. The backgrounds of 12,652 officers who were on active duty on January 1, 1861, were investigated in the inquiry. The proportion of officers in this sample, because of the inclusion of the Guards and the artillery, who had completed their studies in the cadet corps was quite high at 32.6 percent.[21] The bulk of the officers had entered the army as junkers or volunteers,[22] making up 65.5 percent of the total. About 5.8 percent of the latter group had been among the conscripts and had come up from the ranks.[23]

The over-all results were similar to those of the earlier study. As few as 4.5 percent of those commissioned from among the junkers and volunteers had completed a secondary or higher school. Only 15.3 percent of this same group had even studied at a secondary school, while the remaining 84.7 percent had only an elementary education or home instruction.[24] Those coming from among the gentry tended to be somewhat better educated than those from other orders of society, undoubtedly because of their greater affluence as a class and the tendency of state-supported schools to favor them by the offer of government sub-

21. About 90.7 percent of the officers in the artillery brigades were drawn from the cadet corps. See, Il'iashevich, "Chisloviia danniia o sostave korpusa ofitserov nashei armii po vospitaniiu i soslovam," *Voennyi Sbornik*, No. 11 (1863), p. 241.

22. Junkers were the sons of hereditary nobles who entered the army as noncommissioned officers with the privilege of becoming officers after two years of active service and the successful passage of an examination. The system, as its name implies, had its roots in the Prussian custom. See in this regard, Kark Demeter, *Das Deutsche Offizierkorps in seine historisch-sozialogischen Grundlagen*. The volunteers could also become officers after passing an examination, but they had to wait for longer periods of time, depending upon their particular category. The first category included the sons of personal nobles, priests, upper guild merchants, etc., and had the privilege of becoming officers after four years of service. Those in the second category, which included the sons of merchants, townsmen, nonnoble foreigners, etc., became eligible after six years of service, while those in the third category which included those elements of society liable to conscription had to wait for twelve years.

23. Il'iashevich, "Chisloviia danniia o sostave korpusa ofitserov nashei armii po vospitaniiu i soslovam," *Voennyi Sbornik*, No. 11 (1863), p. 238.

24. *Ibid.*, p. 246.

sidies. The army did not particularly suffer from this situation because from 85 to 95 percent of the officer corps was drawn from among the gentry.[25]

Miliutin was very early aware of the weaknesses in the education and training of the Russian officer corps. His own experience as a junker had been more than enough to demonstrate to him the lack of relevance of the training given to future officers. While still a young officer he marked the lacklustre and narrow pedantry of his fellow officers and noted in his diary that this was without doubt a consequence of the narrowness of their training:

> Our officers are trained just like parrots; prior to commissioning they are kept in a cage and incessantly plagued with: "Polly, Left turn, march!," and Polly repeats: "Left turn, March!" "Polly, Present arms!" and Polly repeats it. When Polly gets to the stage that he remembers all of these words, besides learning to be held by one claw, they give him epaulets, open the cage, and he joyfully leaves it with hate toward it and his former teachers. . . .[26]

There is no reason to suspect that Miliutin's views changed substantially in the twenty years between his writing this and his becoming War Minister. His distaste for pedantic formalism remained with him throughout his life.

The question of training a competent officer corps was broached very soon after Miliutin became the Minister of War. He introduced his ideas on the subject to the Emperor in his report of January 15, 1862, and amplified them in a memorandum submitted a few weeks later on February 10, 1862. He recognized that an effective military force was absolutely dependent upon the success of education:

> The improvement of the army is based for the most part upon the education of individuals, their character, and upon the development of their natural talents, not only physical, but also intellectual.[27]

His views were predicated upon the assumption that an army or any other organization was only as good as the men who composed it. Therefore, the one thing that the army needed most was the means for providing

---

25. *Ibid.*, p. 248. Cf. "K istorii voenno-uchebnoi reformy imperatora Aleksandra II," *Russkaia Starina*, No. 5 (1887), p. 356.

26. *Dnevnik*, I., 27.

27. *Doklad* (January 15, 1862), p. 92. Cf. N. Zherve, *Graf D. A. Miliutin*, p. 2.

educated and mature professional officers who could work freely together within the framework of military discipline.

Miliutin noted the changes that had taken place in the nature of warfare during the preceding half-century and recognized that commensurate changes had to be made in the training of soldiers. Forces in the field more than ever had to be capable of operating independently and with maximum resourcefulness. The long night that was the reign of Nicholas I had instilled a fatal malaise in the spirit of the Russian officer. A new spirit had to be generated, and this could only come from proper leadership:

> In the military art there are two aspects; material and moral. Troops are not merely physical forces, a mass serving as the instrument for military operations, but they are human beings endowed with intelligence and warmth. Moral force plays an important role in every consideration and calculation of the commander and, consequently, it is insufficient for the latter only to control the army as a machine; he must know how to control a man, how to bind a soldier to himself and how to fortify his conventional power over the soldier with his own moral strength.[28]

Yet the officer needed more than his own moral power over the soldier. He needed practical knowledge conforming to actual conditions and needs; he needed technical competence. Miliutin was an ardent exponent of the value of training young officers in a manner making them capable of acting in real situations and enabling them to improvise. Dry pedantry and abstract theory were among the sources of past failure. To Miliutin, it seemed

> that the insufficient practicality and the predominance of theoretical training constitutes a weak aspect of our Russian education in all fields; all our special educational institutions are guilty in that they are more concerned with broad scholarly training than with the preparation of expert practitioners.[29]

Miliutin, himself a successful historian, was not opposed to the value of a theoretical education, but he felt that the greatest need of Russian society in general and the army in particular was for people capable of fulfilling routine tasks. Miliutin's later spirited defense of the *Realschulen* was based upon the same premise—that Russia's needs were

28. P. A. Zaionchkovskii, *Voennye reformy 1860–1870 v Rossii*, pp. 49–50.
29. *Ibid.*, p. 237.

for competent officials, technicians, and teachers, not for impractical theoreticians.

In his report of January 15, 1862, to the Emperor, Miliutin suggested that a special committee be appointed to draft a comprehensive program for the junker schools since the bulk of the officer corps was being drawn from the junkers and volunteers. He pointed out that whatever was devised, it could not be allowed to impose any further financial burdens upon the resources of the state. As a model for what he had in mind, he singled out the junker school in Helsinki, Finland. This institution was the only truly comprehensive junker school in the Empire, in that it bridged the functions of both the cadet corps and the training of junkers. The school admitted junkers from the army division stationed there and also accepted the sons of Russian and Finnish functionaries employed in Finland.[30] If Miliutin's statement is interpreted correctly, it may be that his original plan was to merge the functions of the cadet corps into a comprehensive system of junker schools, thereby liquidating the cadet corps altogether. He cited the high degree of success already achieved by some of the temporary junker schools created before he came into office, particularly those in the First and Fourth Corps, and recommended the creation of schools of this type on a permanent basis throughout the army.

Miliutin became more explicit in his views on the question of military education in the special memorandum he submitted to the Emperor on February 10, 1862. He opened his statement with the observation that

In the past few years, the opinion has been very strongly expressed that the military institutions of education, in their present form, do not conform to the current requirements for a valid distribution in the nature of education, both *general* and *military*, and they do not satisfy even their own special purpose.[31]

Nothing short of sweeping reform would suffice in the field of military education. First, he noted, it was necessary to examine the precise contributions made to the state by the military schools and the use made of the appropriations for training officers.

In doing this, Miliutin placed the cadet corps under heavy attack on

30. *Doklad*, January 15, 1862, pp. 94–95.
31. *Stoletie*, X., Part III, 188. The memorandum by Miliutin is reproduced in its entirety.

grounds both of economy and efficiency. The cadet corps were an expensive luxury. The state treasury appropriated in 1860, for example, 3,353,749 silver rubles, and another 1,019,510 silver rubles came from other sources (largely income from investments), making a total of 4,372,601 rubles. The subsidy for the maintenance of buildings and other income pushed the total cost of the cadet corps for 1860 up to an enormous 5,352,662 silver rubles.[32] When drafting this memorandum, Miliutin had not yet received complete figures for the year 1862, but the best estimates were that they would reach a total of 4,712,000 silver rubles.

Next to this budget sheet, Miliutin pointed out the relatively insignificant returns from the cadet corps.[33] Taking as examples the two years, 1860 and 1861, he computed the number of graduates for each year and noted where they went after their graduation:

Destination of graduates	In 1860	In 1861	Avg. for the two years
Into the Guards, Artillery, Sappers and Army	411	546	478
Into the Cossack Forces	2	29	15
Into the Line Battalions and the Corps of the Domestic Watch	84	119	101
Into the Civil Service	9	25	17
	506	719	612[34]

Miliutin therefore reasoned that if an average of 612 men finished the course in the cadet corps each year at an average annual cost of 4,712,000 rubles, then the average cost per man was 7,700 rubles, surely an exorbitant investment in an individual. But even this figure was misleading. Not all those completing the course in a cadet corps actually entered the army. Some, as indicated in the table above, went into the civil service, the Domestic Watch, etc. This, to Miliutin, was another indication that the corps were not fulfilling their purpose of providing the

32. *Ibid., loc. cit.*

33. Miliutin demonstrated clearly that costs had already been cut by half in the four years before he became War Minister. This had been achieved by reducing the number of students on state subsidies. *Ibid.,* p. 189*n.*

34. *Ibid.,* p. 189.

army with officers. The graduates of the cadet corps who actually entered the army, in the estimation of the War Minister, actually cost the army 9,538 rubles apiece.

Nor was this the end of their cost. If they were posted to serve in one or another of the special branches of service, they still had to attend one of the professional academies to acquire the necessary specialized training. The matriculation of these officers into one or another of the academies meant that they were lost for a time from active service, further pushing up the cost of officers entering active service from 12,000 to 13,000 rubles.[35] In addition, a disproportionately large part of the cadet corps were siphoned off into the elite units, so that there were entire regiments in the regular army with only two or three officers, out of a normal complement of sixty, who had received their education in a cadet corps.[36]

But the high costs were only one aspect of the problem. Miliutin noted that those who had completed their education in the cadet corps were usually deficient in their level of knowledge and tended to have an entirely false sense of reality. Their quality, therefore, in no way justified the expenditures. Commenting on this aspect of the problem in July 1862, Miliutin wrote,

The cadet corps and the Sharpshooters' School, just as the three academies, have in the course of the last year graduated into the forces a group of young officers with such a false and noxious attitude that their evil influence, according to the declarations of all the top commanders, is sown among the troops, especially in the special branches of the service, with the exception of the cavalry.[37]

In addition to the general question of morale, such deficiencies adversely affected the initial period of an officer's service, there being "quite an ignorance of military custom, discipline, and the duties of an officer."[38]

35. The Institutions of Military Education cost the government each year roughly the same amount as that spent for all civilian schools while continuing to meet, at the most generous estimate, from one quarter to one third of the army's needs. See "1863 dlia russkoi armii: Preobrazovaniia v voenno-uchebnykh zavedeniiakh," *Russkii Invalid*, No. 116 (1864).

36. "K istorii voenno-uchebnoi reformy imperatora Aleksandra II-go," *Russkaia Starina*, No. 5 (1887), p. 356. Cf. L. K., "Vzgliad' na stepen' obrazovaniia russkish ofitserov v armii, *Voennyi Sbornik*, No. 1 (1858), p. 147, and, "Komplektovanie ofitserami russkoi armii," *Russkii Invalid*, No. 81 (1863).

37. P. A. Zaionchkovskii, *Voennye reformy 1860–1870 godov v Rossii* (Moscow, 1952), p. 222.

38. *Stoletie*, X., Part III, 190–191.

The army had to undertake the basic instruction of these officers after they were already commissioned.

The War Minister declared that the young officers had not yet developed sufficient independence of character and were thus unable to make mature decisions. Quite on the contrary, rather than becoming reliable aides or troop leaders, they were in need of tutors themselves. In the light of this, Miliutin noted that of late the greater part of the troop commanders had begun to show a definite preference for officers drawn from among the junkers, because they were more practical and were more accustomed to the actual conditions of military life.

The unsatisfactory results were not attributable to any single event or individual. Miliutin held that the fault lay with the nature of the system itself and with the structure of the cadet corps. While it was assumed that the basic purpose of the corps was to train officers for the army, they had another, more subtle aim—that of providing the means for educating the sons of those individuals who either were or had been serving the state and of those gentry who did not possess the resources to send their offspring to school. Miliutin admitted that this was most charitable, but he felt that the manner in which the latter motive contributed to the fulfillment of the primary task of training officers was worthy of a close scrutiny and, perhaps, a complete reappraisal.

Miliutin also questioned the pedagogical soundness of the curriculum of the cadet corps and the length of the course. More specifically, he was concerned about the desirability of educating children in military schools:

> For young people already developed physically and morally, it is quite easy to make themselves acquainted with the specialty of military matters, especially for those who are inclined toward that vocation. Within two or three years, they are able to assimilate all basic military knowledge. The cadet corps prepare their charges for officer status over a period of seven to eight years, while in the Alexandrovskii Corps for those of especially young ages, some have been preparing for sixteen years or more.[39]

Miliutin had grave doubts about the soundness of this practice:

> Is it not reputed that this long-term training in the cadet corps is fundamentally to acquaint the cadet with his future duties? But it is never really possible to acquaint him with his duty outside of actual service. How do you

39. *Ibid.*, pp. 191–192.

explain his future to a cadet when he does not yet have an understanding either of soldiers or of a soldier's life?[40]

The pedagogical argument supporting the system of long-term military education from childhood was that it formed in the young a character which later conformed to the needs of military service. A former cadet was supposed to take more readily to military discipline because he had had such training since his tender years. Miliutin pointed out that even if the theory were valid it was impossible to get the kind of instructors that would make of the dream a reality.

Miliutin argued that "Discipline is the foundation of military service; it inescapably must be the basis of military training."[41] He believed that discipline would invigorate a mature person but that it would stultify an individual whose character had not yet begun to develop. The War Minister hypothesized that a strict application of discipline to the training of children would lead to one of two things. Either the students would develop a spartan notion of morality and would be encouraged to be crafty or treacherous, to brawl, to steal, or the development of an independent character in children was, to Miliutin, quite impossible. Neither one purpose nor the other would be served.

The War Minister noted another, lesser flaw in the cadet corps. This was the failure of the corps to teach the cadets to conduct themselves in life. The boys lived a completely sheltered life, and when they left they were totally lost, knowing neither how to deport themselves nor how to live within their incomes.

Miliutin then turned to the proposal of some concrete solutions to these problems. Some steps, he noted, had already been taken by the cadet corps themselves, particularly in respect to educating the very young. A system of day schools had been instituted and materials for home study had been distributed, allowing the smaller boys to live at home and remain under the influence of their own families. This provided a primary education for those too young to benefit from the regular training in the cadet corps, and while not without merit it was insufficient to solve any basic problem. Miliutin proposed, first, that the general education of boys be handled either at home or at civilian institutions.

40. *Ibid.*, p. 192.
41. *Ibid.*, *loc. cit.*

Military schools had only one reason for existence and that was to provide professional training for those young men who felt themselves called to a military career. Secondly, he noted that the cadet corps could not provide enough graduates to satisfy the needs of the army so he turned elsewhere:

> The primary material for the training of officers must be the junkers accepted for service upon the completion of their education at home or in some kind of civilian institution, and upon their passing an examination in the general sciences, no lower than the level of the *gymnazium* course.[42]

Miliutin's proposals were revolutionary. They expressed the hope that the army could dispense with the burden of providing a general education for the sons of the gentry and of government officials. Moreover, he recommended the employment of the junker schools of the type already functioning within some units of the armed forces as the basic institution for the training of officers. By ridding itself of the problem of general education, the army could devote itself to providing professional education to aspirants already possessing a general education.

The key to Miliutin's program was the role to be given to the junker schools. The idea behind the establishment of junker schools in Russia was usually attributed to Rüdiger, who had in 1822 or 1823 submitted a memorandum on the subject to General Diebitsch. He recommended that those junkers who were presently preparing for their officers' examinations be assembled at their respective corps or army headquarters

---

42. *Ibid.*, p. 194. This scheme suggests the general direction of Miliutin's thinking on the military schools with one important deletion. An article appearing three years later in the *Russkii Invalid* and which most certainly reflected the thinking of the War Minister, suggested that class privilege was a handicap for the War Ministry in procuring properly qualified officers:

> Theoretically the best method of preparing officers should be without class distinction, with sufficient general education, and as a consequence there would be achieved a specialized military sophistication in the firm union of theory and practice. The obligation to the state and expenditures would be small.

The article then went on to note, however, that this was not possible within the context of Russian history and that the gentry role as a service nobility had to continue to be observed. The gentry on their part had to fit themselves for that role by acquiring an adequate general educational background. See "1863 god dlia russkoi armii: Preobrazovaniia v voenno-uchebnykh zavedeniakh," *Russkii Invalid*, No. 116 (1864).

and there receive instruction in basic academic and military subjects.[43] As a consequence, such schools soon appeared in several units of the army, particularly in the headquarters of the First and Second Armies, and in the Fourth and Fifth Corps. These schools lasted for several years until the wars with Turkey and Poland at the end of the decade forced the army to redeploy, at which time the schools were closed.

One of the schools was at Mogilev, the headquarters of the First Army. It was open only to the members of the gentry class serving as noncommissioned officers, thereby excluding those who were sons of officers and volunteers. An average of 120 were enrolled at any one time, and while at the school they were organized into a company made up of four platoons. For academic purposes, the school was under the jurisdiction of the Institutions of Military Instruction, but its effective supervisor was the Chief of Staff of the First Army.[44] This school set for itself the goal of training officers capable of going on to more advanced studies in preparation for duty in the General Staff or the artillery. The two-year program was divided into two classes with basically military subjects: tactics, fortifications, topography, and the like. The only academic subjects were mathematics and the Russian language, both professionally useful for officers. The hours of instruction were exceedingly long and the methods were pedantic.[45] The courses continued on a year-around basis with the pressure on the students letting up only a few days before they were to take their final examinations. Those achieving the highest scores were commissioned immediately and posted to more advanced schools. Graduates with lower scores returned to their own units to await vacancies before being advanced to officer rank. Students who failed went through the course again.[46]

Despite the narrowness of its curriculum, the school succeeded in producing adequately trained officers at a very modest cost. The annual budget for the Mogilev school was only 15,291 assignat rubles, and the

43. P. Bobrovskii, "Ob uchrezhdenii iunkerskikh uchilishch," *Voennyi Sbornik*, No. 11 (1864), p. 92. The Prussians again furnished the prototypes for this system. Junker schools were founded at the several divisional headquarters and subsequently became associated with the city or town in which they were located.
44. *Ibid.*, p. 95.
45. *Ibid.*, pp. 96–97.
46. *Ibid.*, p. 98.

average cost of each officer graduated from the program was 128 rubles, of which 54 rubles was the expense of feeding him.[47]

The Junker School of the Second Army was of a somewhat different character. It aimed at providing the student with a more general education. The students were not so well prepared and the requirements for admission were necessarily quite low. The candidate needed only to know how to read and write the Russian language and to be in good health and of good moral character.[48] The curriculum included general as well as military subjects, and the students were divided into three classes instead of two as in the First Army. In order for the junkers to proceed from one class to the next, they had to pass annual examinations.[49] Officers trained in this school were not posted to the more elite units, as were those from the Mogilev school, but were routinely returned to their own units to await vacancies.

The costs of training officers in the Second Army Junker School was even more modest than in the First Army. The annual budget was only 8,860 assignat rubles, with each graduate costing 99 rubles, $33^1/_3$ kopecks.[50] The other junker schools were similar in nature to this one and also operated on very small budgets. But since all of them were located at the headquarters of tactical units, they were always forced to shut down when some emergency caused the army to redeploy. During the thirties and forties the schools were only briefly revived in the Fourth and Fifth Corps. But they had demonstrated what could be done with very little money, and they served as models for the future.

The poor performance and obvious failings of the officer corps during the Crimean War reopened the question of their existence. Field commanders began to open junker schools within their own units and such people as Rüdiger suggested to the War Minister and to the Emperor that a comprehensive system of junker schools be instituted within the armed forces. Prince M. D. Gorchakov, the commander of the First Army during the war, asked the Emperor in a memorandum drafted even before the cessation of hostilities to open two categories of schools,

47. *Ibid.*, p. 99.
48. *Ibid.*, p. 101.
49. *Ibid.*, p. 102.
50. *Ibid.*, p. 104. This figure did not include the cost of maintaining the junker.

each with a one-year course. The first type was to be a regimental junker school to make up for deficiencies in the junker's general education, and the second would be schools at the divisional level, open to those completing a regimental school or possessing a secondary education.[51]

Other experienced field commanders, such as Rüdiger, A. N. Lüders and P. A. Dannenberg, looked to the earlier junker schools as models. So great was their confidence in them that they were willing to see the successful completion of the course in such a school as the sole criterion for commissioning junkers and volunteers. Apparently their views ran counter to a significant proportion of the officer corps who saw in such a system an abridgement of their class privileges.[52] The Crimean War in this case was, however, too powerful a catalyst, and questions of class privilege had to give way.

Rüdiger raised the question with Alexander II immediately upon his accession to the throne.[53] He noted the poor quality of the officer corps and proposed the establishment of junker schools in the various corps headquarters as well as in certain divisions (those in Orenburg, Siberia, and Finland and in the seven cavalry divisions). The program as Rüdiger saw it would comprise eight cavalry and eleven infantry schools which could enroll a total of about 3,000 junkers and volunteers. In effect, he was asking for the comprehensive implementation of junker schools like those that had existed before 1830.[54]

To be eligible for admission to one of these schools, a junker had to pass an entrance examination and then serve two months in a regular regiment to receive basic training. The course in the school would be for two years and would be designed to provide the junker with both general and professional training. He would study the Russian language, mathematics (including elementary algebra and geometry), history, and geography. In addition, the junker would attend classes in tactics, the use of weapons, fortifications, and other military skills. After the annual ex-

51. "K istorii voenno-uchebnoi reformy imperatora Aleksandra II," *Russkaia Starina*, No. 5 (1887), p. 363.
52. *Ibid.*, p. 359.
53. The memorandum was dated March 28, 1855.
54. P. O. Bobrovskii, "Ob uchrezhdenii iunkerskikh uchilishch," *Voennyi Sbornik*, No. 11 (1864), p. 111.

aminations each May, the junkers would be posted back to their regiments for summer field exercises. Those who successfully completed the senior class should, in Rüdiger's opinion, be commissioned whether or not they had completed their terms of service according to their individual class privilege.[55] He estimated the annual cost of training 3,000 junkers at 180,330 rubles.[56]

Alexander approved Rüdiger's proposals and appointed a committee under the latter's chairmanship to work out the details. Included as a member of this committee was Major General of His Majesty's Own Suite Dmitrii Alexeevich Miliutin.[57] Rüdiger died soon afterward, but the committee carried on after his death and submitted its report to the Emperor who approved them on May 1, 1856.[58] But with the end of the war and the death of Rüdiger the momentum of the project was lost, and when Miliutin departed for the Caucasus the prospects for the reform suffered another blow. Despite this, the recommendations of the committee were submitted to the War Ministry in May 1857 and were discussed in the War Council. This body found the program to be sound and appropriated 200,000 rubles for its implementation.[59]

But the junker school system proposed by the Rüdiger committee suffered from too many defects. One of the most important was that the schools were to be established at the headquarters of tactical units, which meant that they would face dissolution with every crisis demanding the mobilization of the army. Also, the concept of class privilege inhibited the establishment of the successful completion of the course in a junker school as the sole criterion for commissioning officers. So long as legal differences existed among the classes, graduation from a junker school would have a difficult time over-riding the specific privileges accorded to any particular group.

Perhaps more basic than either of these issues was the question of money. The War Council, noting the straitened circumstances of the

55. *Ibid.*, p. 112.
56. *Ibid.*, p. 113.
57. *Ibid.*, 111*n*.
58. *Ibid.*, 113*n*.
59. "K istorii voenno-uchebnoi reformy imperatora Aleksandra II," *Russkaia Starina*, No. 5 (1887), p. 351.

budget, came to the conclusion that the sums needed for implementing the program were not available at that time.[60] The fiscal distress proved decisive. The project was not dropped but was suspended, and the matter lay in limbo until Miliutin became the Minister of War.

But even if the War Ministry was unable to establish a comprehensive school system, some of the field commanders did create them within their own units. The Commander of the Second Army during the Crimean War, General Lüders, gave oral instructions to the commander of the Fourth Corps, General-of-Cavalry Hilfreich, to establish at his headquarters in Voronezh a school for the training of junkers. Lüders was clearly motivated by his own experiences as a combat commander and perhaps felt that at least part of the disaster of the Crimean War might have been averted had Russia possessed a better trained officer corps. He wanted each regiment within the corps to send to the school ten or twelve junkers with only a year or two remaining before being commissioned. Each junker would be equipped by his own regiment while the divisions would supply drill officers as well as cooks, tailors, cobblers, carpenters, and orderlies.[61]

The school in Voronezh opened its doors on August 10, 1856. The junkers were selected by the regimental commanders and included besides members of the gentry, volunteers of the first and second categories (that is, the sons of nonnoble families with the right to be commissioned after four and six years, respectively). The appointment of all of these junkers was contingent upon their having passed the examination for officer's rank (an examination instituted by Nicholas I on May 6, 1844, and referred to by that date), and upon the demonstration of good moral character.

The initial contingents of junkers represented a wide variety of educational backgrounds, distinguished chiefly by their meagreness. Figures for the academic year 1861–1862 graphically illustrate just how low this level was. Of those enrolled during that year, 24.7 percent had enrolled in but had not completed the course in a *gymnazium*. A very small group had gone only to a district primary school and most of these

60. P. O. Bobrovskii, *Voennyi Sbornik*, No. 11 (1864), p. 114.

61. P. Bobrovskii, "Uchilishche podpraporshchikov byvshee v Voronezhe s 1856 po 1863 god," *Voennyi Sbornik*, No. 7 (1864), p. 156.

had completed only the second or third grade. An even smaller proportion was reasonably well educated, a very few having completed the course in a seminary. The primary schools of the War Ministry had provided another 5.55 percent with an elementary education, and another 18.52 percent had been enrolled in a cadet corps but had been dismissed either for obesity or for some offense. But this generally gloomy picture was of the better educated junkers. The majority had for the most part received only a home education, which meant that the education of the bulk of them was very limited indeed.[62]

But if the academic backgrounds of the junkers was poor, it was in part offset by the fact that they all had already spent some time on active service as noncommissioned officers. They therefore had a first-hand knowledge of a soldier's life and of military custom, and some even had had combat experience.[63] This allowed the schools to devote a greater part of their time to giving the junkers a better general education.

The academic year in the Voronezh School ran from the beginning of September to the first of July with annual examinations held during June and mid-year examinations taking place in December. The course was two years in length and was divided into two classes: junior and senior. Those students who possessed better academic preparation and those who had successfully completed the junior class were admitted into the senior class. The curriculum was originally intended to include the same courses in both classes, with the exception of topography which would be taught only in the second year.[64]

Religion occupied a prominent place in the curriculum. The Empire placed great stress on the moral training of youth, and the junker schools were no exception. Moral regeneration lay at the heart of the plan for the revival of the efficiency of the officer corps. The students studied intensively the meaning of daily devotions as well as the history of the Orthodox Church. The low level of literacy caused the schools to offer an intensive program in the study of the Russian language. Exercises in reading, writing, and grammar received great emphasis. The curriculum

62. *Ibid.*, p. 161, and, N. Maslov, "Iunkerskiia shkoly v armii," *Voennyi Sbornik*, No. 6 (1861), p. 384.
63. P. Bobrovskii, *Voennyi Sbornik*, No. 7 (1864), p. 158.
64. *Ibid.*, p. 159.

was rounded out by courses in mathematics (including arithmetic and simplified programs in algebra, geometry, and trigonometry), fortifications, tactics, topography, and gunnery.[65]

In addition to these academic and military subjects, the school also offered courses in law and government, including such matters as civil and military law, military court procedure, the structure of the War Ministry and of the military administration, and the army order-of-battle. The history of all ages was an integral part of the curriculum as was geography, but the poor preparation of the students imposed severe limitations upon the scope of these subjects and Russian history came to be emphasized at the expense of other areas. Other adjustments had to be made to compensate for the poor academic backgrounds of the junkers. The courses in law, gunnery, and fortifications had to be limited to the senior class, while geography was studied only in the junior class.[66] The programs in the Russian language and in mathematics were more highly stressed, since the mastery of these subjects was the basis for all other studies.

Because of the low level of their preparation, the failure rate among the junkers was high. But during the seven years of its existence, the school graduated 219 junkers. All this was accomplished at a modest cost. The Fourth Corps expended annually a sum of 12,724 rubles on the school, with the average cost per junker being at the most about 300 rubles.[67] The lesson that this experience taught was that 300,000 rubles a year should be sufficient to guarantee the army at least 1,000 well-trained officers annually. This would materially assist the bridging of the gap between the army's needs and the inadequate system of Russian education.

The school at Voronezh was not the only junker school to appear after the Crimean War. It served as the living model for the establishment of several similar institutions.[68] Among the first to imitate the Fourth

65. *Ibid.*, p. 160.
66. *Ibid.*, p. 161.
67. *Ibid.*, p. 178. For an incomplete study of the expenses of the school during 1859, see the letter of Major General A. I. Del'vig in N. Maslov, "Iunkerskiia shkoly v armii," *Voennyi Sbornik*, No. 6 (1861), p. 386.
68. For a list of other units requesting information concerning the school at Voronezh, see, P. Bobrovskii, *Voennyi Sbornik*, No. 7 (1864), p. 158n.

Corps' example was the Independent Grenadier Corps which founded several temporary schools at the divisional level but offering a similar program of study. In 1859, the Eleventh Infantry Division, a part of the Fourth Corps, established a preparatory school for junkers aspiring to go to the school at Voronezh. On January 1, 1860, the headquarters staff of the Third Corps at Zhitomir opened its own junker school with a curriculum resembling that at Voronezh and with much the same results, with the exception that the Zhitomir students were apparently a little better prepared and were able to handle a slightly more sophisticated program.[69]

In September 1860, the Independent Siberian Corps started some temporary junker classes at Tobolsk with a rather elementary program of study.[70] The following month saw the Second Corps open its own school at Warsaw with a complement of 200 students. This latter school offered a comprehensive program which included, in addition to the usual subjects, military communications, military administration, and the comparison of Russian military practices with those abroad. The course was pitched at a sufficiently high level that its graduates could hope to pass the examinations admitting them to study at the Nikolaevskii Academy of the General Staff. The annual budget of the Warsaw school was 16,287 rubles, 96³/₄ kopecks, of which 13,420 rubles were granted to the school out of the budget of the War Ministry,[71] which by this time was capable of lending some modest financial support to the junker schools.

This pattern of tactical units establishing their own junker schools continued with the establishment by the First Corps of its own school at Vilno in January 1861. This institution, also modeled on the school at Voronezh, was designed to accommodate two hundred junkers at an annual cost of 13,420 rubles. But, this school never got off the ground. No sooner had it assembled one hundred students for its first class than, in April 1861, the corps mobilized because of the growing tensions in Poland, and the school was forced to disband.[72] In the late summer of the

69. "Shkoly i uchebnyia komandy v armii," *Voennyi Sbornik*, No. 6 (1862), pp. 349–360.

70. *Ibid.*, p. 362.

71. *Ibid.*, pp. 347–349.

72. *Ibid.*, pp. 345–346.

same year, the War Ministry reformed the military school (*voennaia shkola*) at Helsinki into a junker school. After its reform, it functioned not only as a junker school for the Twenty-Second Infantry Division deployed in Finland but also fulfilled some of the obligations normally discharged by a cadet corps. It accepted as students the sons of Finns or Russians who were in either the civil or military service within the Grand Duchy, thereby providing these functionaries with the same fringe benefits enjoyed by officers and civil servants elsewhere in the Empire. Since many of the junkers in this school were not of Russian origin and few schools in Finland taught in the Russian language, extraordinary attention was paid in this school to the teaching of Russian.[73]

The War Ministry itself, while providing a minimum of help and leadership in the creation of these junker schools, did try to insure that minimum standards were maintained. In one case, for example, the Ministry issued an order (No. 131, June 1, 1860) in which the War Minister specifically forbad the commissioning of any junker or volunteer who had not first passed the examination according to the formula of May 6, 1844. Moreover, he ordered that those junkers who were awaiting vacancies in their regiments before becoming officers be commissioned in an order of preference based upon their examination scores. This injunction placed a premium on attendance at a junker school by forcing those with deficient preparation to achieve a minimum standard if they expected to become officers.[74]

Therefore, by the time that Miliutin became Minister of War, the armed forces themselves had already begun the creation of their own junker schools while the question lay relatively dormant within the Ministry. The one large unsolved problem was that of providing continuity for the schools, since each was located within a tactical unit and any mobilization or redeployment of the army necessitated their being disbanded. It was left to Miliutin to assure their permanent integration into the armed forces, and, perhaps more important, it was left to the War Minister to define the precise role the junker schools were to play.

73. *Ibid.*, pp. 364–365. Cf. *Doklad* (January, 15, 1862), p. 95.
74. N. Maslov, "Iunkerskiia shkoly v armii," *Voennyi Sbornik*, No. 6 (1861), pp. 380–381. It should be remembered that N. O. Sukhozanet was still War Minister at this time.

The system had already demonstrated its viability and particularly its capacity to perform efficiently with quite limited fiscal resources.

On the basis of his own thinking and the experience of those schools already in operation, Miliutin made a number of suggestions concerning the curriculum of the junker schools. He, above all, wanted the junkers to have a practical acquaintanceship with all the requirements and conditions of actual military service, as well as a mastery of all the necessary academic skills. Upon the completion of his course of training, each junker would be required to pass an examination qualifying him as an officer in his particular branch of service. Those receiving commissions in the infantry or cavalry were to be posted immediately to active duty, while junkers who became officers in the artillery, or sappers, were to continue their training, as officers, in the academy appropriate to their specialty. This advanced training was to last from one to three years. There would also be extended to all officers who completed four years of active service an opportunity to attend the Nikolaevskii Academy of the General Staff.

Miliutin also addressed himself to the problem that had plagued the junker schools of the past: the necessity to disband in the event of mobilization. This would be solved easily by taking the schools out of the headquarters of tactical units and locating them instead at the headquarters of the new military district administrations. Since the latter remained unaffected by the mobilization of the active army, the presence of the schools within them would guarantee their continuity, even in wartime. The size of each military district junker school would be governed by the number of troops deployed within that particular district.

The War Minister accepted the general program which had proven its value in the earlier junker schools. The course of studies would be two years, with the academic year beginning the first of October and continuing until April or May. The junkers would spend the other five or six months on active field service with their own tactical units. The internal structure of the junker schools would be organized along strict military lines in accordance with practice in the active forces. The course was to be subordinated to the one goal of providing professional military training within an atmosphere duplicating as closely as possible regular service.

Miliutin calculated that if the cost of educating one junker was 71 silver rubles per year, then the total cost for 3,000 junkers would not exceed 700,000 to 800,000 rubles per year. The advantages of the junker school system over the cadet corps were several:

(1) The successful provision of the army with officers trained and adapted to its needs, of which the junker schools would annually produce 1,500.

(2) The provision of those officers for the army at a comparably small outlay for the state, inasmuch as it would obtain them for 800,000 instead of 3,832,000 silver rubles.

(3) The possibility to develop out of these savings the means for public education by reforming the cadet corps into *gymnazii* or *realschulen*, and as a consequence restore a more normal proportion to the allotment of the means of the state to general education rather than to specialized military education.

(4) The possibility of distributing the charitableness of the state to an incomparably larger number of the needy. . . . Inasmuch as there are now in that number who do receive an education 7,641 (this represents the average of the two years, 1860 and 1861), it would be possible with the most generous subsidies (up to 200 rubles per person) to guarantee an education to 19,160 people.[75]

Miliutin's object at this stage seems to have been nothing less than the complete destruction of the cadet corps. The savings accrued from this would provide all the necessary funds for the development of the junker school system and would also be sufficient to endow a far more ambitious system of general education to be founded on the remains of the old cadet corps. The army could get out of the business of running a general school system; it could at the same time be assured of sufficient numbers of adequately trained officers, and the nagging problem of general civilian education would receive a shot in the arm.

But any reform usually strikes at vested interests. Those people who were used to having their sons educated in the cadet corps and at the expense of the state were bound to resist. The same could be said of officers who had been educated in the cadet corps and who were able to bring all the vehemence of alumni to bear on any suggestion that their old school was bound for the dust heap. On the other hand, the field

75. *Stoletie*, X., Part III., 195.

commanders who had practical experience with the inadequately trained officers coming out of the cadet corps were likely to support the War Minister. In order to insure the success of his plan, Miliutin needed, however, to round up more support, particularly from people in high places.

Miliutin found one such supporter in General-Adjutant Count S. G. Stroganov, a Senator and member of the State Council. Stroganov's memorandum, which he submitted to the Emperor, was both diffuse and moralistic and was couched in heavy prose.[76] But despite his faults of style, he seconded many of Miliutin's proposals. Recognizing that the basic task of the military schools was to provide a military education for those who expected to become officers, Stroganov was indignant over the secondary task of educating the children of impoverished gentry.[77] This, to his mind, constituted a pernicious influence upon Russian family life. He argued that this freed parents from fulfilling their normal obligations toward their own offspring and that the consequent moral degeneration was causing them to treat the serious matter of education altogether too lightly. This was ominous for the future of the moral fiber of Russia; even worse was the thought that the only home these children had was the comfortless barrack. What kind of officers would they become, asked Stroganov, reared as they were in so narrow and inhuman an atmosphere?

Worse than the threat to the moral strength of the Empire, however, was the unhappy marriage of general and military education. Stroganov's complaint, similar to that of Miliutin, was that children of ten or twelve years had to devote a significant part of their time to learning tactics and the use of arms just when they should be devoting their maximum efforts to their academic studies.[78] Stroganov proposed that the programs of general education be separated from the military training by dividing the cadet corps into two parts, general and specialized.[79] The military organization was to be eliminated entirely in the general classes, and in the

---

76. Apparently the "heaviness" of Stroganov's approach was usual with him. In his diary, Miliutin refers to Stroganov's "usual awkward logic." *Dnevnik*, I., 111.
77. *Stoletie*, X., Part III, 196.
78. *Ibid.*, pp. 196–197.
79. *Ibid.*, pp. 197 and 203.

military schools the students would be able to concentrate on those specialized subjects which they needed to become officers. Moreover, these military schools were to be open to *anyone* who had already completed a program of general studies and who wished to pursue a military career. As model for these schools, Stroganov suggested the already existing Konstantinovskii Military School.[80]

Because of the apparent need for the War Ministry to continue to provide for some time a general education, Stroganov suggested some changes in approach that would insure the proper moral development of the young. This was to be achieved by insulating them from the corrupting influences of the outside world and by the reconstitution of the schools, eliminating their military organization and replacing company commanders with faculty members. Not only would the latter have a salutory effect upon the moral development of the young people, but some savings could be effected, since the salaries and maintenance costs of the officers dismissed in this way would be spared.[81]

Stroganov's views tended to be far more moralistic than those of Miliutin, but both men agreed that the education of children was incompatible with the training of officers. But Stroganov's arguments, from a more positive standpoint, indicate a compromise. Miliutin's plans had only foreseen the conversion of the cadet corps into *gymnazia* or *realschulen* operated by civilian authorities. Stroganov represented a point of view which was quite close to the situation that actually developed. He talked of retaining part of the corps to provide professional military training, and while maintaining control of the classes offering general education, these would lose all their military character. Stroganov's views represented the kind of compromise that in the long run made Miliutin's reform possible.

The War Minister also found support in other quarters, most particularly from his old friend the Minister of Public Instruction, A. V. Golovnin.[82] Golovnin was himself embarking upon an ambitious program of

80. *Ibid.*, pp. 197–198.
81. *Ibid.*, pp. 202–203. One should recall that this was written during a grave crisis in the Russian universities.
82. See, for example, Golovnin's views of Miliutin in Zisserman, II, 59. This cordiality was not to last, however, and their relationship soon became strained. Cf. M. Lemke, *Epokha tsenzurnykh reform, 1859–1865 godov*, pp. 83–85.

reform of the civil school system[83] and was keenly interested in this reform of the military schools. He submitted to the Emperor on July 26, 1862, a memorandum in which he set forth his views on Miliutin's reform proposals, agreeing in many respects with the ideas both of the War Minister and Count Stroganov. Specifically, he agreed that general education and specialized professional training had to be separated, noting that a broad academic foundation was the indispensable basis for any more advanced training:

> If it is important for the state that we have trained people who know the business of artillerymen or engineers, then it is still more important that these artillerymen and engineers should first of all be people with mature understanding, with insight, and be capable of considering questions maturely and in all their aspects.[84]

Golovnin also subscribed to Miliutin's view that the extreme youth of students in the cadet corps precluded their becoming acquainted with the actual needs of the military service. His solution also was similar to that of Miliutin. The *gymnazium* should furnish the basic general education and the army should create institutions to provide the professional training.[85] He estimated that with three million rubles per year (the general amount that could be expected if the cadet corps were liquidated minus the amount necessary for a comprehensive system of junker schools), the state could open as many as 150 *gymnazia* with an annual budget of 20,000 rubles for each. A general education could be provided for as many as 45,000 young men.[86] It is clear that Golovnin also looked to the destruction of the cadet corps with part of its funds then being given over to his Ministry for the further development of civil

83. The degree of collusion between Golovnin and Miliutin, if any, cannot be determined, but certainly in the early years of the Miliutin reforms the civil school system was to be the beneficiary of the War Ministry's plan to divest itself of all obligation to provide a general education.

84. N. F. Pavlovskii, "Aleksandr Vasilevich Golovnin, ego uchastie v preobrazovanii voenno-uchebnykh zavedenii," *Russkaia Starina*, No. 9 (1887), p. 664.

85. *Ibid.*, p. 665.

86. *Ibid.*, p. 666. In 1862, the Ministry of Public Instruction spent 3,394,000 rubles on schools of all kinds, of which 1,240,825 rubles went to *gymnazia* and *pro-gymnazia*. During the years 1863, 1864, and 1865, the outlay for these secondary schools was 2,374,730 rubles, 2,401,935 rubles, and 2,350,814 rubles, respectively. The expenditures for general education were indeed modest.

education. In his view, the money being spent for the cadet corps could be used to educate five times as many students in civil schools.

The possibilities for action in the reform of the system of military education seemed especially propitious when Miliutin came to office. Since 1860, a special committee under the chairmanship of the Emperor himself had been studying the problem. This group had been exploring the possibility of dividing the course in the cadet corps into five general and two professional classes. The committee had issued an interim report in 1861 making a number of recommendations similar to the views of Miliutin, Stroganov, and Golovnin, specifically that the professional classes had to develop adequately the students' practical skills and that a general education had to be the basis for all specialized training. The committee was also concerned that standards not be set by the gifted exceptions, but by the average students. This body continued to deliberate until it disbanded in August 1862.[87]

At this time the entire question was placed in the hands of a new Special Committee for Military Education. Chairman of this new body was the Grand Duke Michael Nikolaevich. The committee included members appointed by both Miliutin and Golovnin: General-Adjutants A. A. Barantsev, Count O. L. Hayden and N. A. Kryzhanovskii, Lieutenant Generals V. P. Zheltukhin and A. I. Verigen, Privy Councillors A. F. Postels and A. S. Voronov, Major Generals K. P. von Kaufman I, N. V. Korsakov, P. P. Kinovich, M. P. von Kaufman II, and P. S. Vannovskii, Colonels G. G. Danilovich, I. A. Birilev and S. A. Slutskii, and Court Councillors E. Th. Eward and I. E. Andreevskii.[88] The committee was to discuss the simplification of the curriculum in the military schools, and the *prikaz* creating the body directed it to separate the general from the specialized classes. Every possibility of reducing expenses[89] would be explored and some formula devised for the diversion of

87. Major General M. Lalaev, *Istoricheskii ocherk voenno-uchebnykh zavedenii podvedomstvennykh glavnomu ikh upravleniiu: Ot osnovaniia v Rossii voennykh shkol do iskhoda pervogo dvadtsatipiatiletiia blagopoluchnogo tsarstvovaniia Gosudaria Imperatora Alexsandra Nikolaevicha, 1700–1880*, pp. 118–119.

88. *Stoletie*, X., Part III, 12. Cf. the *prikaz* of the Grand Duke Michael Nikolaevich, dated August 26, 1862, No. 3012, reproduced in *Russkaia Starina*, No. 6 (1887), p. 699.

89. "R.V.O.: Neskol'ko slov o preobrazovanii voenno-uchebnykh zavedenii," *Voennyi Sbornik*, No. 2 (1863), p. 598.

some funds from the Institutions of Military Instruction to the junker schools.[90]

Because such thorough spadework had already been done, the Special Committee proceeded very rapidly and submitted its report to the Emperor in November 1862. The results were very much as expected. The cadet corps were to be retained for the training of officer candidates and designed to provide the professional and general training needed by potential officers. There can be little doubt that this decision was a compromise, since both Miliutin and Golovnin had favored the abolition of the cadet corps. The new Military Schools would be geared to produce 400 to 500 officers annually. The lower classes of the cadet corps would be reorganized into military *gymnazia* offering only general studies, with all professional subjects being taught only in the Military Schools. These latter would admit any students successfully completing either civilian or military *gymnazia* or their equivalent. The number of schools offering general studies would gradually be reduced by turning them over to the Ministry of Public Instruction. The savings accrued in this manner would be used to support a system of junker schools.[91]

It is interesting to note at this point that the greatest obstacle to reforming the cadet corps was the Emperor himself. He so identified himself with them that he found it difficult to conceive of them in any other form. Miliutin and those who supported him in this matter spent the entire year 1862 trying to persuade him of the necessity for reform.[92] The mounting pressure bore fruit when the Emperor, during an inspection tour of the First Moscow Cadet Corps, had a particularly unhappy experience with a slovenly and disrespectful cadet.[93] This apparently was the last

90. Bogdanovich, III., 139; "R.V.O.," *Voennyi Sbornik*, No. 7 (1863), p. 296, and O., "Obzor' deiatel'nosti voennogo ministerstva," *Voennyi Sbornik*, No. 10 (1865), pp. 252–253.

91. See particularly, "Otchet Glavnogo Upravleniia Voenno-uchebnyi Zavedeniiami," *Vsepoddaneishii otchet Voennogo Ministra za 1863* g., p. 3, and P. A. Zaionchkovskii, *Voennye reformy 1860–1870 godov v Rossii*, pp. 228–229. It was clearly the intention of the War Ministry at this point to get out of the business of providing a general education by gradually turning this function over to the Ministry of Public Instruction.

92. A.E.K., "Mikhail Ivanovich Dragomirov i voenno-uchebnyia zavedeniia," *Russkaia Starina*, No. 10 (1908), p.39.

93. *Ibid.*, p. 41.

straw and he acceded to the advice of the reformers, even though it remained quite painful for him.[94]

Even more difficult to convince than the Emperor was a significant part of the high command. The great military theoretician, M. I. Dragomirov, wrote that during this period Miliutin called together a group of generals to discuss the problem of the military schools. It was found during the course of the meeting that only the War Minister and Generals Dragomirov and Isakov favored the proposed reforms. The rest of the group was made up of men born in the previous century and who as a consequence were less sensitive to the changes that had taken place in the preceding years. They were therefore less disposed toward fundamental reform.[95]

But in the closing days of 1862 the crisis of the cadet corps came to a head when the cadets of the First Moscow Cadet Corps mutinied against their Director, Major General V. N. Lermontov.[96] Clearly, something had to be done, and seeing no alternative the Emperor permitted Miliutin to proceed with his reforms and gave final approval on May 14, 1863, to the plan of the Special Committee for Military Education.[97]

While the retention of the professional classes of the cadet corps as Military Schools was probably a compromise, it is clear that their creation did not prevent Miliutin from successfully achieving most of his other aims. Nor were the Military Schools pedagogically a contradiction of the War Minister's views; quite to the contrary, they would be especially effective professional schools since it could be assumed that all students entering them would already possess sound general educations, an assumption that could not be made in the case of the junker schools. But the Military Schools did consume money that both Miliutin and Golovnin had hoped would be diverted to help build up general education in the Empire. The preservation of vestiges of the cadet corps as Military Schools was in any event not too high a price to pay for the possibility of effecting a generally unpopular reform.

94. *Ibid.*, p. 43.
95. A.E.K., "Mikhail Ivanovich Dragomirov i voenno-uchebnyia zavedeniia," *Russkaia Starina*, No. 11 (1908), p. 369.
96. *Ibid.*, No. 10, pp. 41ff.
97. "R.V.O.: Kratkii obzor' deiatel'nosti voennogo ministerstva v 1863 godu," *Voennyi Sbornik*, No. 4 (1864), p. 156.

The corps were again revived in name, if not in substance, during the reaction under Alexander III, clearly demonstrating the perseverence and depth of the resistance of those opposing the abolition of the cadet corps. From a purely practical standpoint, it is clear that Miliutin got just about all that he could, given the circumstances, and that the resulting system was not an unreasonable compromise.

Sound precedent for the creation of the Military Schools, moreover, already existed. The Konstantinovskii Military School, suggested as a model by Count Stroganov, had grown out of circumstances dating back to 1855. During the course of that year, the Dvorianskii Regiment had reformed itself into the Konstantinovskii Cadet Corps which devoted itself exclusively to the professional training of its cadets. But their poor discipline coupled with the arrogance of the cadets led to difficulties which brought the Corps to the immediate attention of General Adjutant Ia. A. Rostovtsev, the Chief of the Institutions of Military Instruction. After solving the more pressing problems with the use of great tact, Rostovtsev turned to the more fundamental questions which he recognized went much deeper than they seemed.[98] The fact that the cadets as students were not considered to be on active duty meant that they were not liable to military discipline.

If the training in the Corps were to be meaningful, then, Rostovtsev concluded that the students must be considered as soldiers on active duty:

it was necessary to effect a basic reform in the entire way of life of the students, and, first of all, to establish rules of military discipline in order to turn grown students into soldiers and to consider them to be on active duty, just like the junkers in the forces.[99]

In accordance with this view, a number of changes were made in schools along the lines of the already established practices in the Junker School of the Fourth Corps at Voronezh.

During its summer camp in 1858, the Konstantinovskii Military School admitted cadets from several of the cadet corps in the provinces into its more professional program,[100] thereby setting precedents for the admis-

---

98. "K istorii voenno-uchebnoi reformy Imperatora Aleksandra II-go, 1856–1870," *Russkaia Starina*, No. 6 (1887), pp. 693–694.
99. *Ibid.*, pp. 694–695.
100. The Corps was renamed the Konstantinovskii Military School in 1859.

sion of "externals" for specialized training. This right was soon extended
to the graduates of civilian secondary schools who had the right to enter
the service as junkers or volunteers of the first category.[101] The curriculum of the school concentrated upon giving the most professional
training possible, with the assumption that all the cadets (now called
junkers because they were on active duty) already possessed an adequate
general education. At first the course was three years in duration but was
soon cut to two. When the Konstantinovskii School had assumed its final
character, it became the living model for all the subsequent military
schools.[102]

The original plan was to reduce from 6,150 to 3,600 the number of
students in the cadet corps who would be enrolled in three military
schools and nine military *gymnazia*. The number of students attending
the military schools would be regulated by the number of students completing their courses in the military *gymnazia*. The cadet corps that were
not converted would be liquidated.[103]

The actual reform of military education got under way when the
Grand Duke Michael Nikolaevich was posted to the Caucasus, vacating
his position as Chief of the Institutions of Military Instruction. This administration had previously been an independent agency with its chief
enjoying the ministerial right of reporting directly to the Emperor. The
Grand Duke's departure made it possible to incorporate his administra-
tion into the War Ministry so that the entire system of military education
could be properly co-ordinated. Early in 1863, by an Imperial order,
Miliutin issued a *prikaz* (January 21, 1863, no. 21) integrating the
Institutions of Military Instruction into the War Ministry as the Supreme
Administration of the Institutions of Military Instruction. The War
Minister placed this new administration in the charge of a man in whom
he had complete personal confidence, Major General N. V. Isakov.
Isakov acted both as chief of the schools and as the head of their ad-
ministrative and logistical support groups. In the years that followed,
Miliutin worked very closely with Isakov and many of the others who
held positions in the new bureau: G. G. Danilovich, N. V. Korsakov,
P. O. Bobrovskii, M. S. Lalaev, V. P. Kokhovskii, N. K. Wessel, A. N.

101. *Ibid.*, p. 695.
102. *Voennyi Sbornik*, No. 2 (1863), p. 599.
103. "R.V.O.," *Voennyi Sbornik*, No. 7 (1863), p. 302.

Makarov, A. N. Ostrogorskii, P. A. Alekseev, and others. The three academies, the Nikolaevskii Academy of the General Staff, the Engineering Academy, and the Artillery Academy, remained under the control of the heads of their parent branches of the service.[104]

The establishment of the new Supreme Administration set into motion the process of the reform. The Pavlovskii and Alexandrovskii Cadet Corps reformed themselves into Military Schools, taking their place alongside the already existing Konstantinovskii Military School. Nine other cadet corps posted their senior students to these military schools and then reformed themselves into military *gymnazia*.[105] Three cadet corps— the Alexandrovskii in Vilno, the Pavlovskii in St. Petersburg, and the Alexandrinskii-Sirotskii in Moscow—were liquidated. The senior students from the latter three corps enrolled in the military schools while the elementary students apportioned themselves among the military *gymnazia*. The five cadet corps still in existence were left temporarily as they were.[106]

The new military schools were organized along strict military lines with the same discipline as in any field unit. Each school constituted a single battalion with a commander who had direct authority over all students. Each battalion was composed of four companies, each of which was further subdivided into four platoons.[107] Students seeking entry had to be at least sixteen years of age, and in practice most were older. Admission also depended upon both class privilege and the level of the student's education. For example, graduates of a *gymnazium* possessing the *attestat* (the document granting them the right to matriculate in a university) were admitted without examination if they were gentry or if they possessed the right to volunteer with the privileges of the first category. University graduates were admitted without examination, irrespective of their social origins.[108] The military schools generally tended to retain the class character of the cadet corps, despite Miliutin's greater interest in talent as the criterion for responsible service.

The course in the military schools was two years in length and was

---

104. *Stoletie*, X., Part III, 29. Cf. *Voennyi Sbornik*, No. 2 (1863), pp. 596–597.
105. "R.V.O.," *Voennyi Sbornik*, No. 7 (1863), p. 299.
106. See the table in *ibid.*, pp. 303–304.
107. *Ibid.*, pp. 299–300.
108. "Voennyia uchilishcha," *Voennyi Sbornik*, No. 6 (1865), p. 205.

divided into two classes, junior and senior. Students who possessed a
university degree or who had successfully passed a special examination
could be admitted directly into the senior class. The examination demanded a comprehensive knowledge of basic academic subjects as well
as a demonstration of a facility to do freehand drawing.[109] It was expected
that the admission of students with better academic backgrounds would
make possible a more thorough professional training than in the junker
schools and that the military schools would thus contribute better quality
officers to the army.[110] The graduates of these schools entered the army
immediately upon completing the course either as lieutenants or sub-
lieutenants, depending upon how well they succeeded in their final
examinations.[111] Graduates were especially favored for staff assignments
and for attendance at the academies of the more specialized branches
of arms.

The War Ministry in time created two other military schools. The
Nikolaevskii School of Guards Junkers became a military school in 1864
with the special task of training cavalry officers. It was in most respects
similar to the other schools except that it was organized into a cavalry
squadron, and practical cavalry training was of special significance in its
curriculum. In addition, because of the special needs of the school, aspiring students first studied in a preparatory *pension* appended to the
school.[112] An infantry military school also opened at Orenburg in 1867,
but it closed its doors after only two years.[113]

Even His Majesty's Own Corps of Pages, a most elite cadet corps admitting only the sons of the most favored families of the Empire, underwent change. In 1865, the Corps separated its professional courses from
the elementary academic program.[114] The four lower classes became
a military *gymnazium* and the age range for admission was advanced
from a minimum of ten to twelve years and the maximum from fifteen to
seventeen years. Students entering the Corps of Pages enrolled only in

109. *Ibid.*, p. 206.
110. *Ibid.*, p. 209.
111. *Ibid.*, p. 207.
112. "R.V.O.: Russkaia armiia v 1864 godu: V., Voenno-uchebnaia chast'," *Voennyi Sbornik*, No. 11 (1866), p. 22.
113. P. A. Zaionchkovskii, *Voennye reformy 1860–1870 godov v Rossii*, p. 236.
114. "Otdel' ofitsial'nyi" Prikaz Voennogo Ministra, 10 March 1866, No. 85," *Voennyi Sbornik*, No. 6 (1866), p. 119.

the class commensurate with their age, ability, and level of achievement. Officers posted to the Corps were selected on the basis of high leadership and moral qualities as well as military aptitude.[115] The senior classes resembled the military schools in nearly every respect. During the summer, the cadets in the senior classes served in summer camps along with regular noncommissioned officers, while the cadets in the elementary classes went on vacation. The Corps of Pages after its reform was at one and the same time a military *gymnazium* and a military school.

Similarly, the Finnish Cadet Corps at Friedrichsham realigned its table of organization and divided the elementary from the professional courses.[116] This reform, completed in 1865, allowed for a broader base of admission than the other military schools in that students were admitted irrespective of the rank, status, or calling of their fathers. The sole criterion was the passage of an examination.[117]

In the final analysis, the military schools were quite successful. In his annual report to the Emperor in 1873, Miliutin was able to write,

The military schools graduate annually about 50 officers, of which only a very small percentage are retained for duty in army regiments. As a consequence of the higher level of general and military training of these officers graduating from the military schools, a most significant part of them serves in the Guards, in the special branches of service, or they matriculate in an academy to receive a higher military education and are afterwards posted to the various staffs, etc.[118]

This, coupled with the fact that about 70 percent of those entering the military schools at this time were graduates of the military *gymnazia*, meant that the continued monopoly of the command structure of the army by the privileged orders was assured.[119]

115. *Ibid.*, p. 120; "R.V.O.: Preobrazovanie pazheskogo korpusa," *Voennyi Sbornik*, No. 4 (1865), pp. 152–154; and, "Otchet Glavnogo upravleniia Voenno-uchebnykh Zavedenii za 1865 god," *Vsepoddaneishii Otchet Voennogo Ministerstva sa 1865 god*, p. 14.
116. "R.V.O.: Finlandskii Kadetskii Korpus," *Voennyi Sbornik*, No. 6 (1865), p. 210.
117. *Ibid.*, p. 211, and, "Otchet Glavnogo Upravleniia Voenno-uchebnykh Zavedenii, za 1865 god," *Vsepoddaneishii Otchet Voennogo Ministerstva za 1865 god*, pp. 20–22.
118. *Vsepoddaneishii Doklad Voennogo Ministra, January 1, 1873*, p. 41.
119. *Ibid.*, p. 42, and, "R.V.O.: Russkaia armiia v 1864 godu: V., Voenno-uchebnaia chast'," *Voennyi Sbornik*, No. 11 (1866), pp. 21–22.

The military *gymnazia* formed from the elementary classes of the cadet corps were meant to be temporary. The cost of their maintenance imposed a severe strain on the resources of the War Ministry. At the time of their creation, the War Ministry recognized the moral obligation to educate the sons of the privileged already enrolled but hoped that as these completed their studies the schools would be closed or turned over to the Ministry of Public Instruction. While noting the conversion of the Second Cadet Corps into a military *gymnazium*, Miliutin wrote in his annual report to the Emperor on January 1, 1864, that

With the liquidation of its tactical organization, this institution takes on the character of a more purely academic establishment and assumes its own special role—the preparation of children for matriculation into the military schools only until such time as the entry into them of the last of the young people completing the entire *gymnazium* course on their own account, makes possible the gradual elimination of such schools within the War Office, and their gradual transfer to the Ministry of Public Instruction.[120]

In the meantime, they would continue temporarily to provide a fringe benefit to those in the service of the Emperor by accepting without charge the sons of those in military service who did not have the means to educate their children. The *gymnazia* would also be open to others under certain conditions but with the payment of fees.[121]

The *gymnazia* were to assume the character of civilian schools at the secondary level[122] of the type known as *realschulen*.[123] While their major purpose was to prepare students for entry into the military schools, all military organization and exercises were dropped. The *realschule* curriculum was only one part of the schools' character. They also emphasized the moral and intellectual training of the students as well as their physical development through gymnastics, sports, and swimming.[124]

120. Quoted in P. A. Zaionchkovskii, *Voennye reformy 1860–1870 godov v Rossii*, p. 230. Cf., *Voennyi Sbornik*, No. 6 (1864), p. 135, and O., "Obzor' deiatel'nosti voennogo ministerstva," *Voennyi Sbornik*, No. 10 (1865), p. 258.

121. "R.V.O.," *Voennyi Sbornik*, No. 2 (1863), p. 599.

122. "R.V.O.," *Voennyi Sbornik*, No. 7 (1863), p. 302.

123. These were so called because of their emphasis upon modern languages, mathematics, and the natural sciences as opposed to the predominence of the classical languages in the *gymnazia*.

124. For a systematic presentation of their curriculum, see "Otchet Glavnogo Upravleniia Voenno-uchebnykh Zavedenii za 1865 god," *Vsepoddaneishii Otchet Voennogo Ministerstva za 1865 god*, pp. 36–38.

The Second Cadet Corps in St. Petersburg was in 1863 the first to become a military *gymnazium*. Others soon followed, and by 1866 there were twelve such schools in existence. The names of the cadet corps from which they were formed were normally preserved in the names of the *gymnazia* which were formed from them: for example, the First and Second Petersburg Cadet Corps became the First and Second Petersburg Military Gymnazia, etc.[125] The War Ministry closely controlled the enrollments in the schools to insure a proper number of graduates to complement the military schools. At first the War Ministry proposed to maintain a total of about 2,700 students in the *gymnazia*, enough to guarantee 350 to 400 graduates each year from the professional military schools, assuming that a total of about 100 students would enter the military schools from institutions other than the military *gymnazia*.[126] These numbers however proved to be insufficient in practice, and the total number of students enrolled in the military gymnazia rose to 3,700[127]

The original curriculum for the schools as programmed in 1862 proved to be inadequate. Fundamentally, the first program of studies represented a reduction in the types and numbers of the courses formerly taught in the cadet corps. It included religion, the Russian language and literature, a choice of one of two foreign languages, geography, history, arithmetic, elementary algebra, geometry, trigonometry, physics, and the elements of inorganic chemistry, but lacked courses in the history of literature, zoology, botany, statistics, and military history. The original conception that the schools would be transitional mitigated any basic reform in their curriculum, and the War Ministry felt that the students would be able to study these latter subjects within the existing courses: a knowledge of the natural sciences and statistics would be learned in the geography course, and the history of literature would be part of the instruction in literature.[128]

125. *Voennyi Sbornik*, No. 6 (1864), p. 136.
126. "R.V.O.," *Voennyi Sbornik*, No. 7 (1863), p. 298. The War Ministry did not surrender its ultimate hope that those young men aspiring to become officers would see to their own general education. See N. Wessel, "Voennyia uchilischa i voennyia gimnazii," *Pedagogicheskii Sbornik*, No. 1 (1867), pp. 111–112.
127. "Otchet Glavnogo Upravleniia Voenno-uchebnykh Zavedenii za 1865 god," *Vsepoddaneishii Otchet Voennogo Ministerstva za 1865 god*, p. 13. This raised the total annual budget of the military *gymnazia* from 1,366,699 rubles to 1,499,144 rubles but decreased the average cost per student.
128. Lalaev, pp. 119–120.

By 1870, however, when it became clear that the War Ministry was going to continue the operation of the military *gymnazia* indefinitely, Miliutin began a reform of their academic program with the aim of broadening its scope and altering its character to conform more nearly to that of the civilian secondary schools. The War Minister hoped that this would free the military schools from having to fill in gaps in their students' general education.[129] When he issued the draft of the new academic program, he wrote,

the military *gymnazii*, [which] by choice complements the military schools with their students, have not yet, because of their recent founding, succeeded in introducing within themselves a full program of general education of a *real* (*real'nogo*) character; this situation has been reflected in the curriculum of the military schools by the need to include in them that portion of the *gymnazium* course not fulfilled by the *gymnazii*. For this reason, the professional subjects in the military schools have suffered. . . .[130]

The new curriculum of the *gymnazia*, as planned by the Supreme Military Education Committee and promulgated by the War Council, included the usual subjects of religion and the Russian language (including both Church Slavonic and grammar). A knowledge of both German and French became mandatory, with the student required to know one well enough to translate without the aid of a dictionary.

The mathematics requirement was expanded to include algebraic geometry and analytical geometry. In addition, the new program included a course in general political history to 1789,[131] the geography of Russia and the world, physics and astronomy, natural history, physiology, and freehand drawing. The transition to this new course of study was gradual, with its final implementation set for 1874.

One of the more interesting aspects of this reform was the new provision for those who would enter the military schools from other institutions. Miliutin's *prikaz* stipulated that

For entrants into these military schools from among those completing the course in civilian secondary schools or those possessing a certificate of having

129. *Vsepoddaneishii Doklad Voennogo Ministra, January 1, 1873*, p. 43.
130. "Chast' ofitsial'naia: Prikaz po voennomu vedomstvu: S - Petersburg, February 13-go dnia 1870 goda, No. 40," *Pedagogicheskii Sbornik*, No. 2 (1870), p. 43.
131. This interesting terminal date may be interpreted as an attempt to avoid any entanglements with revolutionary questions and the political upheavals of the nineteenth century.

passed an equivalent examination in these institutions, the failure of examinations in the ancient languages would not be an obstacle to matriculation into the military schools.[132]

Miliutin's position between those struggling for parity in Russia between the *realschulen* and the classical schools will be treated in a subsequent chapter, but his motive aside from that quarrel is in this case quite clear. The quality he wanted in a student who was about to begin his professional training in a military school was an acquaintance with a broad range of practical subjects. The level of competence which he sought was that of the *realschulen* (*grazhdanskie real'nye gimnazii*),[133] and subjects, therefore, which were not of practical value could count neither for nor against an aspirant to a military school.

The basic source for trained officers was not, however, the military schools but the junker schools. While the former without a doubt were successful in that they did produce well-trained and capable officers, they graduated too few and the costs were very high. Besides, most of their graduates were posted to the elite units and only occasionally did they go into the regular army formations. Each officer completing the entire course in a military *gymnazium* and in a military school cost the state 6,000 rubles. Moreover, the cadet corps had never been capable of producing enough officers (in the eleven years 1853–1863 they had turned out only 8,199, or an average of 745 a year).[134] The question of training officers in sufficient numbers was resolved by the creation of a comprehensive system of junker schools based upon the military districts.

The struggle over the fate of the cadet corps and their subsequent reconstitution as military *gymnazia* and military schools did not divert Miliutin from the urgency of developing a system of junker schools as the means for training the bulk of the officer corps without imposing any further burden upon the fiscal resources of the state. The problem was critical, and delay, he felt, would be at Russia's peril. In 1864 he forwarded to the Emperor a memorandum in which he wrote:

> The urgency for the establishment of the junker schools is a consequence of the enormous number of those young men, who entering directly into

132. *Ibid.*, p. 44.
133. *Vsepoddaneishii Doklad Voennogo Ministra, January 1, 1871*, p. 32.
134. P. Bobrovskii, "Ob uchrezhdenii iunkerskish uchilishch," *Voennyi Sbornik*, No. 11 (1864), pp. 135–136.

regiments by means of the several ways in which they can become officers, bring into the forces a complete lack of general and, worse than that, military education. With the liquidation of several cadet corps and the reduction of the normal number of officers graduating from them, the number of these individuals must grow still larger and, therefore, at the present time it is more urgently necessary than ever to come to their assistance and to extend to them the means for their preparation in conformity with the needs of the service.[135]

But the problem was more basic than merely that of meeting an emergency, as Miliutin noted in his 1865 annual report to Alexander,

Within the junker schools is encompassed the future of our army. If their establishment succeeds in practice, then the army will be secured by line officers with a level of development sufficient for strictly service aims. Other military educational establishments have other aims, but the elevation of the moral and intellectual level of the *mass* of officers, we must expect only from the junker schools.[136]

As a consequence, the curriculum of the junker schools was a matter for the most careful consideration as was the status of those being graduated by them. While a junker would be expected to pass an examination qualifying himself as an officer in his own branch of arms, those entering the artillery or sappers would be posted to the appropriate academy as a matter of course, and qualified officers would have the privilege of attending the Nikolaevskii Academy of the General Staff after completing four years of active service.[137] There can be little doubt that by these means Miliutin intended to keep all channels open to talent, whatever its source, and to mitigate somewhat the monopoly the elite and special branches enjoyed in obtaining the graduates of the military schools.

Miliutin wanted a study program in the junker schools adhering to the pattern of the already existing practices. He called for a two-year course with classroom studies occupying the fall and winter months, while the summer months would be spent in field exercises with the regular armed forces. In response to the War Minister's proposals, Alexander II created

135. Quoted in P. A. Zaionchkovskii, *Voennye reformy 1860–1870 godov v Rossii*, p. 242.

136. *Ibid.*, p. 243. Italics in the original.

137. O., "Obzor' deiatel'nosti voennogo ministerstva," *Voennyi Sbornik*, No. 10 (1865), p. 236, and, "Iunkerskiia uchilishcha," *Voennyi Sbornik*, No. 10 (1864), p. 264.

a special commission under Major General of His Majesty's Own Suite Count E. E. Sievers[138] and charged it with the implementation of the junker school program. The matter moved rapidly and soon the first two new junker schools opened their doors.

The first to open was the school at Moscow,[139] the headquarters of the Moscow Military District, on October 1, 1864, followed a month later by the school at Vilno.[140] The conversion of the already existing schools at Warsaw and Helsinki quickly followed after Miliutin issued the necessary orders in September 1864. Because of the smaller garrison in Finland, the Helsinki Junker School had to be scaled down to accommodate a full complement of only 100 junkers. Moreover, since there was no secondary school in Finland where Russian could be studied and because many of the junkers were either Finnish or Swedish, the course in the Helsinki Junker School was three years in length rather than two to allow the junkers to develop an adequate command of Russian before entering the senior class. Those who already knew Russian were eligible for advanced placement.[141] The school in Warsaw, activated on January 1, 1865, closely resembled in form those at Moscow and Vilno.[142]

From this time forward, the expansion of the junker school system was rapid. As early as July 1864, the Emperor authorized the creation of six more schools which became operative during the following year. Four of these were intended to train infantry officers and the other two were for the cavalry. The infantry schools, located in Chuguev, Odessa, Kiev, and Riga, each had a complement of two hundred junkers, while the cavalry schools in Elizavetgrad and Tver were smaller, having only ninety and sixty trainees, respectively.[143] During the academic year

138. *Ibid.*, p. 262, and, *Stoletie*, X., part III., 194–195.

139. "R.V.O.: Moskovskoe iunkerskoe uchilishche," *Voennyi Sbornik*, No. 4 (1865), p. 159, and, "Otchet Inspektorskogo Departmenta Voennogo Ministerstva za 1865 god," *Vsepoddaneishii Otchet Voennogo Ministerstva za 1865 god*, p. 48.

140. "R.V.O.: Otkrytie vilenskogo iunkerskogo uchilishcha," *Voennyi Sbornik*, No. 12 (1864), pp. 147–148.

141. "R.V.O.: Gel'singforskoe iunkerskoe uchilishche," *Voennyi Sbornik*, No. 4 (1865), p. 155.

142. "R.V.O.: Varshavskoe iunkerskoe uchilishche," *Voennyi Sbornik*, No. 4, 1865, p. 156, and, "Otchet Inspektorskogo Departmenta za 1865 god," *Vsepoddaneishii Otchet Voennogo Ministerstva za 1865 god*, p. 51.

143. *Ibid.*, pp. 48–49.

1866–1867, two more schools opened in Tiflis and Kazan, bringing the number to twelve and enrolling a total of 1,331 junkers.[144] Other additions were made from time to time until in 1874 there were sixteen schools and 4,210 junkers.[145]

Each school became an integral part of the military district in which it was formed, and it was physically located at or near the district headquarters. Each district chief of staff had direct charge of the junker school, but the curriculum was supervised by the Supreme Administration of the Institutions of Military Instruction.[146] Whenever possible, the schools were staffed by officers who had completed the course in Nikolaevskii Academy of the General Staff and who had been posted back to their own units to await vacancies in the general staff. Previously, officers had been allowed to deteriorate in their regiments, waiting in some cases for years before they were able to make use of their specialized training.[147]

The junker schools were an integral part of the officer procurement program. Junkers and volunteers could become officers *only* by successfully completing a course in a junker school or by passing an equivalent examination. Regimental commanders selected junkers for attendance at the schools and were by this practice able to weed out the obviously unfit.[148] An incentive for the regimental commanders to take their obligations seriously was the fact that the newly commissioned officers were returned to their own regiments, even if their units had been transferred out of the military district.[149] In addition to appointment to the school by their regimental commanders, aspirants to the junker schools had to pass a written examination in such general subjects as reading and writing, religion, arithmetic, and geography. If a junker had completed a university or its equivalent, he was eligible to appointment to the senior class of a junker school without examination.[150]

---

144. "Obshchii obzor' glavnogo upravleniia voenno-uchebnykh zavedenii za 1866 god," *Otchet Voennogo Ministerstva za 1866 god*, p. 110.

145. P.B.[obrovskii], "Dvadtsatiletie iunkerskikh uchilisch," *Voennyi Sbornik*, CXC (1889), 121 Cf., "Iunkerskiia uchilischa v 1871 godu," *Russkii Invalid*, No. 184 (1872).

146. "Iunkerskiia uchilishcha," *Voennyi Sbornik*, No. 10 (1864), p. 264.

147. M. Bogdanovich, "O sredstvakh k rasprostraneniiu prosveshcheniia v armii," *Voennyi Sbornik*, No. 1 (1863), p. 142.

148. "Iunkerskiia uchilishcha," *Voennyi Sbornik*, No. 10 (1864), p. 264.

149. P. Bobrovskii, *Voennyi Sbornik*, No. 11 (1864), p. 142.

150. "Iunkerskiia uchilishcha," *Voennyi Sbornik*, No. 10 (1864), p. 264.

The curriculum of the junker schools was closely related to the level of knowledge required of the junkers at the time of their admission and the absolute minimum standard of competence demanded by the War Ministry. The wide range between these two poles put severe demands upon the schools, even to the point that many closely associated with the schools began to think that the level for admission should be raised by requiring the junkers to attend regimental pre-schools.[151] The curriculum of the junker schools was weighted much more toward general subjects than were the military schools because of the generally lower level of academic achievement of the junkers, and more had to be done in this area. Besides, the junkers were already soldiers with some experience, so that the purely military training offered in the schools did not need to be so comprehensive. Junkers studied both religion and the history of the Church as a basis for their moral training. In addition, the use of oral and written Russian was greatly stressed.

Mathematics loomed large in the curriculum as the basis for all scientific studies. Included within this subject were arithmetic, algebra, and applied geometry. Geography was a broad discipline which included physical geography, the political and regional geography of Russia, the hydrography of Russia, and the Empire's climate and population. Special attention was also given to the study of history to cultivate national pride and devotion.[152] In addition, the junkers took basic courses in administrative correspondence, the use of arms, fortifications, and military regulations. Tactics occupied first place in the program of military subjects and included practical analyses of field problems based upon former engagements by the Russian army.[153]

In 1866, the junker schools added a course in elementary chemistry to be taught in the senior class. Not only was this a course useful to the students' general knowledge, but also, in accordance with the strong practical orientation of the junker schools, it helped to improve their technical and engineering skills.[154]

---

151. "S.O.: Programy dlia iunkerskikh uchilishch," *Voennyi Sbornik*, No. 2 (1867), pp. 78–79.

152. *Ibid.*, pp. 81–91.

153. M. Bogdanovich, "O sredstvakh k rasprostraneniiu prosveshcheniia v armii," *Voennyi Sbornik*, No. 1 (1863), p. 142, and, *Voennyi Sbornik*, No. 2 (1867), pp. 155–159.

154. "Obshchii obzor' glavnogo upravleniia voenno-uchebnykh zavedenii za 1866 god," *Vsepoddaneishii Otchet Voennogo Ministerstva za 1866 god*, p. 57.

The junkers underwent a vigorous daily routine. They arose between 5:30 and 6:30, had tea between 7:00 and 7:30, and went to classes at either eight or nine for a period of four or five hours. Classes were followed by at least two hours of tactical exercises which were followed by dinner. The junkers then had some free time to go walking or visiting. Supper was at seven or eight in the evening and taps blew at nine. The junkers could study until eleven when the lights were put out.[155]

From the very beginning, the results from the junker schools were encouraging. Despite the weakness of their preparation at the time of their entry into the schools, the junkers proved to be good students who applied themselves well, and the experience of the first few years enabled the Supreme Administration for Institutions of Military Instruction to declare that the junker schools were academically satisfactory. In one group of 562 junkers, for example, 370 passed their annual examinations. Within this same sample, but including only those in the senior class, 270 out of 297 were successful.[156] Such results were astounding, considering the low level of the academic backgrounds of the junkers and the brevity of their educational program in the junker schools. The level of the examinations surely was not high, but one must consider that previously many became officers who were incapable of passing any at all.

Not only were the junker schools providing a minimum level of competence in both academic and military subjects, but they were also producing officers in sufficient numbers. By 1870, the sixteen junker schools had an enrollment of 3,340 junkers. There were annually between 1,800 and 2,000 vacancies for officers in the army, and the produce of both the junker and military schools was sufficient to meet this deficit.[157] During the early years of the junker schools, the junkers and volunteers had been reluctant to enter them because of their strict discipline and their unflagging campaign against sluggishness, negligence, and other defects. But once the junkers realized that there was no way to earn an officer's commission other than by successfully completing the course in

155. "R.V.O.: O sostoianii iunkerskikh uchilishch," *Voennyi Sbornik*, No. 7 (1866), p. 68.

156. "Obshchii obzor' glavnogo upravleniia voenno-uchebnykh zavedenii za 1866 god," *Vsepoddaneishii Otchet Voennogo Ministerstva za 1866 god*, pp. 110–111.

157. P. B[obrovskii], "K voprosu o razvitii sposobov dlia komplektovaniia armii ofitserami," *Voennyi Sbornik*, No. 10 (1870), pp. 267–268.

a junker school or by passing an equivalent examination, they became more willing to enroll, so that by the academic year 1869–1870, every school had a full complement of students.[158] During the years from 1864 to 1889, the junker schools trained more than 30.000 officers[159] so that by the latter date, the great bulk of officers then in service had been trained in these institutions.

The junker schools, however, did not prove to be as inexpensive as Miliutin had hoped, but on balance they were still a fiscal success. While the education of every officer completing the entire course in a military *gymnazium* and in a military school represented an expenditure of up to 6,000 rubles, those trained in the junker schools cost the state an average of 640 rubles each. The infantry junkers cost the least at 559 rubles for the two-year course (including their salaries, uniforms, equipment, and allowances), while the cavalry and cossack junkers averaged a little higher at 790 and 1,152 rubles, respectively.[160] The 30,000 officers trained in the junker schools between 1864 and 1889 cost less than twenty million rubles. When one recalls that the old cadet corps had spent more than five million rubles a year to produce from 400 to 500 poorly trained officers per annum, the fact that the junker schools were a bargain becomes quite clear.

One of the more significant qualities of the junker schools was their impact upon the social complexion of the Russian officer corps. While the early hope that merit would become the sole criterion for an officer's commission was never realized, Miliutin's emphasis upon real qualifications for admission to the junker schools rather than social origin did produce a trend toward an increase in the proportion of nongentry elements in the officer corps. At the end of the first eight years of the junker schools' existence, the hereditary gentry made up 63.8 percent of all junkers, while the personal gentry comprised another 21.9 percent. The bulk of those remaining were the sons of clergy or merchants, with only 1.36 percent coming from the peasantry. But the percentage of hereditary nobility was gradually declining in favor of the personal gentry and the *raznochintsy*. For example, in the period from 1869 to 1871, the

158. P. B[obrovskii], *Voennyi Sbornik*, CXC (1889), 118 and 121–122.
159. *Ibid.*, p. 117.
160. *Ibid.*, p. 120.

percentage of those from the clergy and the *raznochintsy* had risen from
4 to 12 percent, and those from the personal gentry climbed from 13
to 21 percent.[161] The junker schools were clearly aiding the process of
social mobility, and it appeared to be only a matter of time before classes
other than the gentry would share fully the power and prestige of service
in the officer corps. This elevation of other classes would mean a relative
decline in the position of the gentry class; the good of the nation was
greater than the interests of any one part of society.

As time went on, moreover, the War Ministry did more to improve the
possibilities of education within the purview of the Ministry, thereby
enabling the army to improve greatly its technical capacity and to expand
the academic backgrounds of those entering the junker schools. This
was accomplished by a series of reforms of the schools for the children
of soldiers into a system of *pro-gymnazii* and higher technical schools.

The schools for the children of soldiers dated back to the reign of
Peter I, when in 1721 he ordered that classes be formed within the infantry garrisons to teach the offspring of the soldiers the basic essentials
of grammar, arithmetic, and useful trades. Later, during the reign of
Anna Ivanovna, all nongentry children of officers and other ranks became the property of the War Office, and the government assumed the
obligation of educating them. By the end of the century sixteen thousand
children were receiving an education at the state's expense. Nicholas I
reformed this system, transforming these schools into battalions and
half-battalions of military cantonists. The increase in numbers did not
diminish, however, and by 1842 the number of such cantonists reached
a total of 300,000 and imposed an immense burden upon the resources
of the state. By the time of the accession of Alexander II, the number
had increased by another 30 percent and was costing the Empire five
million rubles a year.[162]

Soon after the conclusion of the Crimean War, the Emperor freed all
the cantonists except those already on active service. But since these
youngsters had belonged to the War Ministry rather than to their parents,
they in many cases just could not be turned loose to fend for themselves.

161. P. Bobrovskii, "Vyvody iz vos'miletnei deiatel'nosti iunkerskikh uchilishch,"
Russkii Invalid, No. 283 (1872).
162. "Preobrazovanie uchilisch voennogo vedomstva," *Voennyi Sbornik*, No. 8
(1866), p. 199.

The state assumed an obligation toward them and allowed those who desired to do so to enroll in the schools it had created by liquidating the cantonist battalions. An Imperial order of June 10, 1858, opened the Schools of the War Office as they now came to be called, creating twenty-two schools distributed throughout the Empire and accommodating up to 10,000 students.[163] Attrition soon claimed several of these schools, and the total number of students soon declined as the students completed their course of studies. By 1865, only 5,000 remained, and in 1866 this number was halved.[164]

The general purpose of these schools was to provide an elementary education for the sons of noncommissioned officers and to prepare them to perform the various noncombatant functions required by the army. Upon completing the course, they were appointed noncommissioned officers and were assigned directly to their career fields as clerks, artificers, medical aides, engravers, or gymnastics instructors. The schools from the very beginning went beyond accepting only the sons of noncommissioned officers as new students and took in the children of both hereditary and personal gentry, of bureaucrats, of chancellory workers and of priests. Depending upon their particular class rights, those who finished the course were required to serve in the army for a period of ten to twelve years.[165]

During the general reform of military education in 1863, the Schools of the War Office were incorporated into the Institutions of Military Instruction and some changes began. The War Ministry exhibited a curious ambivalence toward these schools. On the one hand, the Ministry felt that the schools were only temporary[166] until the civil school system should become sufficiently effective to provide the needs of both the state and the army, and, on the other, it decided to implement a series of reforms to make these schools pedagogically sound and more in conformity to the needs of the armed forces.

163. *Ibid.*, pp. 200–201. Cf. "R.V.O.: Kratkii obzor' deiatel'nosti voennogo ministerstva v 1863 godu," *Voennyi Sbornik*, No. 4 (1864), p. 158, and P. A. Zaionchkovskii, *Voennye reformy 1860–1870 godov v Rossii*, p. 48.

164. "Voenno-nachal'nyia shkoly," *Voennyi Sbornik*, No. 2 (1867), p. 93.

165. *Ibid.*, p. 92, and, "Preobrazovanie uchilishch voennogo vedomstva," *Voennyi Sbornik*, No. 8 (1866), p. 201.

166. *Ibid.*, pp. 202–203, and, "Voenno-nachal'nyia shkoly," *Voennyi Sbornik*, No. 2 (1867), p. 92.

The War Ministry noted the unequal distribution of students among the schools, the inadequate facilities, the lack of qualified instructors, the paucity and poor quality of the books and materials.[167] Then in June 1863, the War Ministry began to take steps to correct these deficiencies. It imposed limitations upon the number of students in each school, so that the St. Petersburg School would have 200 students, that in Moscow 350, in Kiev 200, and in Voronezh 100.

The character of the St. Petersburg School changed, so that it taught only specialized classes, training students to become engineers, artillery technicians, draftsmen, and military topographers. Conforming to this, military topography was no longer to be taught in the other schools. The War Ministry at the same time began to seek a solution to the problem of obtaining competent instructors by ordering that promising young students within the schools themselves be selected as possible future teachers.[168]

Over the next two years, the number of students declined very rapidly as the former cantonists completed their studies and the War Ministry carefully controlled the number of new students admitted. The Ministry also established in this period a teacher section in the Moscow School which trained fifty new instructors by the end of 1865, materially helping to improve the general quality of instruction in the schools. A special commission within the Chancellory of the War Ministry found it possible with the improving situation to begin to plan a new program of reform for the schools.

Its deliberations were short and to the point. The commission recommended that the training of artillery technicians be given over to the Technical and Pyrotechnical Schools of the artillery branch, that the training of topographers and engineering technicians remain at the St. Petersburg School with its conversion to a military drafting school, that the teacher section of the Moscow School become a teachers' seminary, and that the students in the medical aides' and pharmacists' schools within the hospitals be drawn from the schools of the War Office.[169]

This closer integration of the schools into the education and training

167. "Preobrazovanie uchilishch voennogo vedomstva," *Voennyi Sbornik*, No. 8 (1866), pp. 202–203.

168. *Ibid.*, pp. 203–204.

169. *Ibid.*, pp. 205–206, and, N. S., "Neskol'ko slov o novom ustave dlia gimnazii i progimnazii," *Russkii Invalid*, No. 27 (1865).

system of the War Ministry coincided with a further reduction in the number of schools. When the total number of students dropped to 2,300 in 1866, the War Ministry closed the schools in Novogeorgievsk, Nizhnii Novgorod, Smolensk, Chuguev, Kazan, and Voronezh. This left the schools in Moscow, Iaroslavl', Pskov, Kiev, Saratov, and Perm offering general courses, and the St. Petersburg School and the Teachers' Seminary offering specialized study. With this change, all those schools offering a general education were given the new name of Military Primary Schools.[170]

These Military Primary Schools were still considered temporary by the War Ministry, since their basic purpose was to provide a general elementary education. In the strictest sense, they were not schools at all but military formations. Even in the late sixties they still retained the battalion organization of cantonists and were subdivided into companies commanded by regular army officers. The usual forms of military discipline were present, and despite heroic efforts on the part of the War Ministry to provide competent instructors the bulk of the teachers were soldiers of long service whose academic qualifications were almost nonexistent.[171] However, with the reduction in the number of students and the conviction on the part of the War Ministry that it would likely be a very long time before the national system of education would be adequate to meet the needs of all of Russian society, the Military Primary Schools settled down into a more or less permanent form. Their reform then became both possible and necessary.

Beginning in 1867, the War Ministry began to define more clearly the rights and tasks of each of the schools. The Teachers' Seminary of the Moscow School began on a regular basis to provide a three-year course for those who had finished a Military Primary School and had reached the age of sixteen. Each class was to accept a total of seventy-five students, and, to provide them with practical teaching experience, a free primary school was appended to the Seminary.[172] The War Ministry defined more precisely the curriculum in the other specialized schools

170. "Preobrazovanie uchilishch voennogo vedomstva," *Voennyi Sbornik*, No. 8 (1866), p. 206, and, "Prikaz voennogo ministra za 18 maia, No. 147," *Voennyi Sbornik*, No. 7 (1866), p. 30.

171. "Voenno-nachal'nyia shkoly," *Voennyi Sbornik*, No. 2 (1867), p. 92.

172. *Ibid.*, pp. 94–95, and, "O sostoianii uchitel'skoi seminarii v uchebno-vospitatel'nom otnoshenii," *Pedagogicheskii Sbornik*, No. 7 (1866), pp. 313–394.

to insure high standards.[173] The Military Primary Schools became pre-paratory schools for the more specialized schools and to fulfill this pur-pose offered a four-year elementary program in general subjects. Students were accepted into the schools between the ages of twelve and fifteen, and they generally came from social elements not normally eligible for ma-triculation in the military *gymnazia*.[174]

By 1869, the process of making this system into a permanent part of the military educational program reached a new and final phase. Miliutin ordered that the Military Primary Schools be reconstituted as military *pro-gymnazia*, at once raising their status and giving them permanence. Although the entrance requirements remained much the same after this reform, entering students now had to demonstrate their ability to read, write, and do simple arithmetic. The curriculum of the schools was a bit broader and more advanced and included religion, arithmetic and ele-mentary algebra, beginning geometry, history, geography, calligraphy, drawing, dancing, gymnastics, singing and military drill. The *pro-gymnazia* were no longer to be preparatory schools merely for the higher technical schools of the army, but they now were to provide a reservoir from which students could enter the junker schools.[175] They became to the junker schools what the military *gymnazia* were to the military schools. This was of great significance. Since the students of the *pro-gymnazia* were almost entirely nongentry, they were in effect providing the less privileged elements in Russian society with the means, that of education, to compete on a more nearly equal basis with the gentry for admission into the officer corps.

In summary, it is clear that the failures and problems of military edu-cation and training were a direct consequence of the inability of the civil system of education to satisfy the basic needs of society. The Empire was

173. See, for example, "R.V.O.: Voenno-fel'dsherskiia shkoly," *Voennyi Sbornik*, No. 7 (1869), p. 60, and, "Programa uchebnogo kursa v voenno-chertezhnoi shkole," *Pedagogicheskii Sbornik*, No. 2 (1868), pp. 3–125.

174. "Voenno-nachal'nyia shkoly," *Voennyi Sbornik*, No. 2 (1867), p. 94, and, "Zadacha voenno-nachal'nykh shkol," *Pedagogicheskii Sbornik*, No. 1 (1867), p. 10.

175. "Prikaz voennogo ministra za 6 maia, No. 172," *Russkii Invalid*, No. 58 (1869), and "Voennyia progimnazii," *Voennyi Sbornik*, No. 7 (1869), pp. 58–59. Those who did not choose to go on either to a higher technical school or a junker school could immediately go into active duty with the rank of Clerk of the Second Class and an obligation to serve for a period of six years.

forced to compete with Western European states which had high levels of literacy in all strata of society making possible the creation of modern armies and officer corps responsive to rapid changes in technology and capable of innovation. Miliutin had to make up for the failures in Russian education by having the War Ministry assume the task of providing a general education for its officers and technicians as well as professional and specialized training. The continued inability of the civil schools to meet the needs of the Empire meant that the army had to continue as the school of the nation, despite its desire to relinquish all general studies to the Ministry of Public Instruction.

5

Daniel in the Lions' Den

THE ROLE of Miliutin as a politician was of great significance for the evolution of the Great Reforms. His position as War Minister made him one of the chief advisers to the Emperor and a contributor to the formulation of policy. But his position within that inner circle around Alexander was almost always that of isolation. On particular issues he often would support one or another individual who on any other question was his mortal enemy, and, in turn, individuals would from time to time lend him their support on some matters. Miliutin was nevertheless looked upon as a maverick by his ministerial colleagues, and he was able to remain in office only because of his undoubted loyalty to the Emperor and the fact that no one else appeared who had such obvious qualifications for his post.

Miliutin's loyalty to the crown was closely bound up with his general political convictions. There can be no doubt that he believed in a latter-day form of political enlightened despotism. The autocracy and the state were to him the instruments for reforming Russian society. The Emperor alone had the power to enforce the unity and cohesiveness necessary for the progress of the nation:

Reform [in Russia] may be accomplished only by force. We still have too much dissatisfaction, too varied interests, to expect something good and durable from the initiative of these diverse interests. Further, application to this or that locality damages the unity of the state and fosters separatism and rivalry. . . .[1]

Miliutin's unqualified support of the crown was appreciated by Alexander and provides one of the clues for explaining the War Minister's long tenure of office despite his unpopularity in court circles. Upon one occasion, Count P. A. Valuev, the Minister of Internal Affairs and a member of the planter party, wrote in his diary,

> [Shuvalov] related to me a recent conversation with the War Minister. In respect to the remark that the public is amazed by the firmness of the Emperor in sacrificing his own popularity to retain in their present positions the War Minister. . . his brother, and General Zelenyi, [Miliutin] answered that the Emperor would never dismiss them because they have two great advantages over their opponents: first, they know what they want and are prepared to proclaim it on Admiralty Square, which the others (that is, we) will not do; and secondly, the Emperor knows that they support him completely and wholeheartedly, whereas the others (that is again, we) wish to limit him. The latter thought actually is true in just that precise sense in which His Majesty is thinking. . . .[2]

Miliutin's trust in the autocrat as the instrument of Russian progress was, however, to prove misplaced. After his own retirement, Miliutin reviewed the case and rejected the view that Alexander's reforming activities had

> paused only at that point where they began to touch the very foundation of the autocracy. If [the Emperor] had actually intended sooner or later to touch those foundations, the time for it still had not come; much remained to be done within the strictly administrative sphere. . . . In this respect, there was no necessity to pay any attention to the desires of several of our too-impatient elements, the so-called intelligentsia. The *reasonable* majority acknowledges the inopportuneness of any constitutional reconstruction of Russia. Frightened by the radical minority, it wants only law and order. It also is prepared to support the power of the autocracy *if only* this power would move intelligently along the path of progress.[3]

This implied criticism of the Emperor was made more explicit in other comments on the role and personality of the Tsar-Liberator.

1. *Dnevnik*, I., 31–32.
2. P. A. Valuev, *Dnevnik P. A. Valueva, 1861–1876*, 2 vols., I., 218. Cf. V. V. Garmiza, *Podgotovka zemskoi reformy 1864 goda*, pp. 161–163.
3. *Dnevnik*, IV., 97. The italics are mine.

There is no doubt that Miliutin was personally devoted to Alexander nor that he appreciated the positive achievements of his reign.[4] His grief upon the assassination of the Emperor was real, and for a long time afterwards he was pained by his memory of the tragedy. But while he liked to emphasize Alexander's role as Tsar-Liberator, he recognized that Alexander had allowed his progressive aims to perish.[5] He was, moreover, acutely aware of the flaws in Alexander's character and was often stung by his ingratitude or inconstancy. Miliutin found in an article written by Anatole Leroy-Beaulieu entitled, "L'empereur Alexandre et la mission du noveau Tsar,"[6] an impressive and accurate characterization of Alexander. The writer held that the Emperor was kindly, generous, intelligent, and honorable, but that he lacked resolution. Not possessing firmness himself, he would not seek that quality among his subjects.[7] But even if he had found a Richlieu or a Bismarck, he would not have delegated to him the necessary powers.

Miliutin completely agreed with Leroy-Beaulieu's analysis:

The deceased Emperor received such training and grew up in such an atmosphere that he was not capable in his understanding to rise to the heights of contemporary political questions, and did not possess sufficient character to systematically sustain the reforms begun by him and inspired by one or another of those individuals temporarily enjoying his favor. Actually, he was jealous of his power while temporarily granting influence to this or that person. . . . You have but to recall the times of Count Peter Shuvalov and, at the end, Count Loris-Melikov.[8]

4. *Ibid.*, IV., 25ff.

5. *Ibid.*, I., 120, and *ibid.*, IV., 25 and 30.

6. *Ibid.*, I., 122ff and 193, *ibid.*, IV., 90. The article was in the April 1881 issue of *Revue de deux Mondes.*

7. Feoktistov quotes the poet Tiutchev to the effect that Alexander in the presence of a man of intelligence was like a rheumatic standing in a cold wind. This biting indictment does much to explain the Emperor's behavior, particularly his personal inclination to surround himself as much as possible with "courtiers" rather than the more reflective persons who formed the reform party. E. M. Feoktistov, p. 348.

8. *Dnevnik*, IV., 91*n*. Perhaps no other quality in the Emperor was of greater significance than the Emperor's lack of political perception. He never really understood what the reformers were about, even though they often were carrying out his own instructions. Nowhere is this more clear than in his relations with Nicholas Miliutin.

Leroy-Beaulieu's statement that Alexander did not like to delegate power into the hands of individuals with strong personalities and that he was pleased to have his ministers quarrel among themselves because it made the position of the autocrat stronger, found Miliutin in complete agreement:

> This is quite true; I consider myself a proper person to testify to that. . . . How can I fail to recall in this the difficulties of those periods of struggle with Count Peter Shuvalov, then with Field Marshal Bariatinskii, and later with Count D. Tolstoy, and so on? To the words of the author, I unfortunately may add yet another facet to the character of the departed Emperor; that is his dissimulation, even two-facedness or falsity.[9]

Miliutin, moreover, felt that Alexander had a naturally suspicious nature, resembling in this respect his uncle, the Emperor Alexander I.[10]

Miliutin's insistence upon a strong and unified state remained a characteristic during his entire political career. He consistently opposed all divisive national movements and the assertion of special rights for any particular class. He viewed the reforms as positive moves to foster the general organic unity of the nation.[11] Without doubt, Miliutin believed, as did Pogodin,[12] that the true Russian society was classless and that it was the manifest will of the *narod*, the Russian nation which was of special importance. One often finds allusions in the *Russkii Invalid* to the sense of partnership between the state (epitomized by the autocracy) and the people, with the state assuming the role of the instrument of national progress.[13]

This fundamental attitude underlay the whole range of Miliutin's political and social thinking and brought him into direct conflict with the interests of the gentry class. Such class or other special interests were an anathema to Miliutin. Because he feared that a constitutional government would result in an aristocratic oligarchy in Russia, he opposed the granting of any constitution which would limit the powers of the auto-

---

9. *Ibid.*, IV., 91–92*n* and 93.
10. *Ibid.*, IV., 92.
11. *Russkii Invalid*, No. 192 (1865).
12. N. V. Riasanovsky, *Nicholas I and Official Nationality in Russia, 1825–1855*, p. 143.
13. This is implicit, but see particularly, *Russkii Invalid*, No. 192 (1865), for an editorial defending the basic social and national views of Miliutin's newspaper.

crat. He in fact adhered to the Slavophile view that class privilege was alien to the Russian national experience:

The history of Russia is not at all explained nor is it justified by separate closed classes, each enjoying special privileges. Such classes existed in the West; we never had any of them. The *dvoriane* had formerly the status of serving people; they bore service to the state and for this enjoyed special advantages, but this class was always open to individuals from other classes. . . . The majority of the *dvoriane* carry on no type of service and do not have even a secure status. For this reason, it would hardly be useful for the state to implement reforms introducing enactments which would support a separation of the *dvoriane* from the other classes and would give them new class privileges. . . .[14]

Miliutin underscored the implications of this view in its political sense:

For us, there are two major conditions, *sine qua non*—without which the entire political theory as applied to Russia must be considered as insoluble: first—the [necessity] of the unity and integrity of the state, and, secondly, the legal equality of its members. For the first condition is necessary the strong power and resolute predominance of the Russians. For the second condition, we must cast off all obsolete, out-lived privileges, to dispense once and for all with the rights of one caste over another. Still, strong power does not exclude the personal liberty of the citizen, nor his autonomy; the predominance of the Russian element does not mean the oppression and destruction of other peoples. The removal of old privileges is a long way from leveling or socialism. Thus, he who sincerely wishes good for Russia and the Russian people, and who thinks more about their future than about present egocentric interests, must then resolutely reject everything which may either shake the power of unity and indivisibility, or incite or plot the separation of the several parts, or support the concept of the ascendency of one class over another.[15]

Miliutin had a strong sense of history and its progress. History to him was an organic process governed by general laws. Within the historical process, each people was free to develop in its own way but always in conformity with those general laws.[16] Russia was free to follow her own path but had in the western European states, and particularly

14. Quoted in Garmiza, p. 233.
15. Quoted in *Dnevnik*, I., 32. Cf. B., "Spravedlivy li tolki o separaticheskikh stremleniiakh ostzeiskogo kraiia," *Russkii Invalid*, No. 211 (1864). A paraphrase of the above quotation may be found in an editorial in *Russkii Invalid*, No. 17 (1865).
16. This is implicit in the general editorial policy of the *Russkii Invalid* during the 1860s. For an explicit example, see "Zemskiia uchrezhdeniia," *Russkii Invalid*, No. 184 (1863). Cf. Men'kov, II., 307, and, E. M. Feoktistov, p. 335.

England, the models for her future evolution;[17] any reform had to begin with a study of foreign models but in the end they had to conform to Russian needs and circumstances. Peter the Great had placed Russia on the path of progress, but she had strayed, and Miliutin feared that she might do so again.[18] One can conclude from Miliutin's views that while the West had shown Russia the way of progress it had also taught her the lessons to be learned through error. The convulsions of social and political revolution in western Europe could, he hoped, be avoided in Russia only by maintaining the organic unity of the nation and self-consciously working for progress.

Miliutin viewed the emancipation of the serfs and the Great Reforms against this general background. He saw the emancipation as the most fundamental change in all Russian history. It rivaled the actions of Peter the Great and in one way exceeded them. Peter's reforms had been mechanical, having been limited to the fabrication and recasting of institutions, while Alexander's reforms touched the people, the very roots of society.[19] At the foundation of the reforms lay the peasant question. From the liberation of the serfs came all other reforms and would eventually come the future of Russia.[20]

But in the view of the War Minister, the mass of the people were not yet ready to assume any responsibility for the direction of the state. A long period of education and the gradual acquisition of experience in the conduct of civic affairs would first be necessary.[21] The gentry as a class often possessed the necessary education, but there existed a clear danger that if they alone were brought into the direction of public affairs, they would seek to retain or expand their privileges and would continue to exist as a caste apart, thereby destroying the organic unity of the nation.

17. N., "Neskol'ko slov o proekte zemskikh uchrezhdenii," *Russkii Invalid*, No. 138, 1863. This did not imply, however, that there could be any slavish borrowing; reforms had to be constructed in accordance with Russia's own unique needs and conditions. See, for example, *Russkii Invalid*, No. 182 (1863).

18. D. A. Miliutin, *Vospominaniia*, pp. 414–415, and *Russkii Invalid*, No. 1 (1863).

19. *Ibid., loc. cit.*

20. This view is implicit in every new reform undertaken by the War Ministry. See especially the impassioned and polemical editorial on the emancipation and Russian politics in *Russkii Invalid*, No. 229 (1865).

21. Nowhere is this made more clear than in his comparison of the quality of Russian recruits with those of the western European states. *Despatches*, March 8, 1872.

One of the immediate questions for the reform period, therefore, was that of reconciling the changes that were taking place in respect to the interests of the landowners.[22]

Perhaps the best illustration of Miliutin's views on what specifically needed to be done to reconcile the gentry was in his efforts to shape the new land assemblies or *zemstva* which the government began to establish in the European provinces of Russia beginning in 1864. These elective bodies, which existed at only the district and provincial levels, assumed the responsibility for many local functions including the management of some economic matters, such as education, the building and maintenance of roads and hospitals.[23] While the powers granted to these bodies were quite limited, few failed to understand their potential significance. Without speculating further, Miliutin saw in them the means for the revitalization of the economy of the countryside and a stimulation for both agriculture and industry. He conceived of them as essentially administrative bodies and only secondarily legislative, with their basic purpose being that of promoting economic growth.[24]

Perhaps the knottiest question preceding the establishment of the *zemstva* was that of their composition and the manner of their election. At issue, in the eyes of the War Minister, were the two questions of the unity of the Russian people and of providing the *zemstva* with responsible deputies. An editorial in the War Minister's official newspaper, *Russkii Invalid*, noted just before the opening of the debates on this subject in the State Council:

> The forthcoming debates on this subject in the State Council may pay no more attention to any one thing than this, that at the present time every step on the road to develop the public life of Russian land and the *unity* of its inhabitants provides strength to the Russian state, but to its enemies it suggests an awareness of this strength.[25]

The *zemstva* had to provide the means for the inhabitants to meet together in their common interest but was not to be a vehicle for com-

---

22. *Russkii Invalid*, No. 1 (1863).

23. The restrictive limitations upon the scope and purposes of the *zemstva* found approval in the editorial policy of the *Russkii Invalid* very early. See, for example, the editorial signed by M. Iumatov in No. 4 (1863).

24. *Russkii Invalid*, No. 186 (1863).

25. *Russkii Invalid*, No. 110 (1863).

petition among its elements as in western assemblies. Another editorial recalled that the Russian state had been founded upon the basis of the trust granted to the rulers by the people and that this trust had remained as a fundamental part of Russian national life.[26]

The group which threatened this unity was the gentry. While they could not be excluded from participation in the *zemstva*, their role in the land assemblies had to be on bases other than their privileges as members of a favored caste:

Individuals capable of dealing with economic matters as must be the affairs of the land establishments, are to be found in all classes, and if the mass of all classes are taken into consideration, it may be that the preponderance is not on the side of the *dvoriane*. . . . Without doubt, the chief influence in [the *zemstva*] will be retained by the *dvoriane*, but they will achieve this by their personal qualities, not by social privileges.[27]

Miliutin reinforced this with the further assertion that the Russian gentry, coming as they did from the serving people, were unlike the western nobility. Thus there had been no class struggle in Russia, and there remained no valid historical or legal distinctions among the people which could justify any accommodation for the gentry in the electoral system of the *zemstva*.[28] The *Russkii Invalid* offered the optimistic view that the gentry in the post-emancipation era were willing to live a life in unity with the people and would entrust to them their talents and resources.[29]

In the final analysis, Miliutin was concerned with an elector's sense of responsibility. He therefore rejected what he considered to be the extremes of universal manhood suffrage and electoral elitism and chose instead a middle course which balanced some popular representation against a franchise based upon function. He felt, for example, that those who possessed property or a university-level education would be suffi-

26. N., "Neskol'ko slov o proekte zemskikh uchrezhdenii," *Russkii Invalid*, No. 138 (1863).

27. Quoted in Garmiza, p. 233.

28. This concept is constantly reasserted in the *Russkii Invalid* and was a fundamental tenet of Miliutin's ideological commitment to the organic unity of the Russian people. See, for example, "Zemskiia uchrezhdeniia," *Russkii Invalid*, No. 184 (1863), and, N., "Neskol'ko slov o proekte zemskikh uchrezhdenii," *Russkii Invalid*, No. 138 (1863).

29. "Zemskiia uchrezhdeniia," *Russkii Invalid*, No. 184 (1863), and "O zemskikh uchrezhdeniiakh," *Russkii Invalid*, No. 11 (1864).

ciently responsible to assure the election of a worthy assembly. The deputies had to have particular interests, but they also had to be able to rise above them and to view the needs of society as a whole.[30]

To accomplish this, Miliutin proposed a formula. Within a district, one half of the *zemstvo* would be elected by that part of the population which paid the land tax. By a graduated system, those who paid the highest land taxes were to be favored out of proportion to their numbers, while those who possessed university degrees and the clergy were to be given some representation. The other half of the *zemstvo* would be elected by the rest of the population.[31] This formula gave those few with landed property and higher educations a parity with the great bulk of the population, insuring responsibility and stability in the conduct of the *zemstva* while providing the less affluent elements of society with some voice and the means for gaining experience in the resolution of their own affairs. There is little doubt that the War Minister saw a possibility for social mobility. Individuals acquiring either education or property could move from one category to the other, so that neither group would assume the characteristics of a caste.

Miliutin was not at this time ready to trust any real power, even in the *zemstva*, to the broad base of the population. He wanted some prior demonstration of responsibility as a test for office, since the most immediate value of the land assemblies was the improvement of the economy and the commonwealth of the nation. The gentry class over the short run would probably play the dominant role but they would do this as property owners or as the better educated in society, not as a privileged class.[32] Social mobility was to be possible on an individual basis through the acquisition of property or an education. Despite Miliutin's basic confidence in the future of the Russian people, he did not feel that they yet understood public affairs sufficiently to be given real power.[33]

This attitude on the part of Miliutin was important in other areas as well. In the early sixties, the subject of a constitution for Russia was a matter for lively discussion in the Russian press and in the private salons. Miliutin did favor a constitution as an ultimate objective but

30. "Zemskiia uchrezhdeniia," *Russkii Invalid*, Nos. 184 and 186 (1863).
31. "Zemskiia uchrezhdeniia," *Russkii Invalid*, No. 207 (1863).
32. See above.
33. "Zemskiia uchrezhdeniia," *Russkii Invalid*, No. 186 (1863).

rejected the advisability of any instrument limiting the power of the autocracy in the near future:

I of course do not share these aspirations, not because I am an opponent of constitutions in general—what educated person could condemn this form of government?—but rather because if we should at some time have a constitution, then it must be a real constitution, that is, completely democratic. It is my conviction that granting political rights to one class and not to another would be unjust and harmful.[34]

The gentry threatened to assert its own interests at the expense of the rest of society, while the great mass of the people lacked education and the necessary experience.

Miliutin was not, however, opposed to constitutional schemes which did not limit the power of the autocracy. Count P. A. Valuev presented to the Emperor and a circle of his selected advisers, including the War Minister, on April 13, 1863, a scheme for the integration of representatives from the proposed land assemblies into the State Council.[35] Every effort was made to assure the collected body that their role was to be merely *consultative* and that the members of the Council who had been appointed by the Emperor would retain the initiative of the agenda. Despite the moderate role these *zemstva* representatives were to play, only Miliutin and Prince V. A. Dolgorukov, the former War Minister and presently the Chief of Gendarmes, supported the proposal.[36]

A few years later, the Emperor's brother, the Grand Duke Constantine Nikolaevich, presented a similar proposal for reorganizing the State Council, noting that this did nothing that would affect the powers of the autocracy but would give some satisfaction to those who had a real desire to have some means for their voice to be heard at the throne.[37] These schemes were in no way inconsistent with Miliutin's basic views, since neither limited the autocracy; quite on the contrary, they would serve to provide the links binding the Emperor and the people, thereby making concrete one of the War Minister's most cherished ideas.

34. Feoktistov, p. 327.
35. For the text of Valuev's proposal, see K. L. Bermanskii, " 'Konstitutsionnye' proekty tsarstvovaniia Aleksandra II," *Vestnik Prava*, No. 11 (1905), pp. 225–233.
36. Garmiza, p. 163. Dolgorukov's motives were undoubtedly different from Miliutin's as he was a consistent proponent of the interests of the gentry.
37. Valuev, II., 166.

Miliutin's political gradualism and his sense of the organic unity of the nation were integral parts of his highly developed nationalism. One finds that his nationalist outlook more closely resembled that form of Official Nationality espoused by the historian and publicist M. P. Pogodin than of any other group or person. Miliutin was close to both westernizer and slavophile circles, but was essentially an eclectic in this respect. He, as has already been mentioned above, looked to the evolution of the western European states as the general path of the future but felt that Russia was free to follow its own specific route, although he did not see any unique fate for Russia.[38] His nationalism was in the final analysis a cultural nationalism, and this meant within the Empire the supremacy of Great Russian culture and the close identification of the Empire's cultural advance with that of the other Slavic peoples.

Miliutin held in regard the common culture, institutions, and language of the Slavic peoples. Without doubt the most important of these institutions was the Orthodox Church,[39] which in the sixties assumed a special significance as the epitome of true Slavic culture as opposed to the German-Latin west—in particular that part represented by the apostate Roman Catholic Poles. In the past, the Slavic peoples had been imposed upon by the Mongols and the Germans; the former had retarded them and the latter had tried to absorb them.[40] Their emergence to their rightful place among the peoples of the world was not to be found in either force or war, but by instilling in the minds of the Slavic peoples a consciousness of their own uniqueness, an understanding of their rights and duties, a trust in their own moral strength, and in the solidarity and strength of all the Slavic peoples.[41] This view was not political and did

38. *Dnevnik*, IV., p. 103.

39. The question of the Catholic Church and the view of it as an alien force is implicit in all that Miliutin thought and did about Poland. For some specific examples, see M. Koialovich, "Mistifikatsiia papskikh vozglasov protiv Rossii," *Russkii Invalid*, No. 207 (1864); "Beloe rimskokatolicheskoe dukhovenstvo v Tsarstve Pol'skom," *Russkii Invalid*, No. 288 (1865); the editorial in *Russkii Invalid*, No. 126 (1866); and the editorial on the Uniat Church in *Russkii Invalid*, No. 189 (1866). For Miliutin's views and policies toward the Uniat Church and its reincorporation into Russian national life, see *Dnevnik*, I., *passim*.

40. *Russkii Invalid*, No. 163 (1867).

41. *Ibid., loc. cit.*

not see in the Russian fraternity with the Slavs any plan for expansion to the Elbe and the Adriatic, the frontiers already having been pushed far enough.[42]

The official newspaper of the War Ministry, the *Russkii Invalid*, was Miliutin's chief vehicle for publicizing his views on nationalism. It reminded its readers of the great moments of the past when the Russian nation had arisen in the defense of the fatherland. The population had in those times been enserfed, but with the emancipation they had become free and they could be expected to be even more willing to defend the state.[43]

But without doubt the most thorough exposition of Miliutin's national sentiments was to be found in his attitudes toward the Poles and the Baltic Germans. Miliutin came to the War Ministry just as the crisis which was to lead to the Polish Insurrection of 1863 was building. The deep roots of this revolt went back to the partitions in the eighteenth century when the Polish state was divided among its three neighbors— Prussia, Austria and Russia. The Russian share, together with some other bits of territory, was constituted by the Congress of Vienna as the Kingdom of Poland with the Russian Emperor as king. After a revolt in 1830–31, Nicholas I canceled its constitution and gradually began to incorporate Poland organically into the Empire.[44] New troubles erupted when, in the reign of Alexander II, the Russian government began to seek some accommodation with Polish national feelings. The raised hopes of the Poles led to a number of demonstrations which tended to grow more violent. The government countered by attempting to conscript the more unruly elements into the army, thereby precipitating the revolt which began in early 1863.[45]

Miliutin came to office just as the Polish question was entering its most difficult stages. In fact, on the day before he assumed his new post he took part in a council of which the Emperor himself was chairman to

---

42. *Ibid., loc. cit.*

43. *Russkii Invalid*, No. 50 (1863), p. 216.

44. For two recent studies of the Polish insurrections, see R. F. Leslie, *Polish Politics and the Revolution of November, 1830*, and R. F. Leslie, *Reform and Insurrection in Russian Poland, 1856–1865.*

45. *Ibid.*, pp. 163–167.

consider policy matters affecting Poland. At this time, Miliutin favored merging the civil and military administrations in Poland to assure stricter control.[46] The government was pursuing a policy of conciliation at the time, however, and looked to a Polish nobleman, the Marquis Alexander Wielopolski, serving as the highest civil administrator in Poland, to act as an intermediary and to appeal to the more moderate elements in Polish society. Miliutin maintained a hearty dislike of Wielopolski and distrusted him:

> Ideologically he was old Poland, *szlachta*, and clerical; in all his projects, Wielopolski systematically promoted the interests and influence of the Catholic Church.[47]

In high policy meetings Miliutin consistently refused to support Wielopolski and the policy for which he stood. Upon one occasion, he expressed his feelings toward the Poles by quoting his former commander in the Caucasus, Prince Bariatinskii, to the effect that the best thing that Russia could do about Poland would be simply to get rid of it altogether, since nothing that Russia could do would likely effect any sort of reconciliation with the Poles.[48] Since this approach was not practical, the only alternative was repression.

On September 20, 1862, the Emperor created a special committee to review the events taking place in Poland and the western provinces.[49] This body, which lasted until 1865, included many of the ministers whose portfolios in one way or another made them interested parties in the developments in the area, with the President of the Council of Ministers, Prince P. P. Gagarin, as chairman. This group advised the Emperor on a day-to-day basis on the progress of affairs during the insurrection and the settlement which followed. Miliutin of course played an important role in this committee,[50] but his contributions were more spectacular in other areas.

Miliutin was in a difficult situation because of the revolt. He had only

46. Valuev, I., 126.
47. Quoted in B. G. Revunenkov, *Pol'skoe vosstanie 1863 g. i evropeiskaia diplomatiia*, p. 89. Cf. Valuev, I., 166.
48. *Ibid.*, p. 265, and Feoktistov, p. 345.
49. Valuev, I., 393–394.
50. Valuev, I., *passim*.

just come to office, and the reforms he was conducting in the army had only just begun. The Russian army was in no condition to carry on a major war,[51] and during its entire course the Polish Insurrection threatened to precipitate an intervention by one or more of the European powers. Much of European opinion was hostile to Russia,[52] and the creation by the powers of the Kingdom of Poland at the Congress of Vienna posed a tricky legal question. The problem therefore was to conduct military operations in Poland and to suppress the revolt, while at the same time preventing European opinion from forcing one or another power to yield to the temptation to intervene. Miliutin lived in fear that the Polish situation would involve Russia in a war for which she had neither the military nor financial resources. In his memoirs he reviewed the gravity of the situation in most somber tones:

> It was necessary that we avoid any possibility of war, which at that time would have been disastrous. Our armed forces were not ready for war. Therefore, our diplomats were directed to employ all their arts in stalling so that without sacrificing the integrity of Russia, we would not be locked in a war with the largest part of Europe.[53]

The task was not easy, and several times during the crisis disaster seemed to be imminent.

In this atmosphere of great anxiety, while the armed forces were proceeding with the pacification of Poland, Miliutin turned to one of his most potent weapons, the printing press. The War Minister's understanding of the power of the written word led him to transform the official newspaper of the War Ministry, the *Russkii Invalid*, from a narrowly military organ to a wide-ranging forum for the discussion of questions affecting the whole of Russian society and of foreign affairs. When Miliutin became War Minister, the newspaper was not even published within the Ministry but was contracted out. This soon changed, however, and on January 19, 1862, the Inspectorate of the War Ministry issued a circular announcing that beginning on January 1, 1863, the War Ministry would resume publication. The announcement further noted that the

---

51. *Doklad*, January 15, 1862, *Stoletie*, I., 73ff.
52. See, for example, the assessment of European opinion and the possible policies open to the western powers in the editorial in *Russkii Invalid*, No. 105 (1863).
53. Quoted in Revunenkov, pp. 257–258.

Russkii Invalid would be an official publication of the War Ministry in its official section only and that the rest of the newspaper would be devoted to news of broader interest.[54]

The first editors of the *Russkii Invalid* were Colonel of the General Staff D. I. Romanovskii and A. N. Beketov, a professor at St. Petersburg University. The latter served only a short time, and when he left he was replaced as assistant editor by a brilliant young staff officer, S. P. Zykov. In 1865, Zykov replaced Romanovskii as editor and held that post until the newspaper was forced to revert to being a narrowly official organ of the War Ministry at the end of 1868.[55]

The newspaper was explicitly political in its new form. It was similar in this respect to several other newspapers serving other ministries. The Minister of Education, A. V. Golovnin, for example, had subsidized and helped to found the newspaper *Golos*,[56] which in turn gave his views and policies wide publicity. At the same time, the Minister of Internal Affairs, Valuev, founded the *Severnaia Pochta* as an official organ of his Ministry and carefully controlled its editorial policy.[57] But the *Russkii Invalid*, because it served the War Minister, and because its editorial policy accepted the reforms and wanted to see them extended, became the target of all those who resented the nineteenth of February or who wished to see the reforms ended or pushed in another direction.

The editors and contributors of the *Russkii Invalid* represented an aggregation of very fine minds. Included were A. V. Bushen, V. P. Burenin, the pan-slavist A. F. Hilferding, A. P. Zablotskii-Desiatovskii (who later was biographer for Miliutin's uncle, Count P. D. Kiselev), Professor M. I. Koialovich, A. I. Levshin, Prince V. P. Meshcherskii, V. I. Lamanskii, the brother of the War Minister, N. A. Miliutin, A. S. Suvorin, and E. M. Feoktistov (who later edited the Journal of the Ministry of Public Instruction).[58]

The regular staff took its job very seriously and worked each day from

54. S. P. Zykov, "Nabroski iz moei zhizni," *Russakaia Starina*, No. 6 (1910), p. 483.
55. *Ibid.*, pp. 483–484.
56. M. Lemke, *Epokha tsenzurnykh reform, 1859–1865*, pp. 83–85.
57. See A. V. Nikitenko, *Dnevnik*, 3 vols., II., *passim*.
58. S. P. Zykov, "Nabroski iz moei zhizni," *Russkaia Starina*, No. 6 (1910), p. 484.

early in the morning to late in the evening. The War Minister maintained close control over editorial policy, particularly in matters affecting foreign policy. Editors were liable to be called at any hour to the War Minister's office to allow Miliutin to read and approve articles before their publication.[59]

During its years of publication, the newspaper maintained a consistency of viewpoint possible only because of the War Minister's careful direction of its policy—and his deliberate use of it as a political weapon. Alexander himself chose from time to time to insert articles, much to the frustration of the censor assigned to the newspaper, a certain Colonel Stürmer.[60] Often, the intervention of the Minister himself was necessary to override the censor's objections and to allow the publication of an item inserted by the Emperor.

The *Russkii Invalid* began its new program of publication just at the time that the shooting started in Poland. The newspaper sought to keep the public well informed on the progress of military operations in Poland. To accommodate this new role, the editorship decided to publish mornings so that the telegraphed bulletins arriving late at night from the battle zones could reach the streets with a minimum of delay.[61] In addition, in those periods when the military action became most intense and telegraphed dispatches were coming in around the clock, the *Russkii Invalid* issued tabloid-size supplements with its regular editions so that the public could be assured of receiving the very latest news.

Other newspapers in the capital, not having the special advantages enjoyed by the *Russkii Invalid* as an organ of the War Ministry, were understandably upset by what they considered to be unfair competition.[62] On one occasion, the editorship felt compelled to answer charges made by *Birzhevye Vedomosti* that great events were also taking place in Schleswig-Holstein, Italy, and the Danubian Principalities which demanded attention in the Russian press equal to that devoted to Poland.[63]

---

59. *Ibid., loc. cit.* Cf. Feoktistov, p. 335, and P. K. Men'kov, *Zapiski Petra Konovicha Men'kova*, 3 vols., II, 307.

60. S. P. Zykov, "Nabroski iz moei zhizni," *Russkaia Starina*, No. 4 (1910), p. 143.

61. *Russkii Invalid*, No. 49 (1863).

62. See, for example, the sarcastic editorial in *Birzhevye Vedomosti*, No. 50 (1863).

63. *Russkii Invalid*, No. 262 (1863).

Nevertheless, the *Russkii Invalid* persisted in its policy of closely covering the events in Poland until early in 1864, by which time the insurrection had been suppressed and the danger of European intervention had
passed.

But the purpose of the *Russkii Invalid* was not merely to keep the
public informed of events. It sought to explain the actions of the Russian
government and to persuade both domestic and foreign readers of the
justice of Russian policy. The newspaper maintained the view that the
insurrection in Poland was not a national revolt. The peasantry in particular did not go along with the movement and in fact often actively
opposed it.[64] The revolt was the work of a relatively small group composed of the great magnates of Poland, the *szlachta*, the priesthood, some
civil functionaries, and a small segment of Jews.[65]

The editorship pointed out that legal means for reform had been placed
at the disposal of the Poles, but the lack of any Polish aptitude for orderly
government had made the use of these means impossible.[66] Later on,
in answer to charges that Russia had suppressed a *national* revolution in
Poland by fomenting a *social* revolution and pitting the lower against
the upper classes, the *Russkii Invalid* affirmed that the so-called national
revolution was restrictive in its social complexion and that the people,
that is the *nation*, had remained apart.[67]

The newspaper consistently maintained this point of view, adhering to
it long after the cessation of hostilities.[68] There is little doubt that this
was Dmitrii Miliutin's own view as well as that of his brother Nicholas
and that this concept underlay the settlement that the latter was instrumental in making in Poland after the conclusion of the revolt.[69]

The *Russkii Invalid* carried on a vigorous dialogue with the domestic
press on the Polish question, lecturing them on patriotism and on the

64. See particularly, *Russkii Invalid*, No. 100 (1863), and -v, "Po povodu
osvobozhdeniia litovskikh krest'ian," *Russkii Invalid*, No. 73 (1863).

65. *Russkii Invalid*, No. 27 (1863).

66. *Ibid., loc. cit.*, and *Russkii Invalid*, No. 105 (1863).

67. *Russkii Invalid*, No. 16 (1864).

68. See, for example, the editorial in *Russkii Invalid*, No. 142 (1865).

69. For an analysis of Nicholas Miliutin's views on Poland, see Stanley J.
Zyzniewski, "Miliutin and the Polish Question," *Harvard Slavic Studies*, IV.,
237–248.

broader significance of the Polish question. Normal discretion made it difficult for newspapers with more moderate viewpoints to defend themselves from the militancy of the *Russkii Invalid*. Their most usual counter was the observation that the newspaper was an organ of the War Ministry and should therefore concern itself only with military matters and not with the "Polish question" as such.[70] Despite the weight of such newspapers as the *Severnaia Pochta, Golos', Birzhevye Vedomosti*, and *Vest'*, which opposed in one way or another the policies of the *Russkii Invalid*, it found a firm ally in M. N. Katkov's *Moskovskie Vedomosti*.

This latter newspaper took its cue from the *Russkii Invalid*[71] and soon became an even more shrill defender of the Russian national cause in Poland than the organ of the War Ministry. The editorship of the *Russkii Invalid* noted with satisfaction that the outlook of the two papers was often in complete accord on the Polish matter and within the framework of this atmosphere of good feeling heaped praise upon Katkov, and went to great pains to carry the story of a testimonial dinner given in honor of the Moscow editor.[72]

The really pressing problem was not the domestic press, however, but western European opinion and the threat of intervention. The avowed concern of the *Russkii Invalid* was that as the organ of the War Ministry it could obtain full and accurate information, thereby refuting false reports and rumors.[73] There may really have been a naive belief on the part of the War Minister and the editorship that if the public at large and western European opinion only knew the truth and understood the motives of the Russian government, any further difficulties would be forestalled. On one occasion, the *Russkii Invalid* severely questioned the validity of the "third-hand" information upon which the foreign journalists and diplomats based their assumptions. It sharply scored these

70. See the editorial in *Russkii Invalid*, No. 49 (1863) answering charges made by *Birzhevye Vedomosti*. Cf. *Golos*, No. 259 (1863).

71. A comparison of the time table of editorials on the Polish question, suggests that initially the *Moskovskie Vedomosti* followed the *Russkii Invalid* both in time and subject matter. The *Moskovskie Vedomosti* tended to be more extravagant, however, in its views. See, for example, the editorial in *Moskovskie Vedomosti*, No. 107 (1863).

72. "Obed M. N. Katkovu," *Russkii Invalid*, No. 131 (1863).

73. *Russkii Invalid*, No. 29 (1863).

western news stories, calling them "tales of Scheherazade," only with malice.[74]

In its efforts to influence foreign opinion, the *Russkii Invalid* recounted at length the legal bases of Russia's position in Poland, recited the various international agreements governing the constitution of the Kingdom of Poland, and reviewed the history of the entire situation.[75] Among the specific purposes of these articles was the none too subtle attempt to detach Austria from any possible coalition with France and Britain. The *Russkii Invalid* pointed out, for example, that the same international agreements that had given Russia her present position in Poland had also granted Austria the possession of one of Poland's richest provinces. Therefore, the newspaper argued, the Polish question could not be resolved by international conflict but only by peaceful agreement among the three partitioning powers: Austria, Prussia, and Russia.[76] In the same vein, the paper slyly asked the European powers what they expected to gain from going to war over Poland, then gently reminded them of the costs they would incur by resorting to arms.[77]

Besides these efforts to restrain any western impulse to intervene, the *Russkii Invalid* also sought to provide the struggle in Poland with some theoretical significance. During the course of the insurrection, the newspaper opened its pages to such writers as the pan-slavist bureaucrat Alexander Hilferding; Michael I. Koialovich, who was Professor of History at the St. Petersburg Theological Academy and an expert on religious affairs in the western provinces; and Michael P. Pogodin, the journalist and historian. Besides the more formal articles written by such men as these, there were numerous reviews and letters to the editor which added to the argument that Russia's actions in Poland were fulfilling a great historical purpose.

The concensus of these views was that the conflict in Poland was a part of the great continuing struggle between the Orthodox and Slavic east and the Latin-German west. The prize at issue at this particular point in that struggle was the control over the fate of the western prov-

74. *Russkii Invalid*, No. 101 (1863).
75. *Russkii Invalid*, No. 10, (1863).
76. *Russkii Invalid*, No. 145 (1863).
77. *Russkii Invalid*, No. 134 (1863).

inces. These lands were basically those taken by Russia during the first two partitions and in which the Polish population constituted only a small but influential minority.

These provinces had been a part of the Kievan state during the middle ages but for the last several hundred years had fallen under the domination of the Poles. The conflict in this situation stemmed from differences in culture; the Poles by adopting Catholicism had turned to the west and had thus undergone a separate evolution from the other Slavic peoples. The Polish social organization, history, and world view reflected the evolution of the west and made Polish culture alien to that of the other Slavs.[78] But the articles in the *Russkii Invalid* maintained that Polish culture, despite the domination of centuries, had failed to win over the people of the western provinces and that the latter really hungered for their reintegration into the national life of their Russian brothers.[79]

Within this context, it is interesting to note that Miliutin seemed to find the Catholic Church the most important factor in this struggle between the two cultures. He was bitterly anti-Catholic and remained so throughout his life. The *Russkii Invalid* consistently placed the priesthood among those most responsible for fomenting the insurrection[80] and accused them of forsaking the spirit of their religion to pursue purely ultramontane goals.[81]

The War Minister saw the chasm between Poland and Russia as so wide that no reconciliation was possible. Any autonomy or constitutional government would only allow the *szlachta* to repeat the events of 1830 and 1863. To meet the demands of the Polish nationalists would be unthinkable in any event, since this could be achieved only by dismembering the Empire[82] and handing over to them the peoples of the western

78. This is implicit, but a representative statement of this general viewpoint may be found in S.Sh., "Polozhenie Pol'shi v srede slavianskikh," *Russkii Invalid*, No. 50 (1863).

79. "Pis'mo iz Vil'na," *Russkii Invalid*, No. 78 (1863).

80. These charges were not limited to the clergy within Poland itself but extended to the Vatican as well. See the charge that the Polish seminary in Rome was used to train propagandists destined to stir up new troubles in Poland in *Russkii Invalid*, No. 252 (1864).

81. *Russkii Invalid*, No. 27 (1863).

82. S.Sh., "Polozhenie Pol'shi v srede slavianskikh," *Russkii Invalid*, No. 50 (1863).

provinces. Consequently, Poland had to be closely bound organically to the Empire. This organic union was to provide the government with the means to cure the ills that beset this troubled area. The state could strike at the roots of the evil, "polonism," and could destroy the *szlachta* as a class while raising the peasantry to the level of that in the rest of the Empire.[83] This social revolution would be accompanied by the emergence of the Orthodox Church from its subordinate position in the area and by the creation of a comprehensive system of elementary schools using one of the "Russian" languages.[84]

Ethnic Poland, on the other hand, would have to endure physical occupation and stern control for a long time. Hilferding maintained that Poland in any event no longer really existed, having died in the eighteenth century at the hands of the *szlachta* and the Jesuits. The bones of a decaying civilization had to be pushed aside to allow new life space in which to grow; Poland had had its moment in history but now it had no future.[85]

But during the months of crisis in 1863, the *Russkii Invalid* proved to be inadequate for all the propaganda purposes of the War Ministry. The concensus among its editorial staff was that the articles on the Polish situation suffered from several liabilities, the most important of which were that they appeared in an official newspaper and that they were published in the Russian language.[86] As a consequence they were neither convincing nor did they lend themselves to being easily read abroad. The conclusion of the editors was that they had to try to reach the western European reader on a more regular basis to counter the propaganda advantage so long enjoyed by the Polish dissidents. Miliutin was personally anxious that the articles written by Hilferding and Koialovich and pub-

83. This view appears frequently in the editorials and articles published in the *Russkii Invalid*; see, for example, No. 16 (1864) and No. 36 (1864). For a more theoretical exposition, see, A. Hilferding, "V chem iskat' razresheniia pol'skomu voprosu," *Russkii Invalid*, No. 166 (1863).

84. For example, *ibid.*, and "O narodnykh shkolakh v Podol'skoi gubernii," *Russkii Invalid*, No. 77 (1864).

85. Hilferding, "Polozhenie i zadacha Rossii v tsarstve Pol'skom," *Russkii Invalid*, No. 255 (1863). The editorship confirmed its concurrence in these views in a spirited defense of this article in No. 273 (1863).

86. S. P. Zykov, "Nabroski iz moei zhizni," *Russkaia Starina*, No. 7 (1910), p. 22.

lished in the *Russkii Invalid* should be translated and circulated abroad.[87]

The War Minister accordingly took this matter to the Emperor and gained permission to conduct studies to discover how best to reach the western European public. Miliutin placed the matter in the hands of S. P. Zykov, one of the editorial staff of the *Russkii Invalid*, who put his ideas in the form of a memorandum to the Emperor. In this draft, he reviewed the need for countering Polish propaganda in western Europe and proposed, therefore, to create a system for supplying on a regular basis news material to the western newspapers which reflected the kind of image that the government wanted to project. The Emperor gave his approval for the editorship to proceed concretely on June 19, 1863, and appropriated 10,000 rubles to cover the costs.[88]

At first the editors thought to issue individual pamphlets containing the articles of Hilferding and Koialovich, in Russian as well as in translation. They soon changed their minds, however, and began to consider the publication of a periodical which would provide the western press with news releases on a regular basis. A certain Baron Kane, a functionary at the Imperial Court, at this point warned that anything known to be emanating from the editorial staff of the War Ministry would be viewed as suspect by foreign journalists and that there was therefore a need to operate clandestinely. Miliutin passed on Baron Kane's comments to Zykov who saw merit in them. Consequently, the War Ministry began to publish secretly within the offices of the *Russkii Invalid* a lithographed newssheet called the *Correspondance Russe*.[89]

This newssheet was printed in a number of languages including English, French, Italian, German, and Dutch. They were taken out of Russia secretly and distributed abroad in such a manner as to conceal their origin in the Russian War Ministry. Despite a rather modest beginning, the articles from the *Correspondance Russe* began to appear in as many as eighty-two western European newspapers, and by 1866, so Zykov asserts, one began to find such material appearing in western newspapers as a matter of course. Its publication in Russia continued to be a well

---

87. *Ibid.*, pp. 22–23.
88. *Ibid.*, p. 24.
89. *Ibid.*, pp. 25–28.

kept secret; no copies were allowed to remain within Russia, and only such people outside the War Ministry as the Foreign Minister and his closest associates were ever aware of its existence.[90]

It is of course impossible to assess what impact the *Correspondance Russe* might have had on the development of foreign opinion (certainly in respect to the Polish insurrection there was almost none, if any), but it did provide the Russian government with some means to be heard abroad. The policies of the Empire could be explained, trial balloons could be sent up, and there did exist at least some means to combat hostile foreign opinion.

The militant attitude of Miliutin and the *Russkii Invalid* toward Poland did not change even after the conclusion of the military operations and the passage of the threat of an European intervention. The War Minister was firm in the belief that any relaxation would only be misunderstood and would lead to further disturbances.[91] He advocated the continuation of a legal state of war in Poland long after the cessation of hostilities, and when in May 1867 the Emperor did end the state of war, Miliutin looked upon it as an act of "unmitigated stupidity."[92] During the succeeding years, however, the Emperor did continue Miliutin's policy of unified civil and military control in Poland.

The War Minister was convinced of the need to reconstitute Polish society so that it could reform itself before force could be withdrawn. Polish society was an anachronism and had to be made to conform to contemporary needs. The Russian government was to effect this change in a variety of ways. The most important of these were the destruction of the Polish landowner class as an effective element in Polish society and the commensurate elevation of the urban and peasant classes.[93]

Closely related to this was the *Russkii Invalid*'s and Miliutin's continuing attacks upon the Catholic Church, not only in Poland but in the Vatican itself. The *Russkii Invalid* saw in the actions of the Church a monstrous conspiracy to promote subversion in Poland and accused the

90. *Ibid.*, pp. 29–32.
91. See, for example, Valuev, II., 155.
92. *Ibid.*, II., 208.
93. *Russkii Invalid*, No. 256 (1863), and "Krestianskii Vopros," *Russkii Invalid*, Nos. 18, 22, 33, and 34 (1864). Cf. *Russkii Invalid*, No. 142 (1865), and *Russkii Invalid*, No. 277 (1866).

Church of preying on other Christians for the sake of power.[94] More important, and symptomatic of the cultural nationalism of Miliutin, was the ardent campaign to reintegrate the Slavic minorities in the western provinces back into Russian life by means of education and the restoration of Uniat churches back into the Orthodox fold. The *Russkii Invalid* accorded to these policies the greatest importance and saw in them the final restoration of their brethren after centuries of attempts to "polonize"[95] them. When some of the Uniats showed some inclination not to be restored, Miliutin did not shrink from the use of force in accomplishing his purpose.[96]

Perhaps nothing illustrates better the militancy of Miliutin's support of a strong policy in Poland than his attitude toward M. N. Muraviev. This vigorous general and member of one the Empire's most illustrious families was named by the Emperor early in the summer of 1863 to pacify the Lithuanian area. Muraviev followed the dual policy of trying to win the support of the peasantry while dealing out summary punishment in the form of hanging to those found engaged in the insurrection.[97] The positive side of his achievements earned for him the surname of "Wilensky," while the harsher aspects of his actions acquired for him the unofficial title of the "hangman." Muraviev-Wilensky's general policies toward the settlement of affairs in the western provinces closely resembled those of the War Minister,[98] but the brutality of his administration and his policy of playing the peasantry off against the landowners cost him much support in court circles.

Nevertheless, Miliutin publically identified himself with Muraviev and took advantage of every opportunity to express his gratitude and support

94. S. P. Zykov, "Nabroski iz moei zhizni," *Russkaia Starina*, No. 7 (1910), p. 7; "Ocherk otnoshenii pol'skogo gosudarstva k pravoslaviiu i pravoslavnoi tserkvy," *Russkii Invalid*, No. 60 (1866); and "Neskol'ko slov o rimsko-katolicheskom dukhovenstve v tsarstve pol'skom," *Russkii Invalid*, No. 16 (1867). Cf. M. Koialovich, "Mistifikatsiia papskish vozglasov protiv Rossii," *Russkii Invalid*, No. 207 (1864), in which the author bitterly attacks what he believes to be papal subversion in Poland, and *Russkii Invalid*, No. 126 (1866).

95. *Russkii Invalid*, No. 175 (1866).

96. See, for example, *Dnevnik*, I., 128.

97. For a brief description of Muraviev's activity as Governor-General, see R. F. Leslie, *Reform and Insurrection in Russian Poland, 1856–1865*, pp. 224ff.

98. Compare with Miliutin's views those contained in a memorandum submitted to the Emperor on May 14, 1864, in Valuev, I., 415.

for the latter's actions.[99] Nicholas Miliutin, the War Minister's brother, was instrumental in securing for Muraviev the hereditary title of Count in reward for his services.[100] When Muraviev resigned because of mounting pressure at court and because of illness, the War Minister and those who supported what he had done were at great pains to get the Emperor to appoint a successor who would continue the same policies.[101] Despite the opposition of the majority of Alexander's advisers, the War Minister was generally successful in controlling the appointments to the post vacated by Muraviev and consequently the policy of stringent russification in the area enjoyed a measure of continuity.[102]

Miliutin and the *Russkii Invalid* demonstrated the consistency of their nationalist principles and their desire for the organic unity of the Russian state in yet another area—the issue of the Baltic Germans. There began in 1864 a newspaper controversy over the relation of those Germans living in the Baltic provinces of Lithuania, Latvia, and Estonia to the rest of the Empire. These Germans had long been a privileged group, having been guaranteed the possession of their lands and ancient privileges at the time of their incorporation into the Russian Empire during the eighteenth century, and with the passage of time they as a class became prominent in the bureaucracy and the officer corps. Often possessing superior educations and unquestioned loyalties to the dynasty, they frequently occupied the highest civil and military posts, but as Russian nationalism began to develop, their privileged position began to become a matter of controversy.

With the suppression of the Polish revolt and the heightened sense of nationalism generated during that trial, and the rapid movement of the reforms following the emancipation of the Russian serfs, the position of the Baltic Germans began to appear more and more anachronistic. Moreover, outside of Russia, the great events leading to the national unification of Germany under the tutelage of Prussia served to raise some doubts about where the real loyalty of the Germans might lie. The more extreme

99. *Russkii Invalid*, No. 265 (1863); *Russkii Invalid*, No. 204 (1863).
100. A. I. Del'vig, *Polveka Russkoi Zhizni: Vospominaniia A. I. Del'viga, 1820–1870*, 2 vols., II., 268–269.
101. *Ibid.*, pp. 268–269.
102. For a contemporary view, see N. I. Kostomarov, *Avtobiografiia*, edited by V. Kotel'nikov, p. 383.

nationalist newspapers of Russia, particularly Ivan Aksakov's *Den'* and Katkov's *Moskovskie Vedomosti,* openly distrusted the Germans and saw separatism in their every action.[103] The *Russkii Invalid* shared some of these sentiments and consequently drew some withering blasts from the German-language newspapers, particularly the *S.-Petersburger Zeitung.*[104]

With this, the attack was joined, and the whole question of German nationalism became a matter for open debate in the press. The *Russkii Invalid* differed from the other nationalist papers in that it was an official publication and it was known that its views were those of the War Minister; therefore, it was at the very center of the controversy until Alexander ordered Miliutin to drop the question of the Baltic Germans.[105]

The position of the *Russkii Invalid,* and consequently of Miliutin, was basically that the issue in the three provinces was neither separatism nor nationalism but rather the class interests of the German landowning nobility that wished to keep the mass of the people in bondage.[106] Despite the fact that the people were legally free, the peasantry was still exploited on the land and the court system remained as the guardian of the rights of the landowners. The medieval guild system and the municipal governments were also the strongholds of the German minority and acted as a brake on the economic development of the area.[107]

But the *Russkii Invalid* affirmed that all classes in Russia were equal and enjoyed equal rights; the enjoyment of a special position by any group denied the rights of others.[108] With some hint of russification, the newspaper observed that the great bulk of the common people were being denied the opportunity to merge with the Russian people.[109] The issue therefore was not one of national separatism but was rather the problem

103. *Russkii Invalid,* No. 76 (1865).

104. S. P. Zykov, "Nabroski iz moei zhizni," *Russkaia Starina,* No. 6 (1910), pp. 502–505.

105. If Zykov is to be believed, Alexander II at this time was in close agreement with Miliutin on the question of the Baltic Germans and only moderated his views in the later stages of the controversy. Zykov, *Ibid.,* pp. 506–507.

106. See, for example, *Russkii Invalid,* No. 76 (1865).

107. B . . . , "Spravedlivy li tolki separatisticheskikh stremleniiakh ostzeiskogo kraia," *Russkii Invalid,* No. 211 (1864).

108. *Russkii Invalid,* No. 76 (1865).

109. B . . . , "Spravedlivy li tolki o separatisticheskikh stremleniiakh ostzeiskogo kraia," *Russkii Invalid,* No. 211 (1864).

of a pocket of social and legal anachronisms that both inhibited the process of achieving organic unity and acted as a brake on the development of the nation.

As a practical politician, Miliutin was utterly dependent upon the favor of the Emperor. This support was generally assured because of the War Minister's undoubted competence and his sincere devotion to the autocracy. Nevertheless, Miliutin was the object of innumerable intrigues as during his official career he increasingly became the chief obstacle in the path of the planter party. The late sixties and early seventies particularly saw him under unremitting attack within the higher court circles as well as in the public press. The general purpose of these assaults by the planter party was to discredit Miliutin with the Emperor and thereby bring about his dismissal. Alexander, who as a matter of policy liked to see his ministers at odds with one another,[110] was insensitive to the plight of his War Minister and to the implications of these intrigues in respect to matters of public policy.

During his tenure as War Minister, Miliutin and his brother Nicholas stood at the center of a "Miliutin party," which, as the reforms began to unfold during the early sixties, emerged from the dialogue between the planters and the reform-minded bureaucrats. The roots of the Miliutin party lay in the fading years of the forties when K. D. Kavelin, the brilliant young historian and former professor at the University of Moscow, came to St. Petersburg and entered the bureaucracy as a functionary in the Economic Department of the Ministry of Internal Affairs. During the next few years he successfully pursued his civil service career and chose as his closest friends the two Miliutins, Nicholas and Dmitrii.

Together with a few other select friends, also from among the bureaucracy, these talented young men formed a circle which habitually met to discusss art and science within an atmosphere of lively good humor. Included in this circle, which often met at the Russian Geographic Society, were A. P. Zablotskii-Desiatovskii, a former associate of Count P. D. Kiselev and ultimately the latter's biographer; K. K. Grot, at this time an associate of Kavelin and Nicholas Miliutin in the Ministry of Internal Affairs and later an official in the Finance Ministry and a member of the State Council; and I. P. Arapetov, a former university classmate

110. *Dnevnik*, IV, 91–92n; 93.

of Herzen, a close associate of many of the literary elite, a bureaucrat, and later a member of the editorial commission for the emancipation of the serfs.[111] Called by contemporaries the "party of Petersburg Progress," the circle saw the causes of Russia's backwardness in the institution of serfdom and stood for its abolition, but looked to the autocracy for the initiative.[112]

When Miliutin became the Minister of War, these same individuals continued their close relationship with him, both politically and personally. During his official career, Miliutin liked to relax on Sundays and to be "at home" to his friends. In addition to those mentioned above, his intimates included the three Botkin brothers, Vasilii, Michael, and Sergei. The first of these was a former member of the Stankevich circle of the thirties and an intimate of many of the leading literary figures of the day, while the latter two were an artist and a professor at the Medical-Surgical Academy, respectively.

In the early years of Miliutin's ministry, the circle also included E. M. Feoktistov who served on the editorial staff of the *Russkii Invalid*, but by the middle of the decade he deserted this association and eventually became the editor of the Journal of the Ministry of Popular Instruction. The circle also included Nicholas Miliutin's close associate during the drafting of the emancipation legislation, Ia. A. Soloviev; Miliutin's sister, Maria Alexeevich; Prince Dmitrii Obolenskii, a member of the State Council and a leading participant in the censor reforms of the sixties; S. M. Zhukovskii, a bureaucrat and a member of several of the commissions which worked on the legislation for the emancipation of the serfs; and the historian, I. P. Kornilov.[113]

Among the military members of Miliutin's circle were P. K. Men'kov, who edited the *Voennyi Sbornik*; General A. Lavrentiev, who succeeded Men'kov as dual editor of the *Voennyi Sbornik* and the *Russkii Invalid*; General N. N. Obruchev, who along with several other of Miliutin's

111. V. N. Rozental', "Ideinye tsentry liberal'nogo dvizheniia v Rossii nakanune revoliutsionnoi situatsii : Peterburgskii kruzhok K. D. Kavelina v 1855–1857gg.," *Revoliutsionnaia situatsiia v Rossii v 1859–1861gg.*, pp. 383–391, and Nikitenko, II, 441.
112. V. N. Rozental', pp. 393–397.
113. *Zapiski Men'kova*, II, 363, and S. P. Zykov, "Nabroski iz moei zhizni," *Russkaia Starina*, No. 7 (1910), p. 22.

military aides, including S. P. Zykov and V. M. Anichkov, was especially hated by the reactionaries as a former associate of the socialist, N. G. Chernyshevskii; General M. I. Dragomirov, a brilliant military theoretician who disagreed with Miliutin now and then; General A. Leer, and so on.[114] Among those occasionally participating in the circle were the famous slavophiles, Iurii Samarin and Prince V. A. Cherkasskii, and the publicist, professor, historian and official nationalist, M. P. Pogodin.[115] Within the Council of Ministers, Miliutin's most consistent ally was A. A. Zelenyi, the Minister of State Domains.[116]

It is interesting to note that the Miliutin party was overwhelmingly composed of bureaucrats and officers from the general staff, and even an intellectual like Kavelin was closely associated with state service. There were few intellectuals among the members; Kavelin and Miliutin himself really were about all, although many of the members were on the fringes of the literary and scholarly circles of the day. This alone is sufficient to suggest why the group was opposed to any revolution but was the reformist party. Many of this group, including the two Miliutins, were leading spirits in one or another aspect of the reforms, generally serving as an official in one of the special committees constituted by the Emperor to draft the terms and specifications of the several reforms. They sought orderly progress through the use of the instruments of government and were not necessarily "liberal" but were progressive and reformist.

Miliutin and those about him evoked the wrath of the planter party. The reforms took place largely at the expense of the privileges and pretensions of the gentry. The bureaucratic clique that the War Minister headed threatened, moreover, to displace the gentry from their historical position. The very argument for the existence of the gentry was their ancient role as the "serving people" who administered and defended Russia in the name of the Tsar.[117] The gentry had been freed

---

114. *Zapiski Men'kova*, II, 364.

115. See, for example, N. Barsukov, *Zhizn' i trudy M. P. Pogodina*, XX, 202–205.

116. For Miliutin's own appreciation of Zelenyi, see *Dnevnik*, I, 117, and III, 138.

117. This view of the gentry class was quite typical of the period in general and of the reform party in particular. Compare, for example, "Zemskiia uchrezhdeniia," *Russkii Invalid*, No. 184 (1863), with K. D. Kavelin, "Dvorianstvo i osvobozhdenie krest'ian," *Sobranie Sochinenii*, II, 115–131.

from obligatory state service in the eighteenth century but the privileges they had enjoyed generally had remained sacrosanct, and the emancipation and the reforms that followed represented the first great assault upon these privileges.

Even before the emancipation of the serfs was drafted into legislation, representatives of the interests of the gentry class were hard at work trying to render the reform as painless as possible, and as time went on the gentry opposition began to coalesce and to become more sharply defined.[118] The American Minister to St. Petersburg in October 1862 reported back to the State Department that he was having difficulty in getting frank answers on the subject of the strength of the dynasty. He saw two elements opposing the reforms by the Emperor: the Left, which hoped to overthrow the regime, and the reactionaries, composed of the gentry and the merchants whose attitude was one of sullen resistance.[119]

One of the first to fall prey to the gentry was Dmitrii Miliutin's brother Nicholas. Nicholas, the chief architect of the emancipation, was dismissed from office only a month after the publication of the act of liberation. The Minister of Internal Affairs, Count S. S. Lanskoi, was beginning to feel his years, so that Alexander allowed him to retire and immediately replaced him with Count P. A. Valuev, a leading advocate for the planters. With this change, the Emperor dismissed Nicholas Miliutin from his post of Deputy Minister of Internal Affairs, saying to him that he was sorry to see him go but that the gentry thought him to be one of the "reds."[120] Dmitrii Miliutin analyzed the situation in his memoirs in this way:

The departure of Lanskoi and especially of my brother was the inevitable consequence of the continuous intrigue carried on by the opponents of the liberation of the peasants. The Emperor resisted these pressures while these

---

118. See, for example, the brief account in W. E. Mosse, *Alexander II* and the Modernization of Russia, pp. 50ff. and *passim*.

119. Bayard Taylor to William Seward, *Despatches*, October 25, 1862.

120. Nicholas Miliutin was understandably most angry at this ungrateful and capricious act of Alexander II and was said by Feoktistov to have remarked to him that: "It is all right that I was dismissed from my post and sent abroad; all this is progress. Under the Empress Anna Ivanovna, my tongue would have been cut out and I would have been sent to Siberia." Feoktistov, p. 343.

individuals were needed to bring the peasant matter to a conclusion, but once this objective had been achieved, the Emperor, in accordance with his character, found it expedient to mollify the dissatisfaction which the *pomiestie* class had toward the great reform and to reconcile as much as possible toward the great reform those individuals whose interests were touched by the worthy government measure. For this, the very implementation of the new law had to be taken out of the hands of those who had incurred the wrath of the *pomiestie* class and entrusted to those individuals who could never possibly be suspected of enmity toward the gentry.[121]

The dichotomy of the Emperor's policies as illustrated in this matter was just what made Miliutin's position in the government so difficult. Alexander pursued an essentially dualist policy throughout his reign— that of pursuing reform without accepting the implications of the change.

The sharp conflicts between Miliutin and the planters were at first only tentative trials of strength, but by the mid-sixties they became deep and bitter. The two events most critically responsible for the transformation were the Polish Insurrection and the attempt in 1866 on the life of the Emperor. The latter was perhaps the most important factor in strengthening the hand of the planter party, because it created a new political relationship within the upper levels of government. Alexander had been badly frightened by the act, and as an immediate consequence he began to make some changes in his government both to suppress active movements and to control what he considered to be the sources of this disaffection.

Prince V. A. Dolgorukov, the Head of the Third Section and the Chief of Gendarmes, went to the Emperor soon after the assassination attempt and tendered his resignation. He was the official responsible for the security of the head of state and in the wake of the attempt on the life of Alexander he felt that he had lost the confidence of the public. When the Emperor asked who should be appointed to replace him, Dolgorukov suggested that he name Count Peter Andreevich Shuvalov.[122]

The latter's father had been Marshal of the Court under Nicholas I and Peter, his brother, and Prince Bariatinskii had been among the future Emperor Alexander's closest companions. When Alexander came to the throne, he appointed his boyhood friend, Peter Shuvalov, to the

121. Valuev, I, 371.
122. Prince V. P. Meshcherskii, *Moi Vospominaniia*, II, 17–18.

post of Police Chief for St. Petersburg, despite the latter's relative youth and lack of experience. Immediately before his elevation to the headship of the Third Section, he served as the Governor-General of the Baltic Province.

Shuvalov became upon his appointment as Chief of Gendarmes the Imperial favorite until his dismissal from the Third Section in 1874, and in the course of this career was, aside from the Emperor, the single most powerful man in Russia. His influence was so strong in virtually every aspect of government that he was known in court circles as an Arakcheev II or a Peter IV, and the poet Tiutchev even composed a little verse to that effect.[123]

The sources of Shuvalov's influence over the Emperor were several. First of all, as Chief of Gendarmes, Shuvalov was able to play on Alexander's fears and could suggest this or that line of policy as in the best interests of security.[124] Moreover, he was not only Alexander's boyhood friend but he was the sort of suave and sophisticated courtier that Alexander liked to have around.[125] But perhaps his most effective means of influencing the Emperor was his ability to insulate him from the intrigues going on about him, thereby creating a sense of harmony and tranquility. Shuvalov also seems to have understood Alexander well enough to anticipate his needs and could therefore make himself indispensible.[126]

Shuvalov seemed to possess all the necessary gifts for the successful statesman at the Russian court. He was strikingly handsome and always was a picture of sartorial elegance. His manner conveyed a sense of great vitality, and his voice was always sympathetic. His mind was clever rather than brilliant, and he always carefully took in all about him. Nevertheless, he conducted himself self-consciously as an aristocrat and

123. The verse appears in F. I. Tiuchev, *Polnoe Sobranie Stikhotvorenii*:
Nad Rossiei rasprostertoi
Vstal vnezapnoiu grozoi
Petr po prozvishchu *chetvertyi*
Arakcheev zhe *vtoroi*.
124. This is Miliutin's own view. See *Dnevnik*, IV, 95–96.
125. A. I. Del'vig, *Polveka russkoi zhizni : Vospominaniia*, II, 431–434. Del'vig could on no account be considered a friendly witness since he himself suffered at Shuvalov's hands. See *ibid.*, II, 483–484.
126. Meshcherskii, II, 64.

always held himself aloof from all those with whom he came into contact.[127]

But Shuvalov, despite his gifts and the great power which he for a time possessed, was shallow and only played at politics.[128] His character was chameleonic, allowing him to adapt to situations rather than act on principle. This characteristic was clearly revealed in an incident that took place before his appointment as the Governor-General of the Baltic Province. In the presence of the Emperor, he railed against the Baltic German nobility, but Alexander severely rebuked him, pointing out to him that they were his loyal subjects.[129] Ever afterward, Shuvalov was careful to be among their most ardent supporters.

This does not mean, however, that Shuvalov was devoid of a point of view. He and his associates masked their views and goals behind a façade of liberalism. Prince V. P. Meshcherskii, who knew Shuvalov and who interviewed him during the height of his power, found that Shuvalov had a sort of "European fatalism" about Russian politics and that he believed in "the vague force of a liberal regime for Russia in the field of domestic politics."[130] He felt that the Russian government was compelled by the force of circumstances to travel along the liberal path and that the time had arrived for Russia to comply with this vague historical law. The only check on this conformity with the spirit of the times was the person of the autocrat.[131]

Shuvalov did not believe in constitutions per se, but he did want an expansion of local autonomy, which would have the effect of delivering more power into the hands of the gentry as a class. He wanted the *zemstva* to have very extensive economic powers and considered these bodies to be the axis of the Empire's economic structure. Most importantly, he wanted the *zemstva* to have the power to rid Russia of the peasant commune and to replace it with the western European system of land tenure.[132] What in effect Shuvalov wanted was for the Emperor

127. *Ibid.*, I, 108, and Feoktistov, p. 107.
128. Valuev, II, 284.
129. Feoktistov, pp. 348–349.
130. Meshcherskii, II, 146.
131. *Ibid.*, II, 147.
132. *Ibid.*, *loc. cit.*

to remain as the autocrat but for most of the actual power to run the country to be delegated to the gentry.

A number of examples suggest that Shuvalov did try to implement such a program. As early as June 1866 he, in concert with Valuev and Zelenyi, submitted to Alexander a memorandum calling for more local powers for the provincial governors, specifically granting them the control over those institutions not directly subordinate to the Ministry of Internal Affairs. The Emperor responded by assembling a special committee under the chairmanship of Prince P. P. Gagarin, the Chairman of the State Council and a dedicated planter, which included in addition to Shuvalov, Valuev and Zelenyi, Count M. N. Muraviev, and Dmitrii Miliutin.[133]

While on the surface this appeared to be quite liberal legislation, Miliutin was not deceived. He tried at first to kill it by maintaining that it should properly be discussed in the State Council and made a part of a larger review of the general problem of supervising local government. Miliutin pointed out, moreover, that the disorder in the provincial administration did not stem from any lack of powers on the part of the local governors but arose from their own stubbornness and lack of respect for the law and for persons. These offices, in his view, were all too often held by individuals who did not possess the requisite qualifications for such high office, and, therefore, merely increasing their powers would not solve the problem.[134] What he did see in the proposal was an attempt by Shuvalov to gain powers and prerogatives for local gentry officials at the expense of the Imperial government.

Shuvalov by means of intrigue and the unprincipled use of his position became the most powerful leader of the planter party. Soon after he himself was named Chief of Gendarmes, he persuaded the Emperor to dismiss the relatively liberal Minister of Public Instruction, A. V. Golovnin, and replace him with Count D. A. Tolstoy, the current procurator of the Holy Synod. The goal was to find a Minister of Public

133. Valuev, II, 467–469.

134. *Ibid.*, II, 137. There is ample evidence that Shuvalov systematically sought to gain control of all the highest offices of the government including the Ministries of War and Foreign Affairs. See N. G. Zalesov, "Zapiski," *Russkaia Starina,* No. 6 (1905), p. 537.

Instruction to whom, as a security measure, the church schools could also be subordinated, and therefore it was necessary to combine this office with that of the Procurator General.[135] In similar fashion, Count K. I. Pahlen became the Minister of Justice in 1867,[136] and after Valuev's resignation from the Ministry of Internal Affairs in 1868 another nominee of Shuvalov, A. E. Timashev, replaced him in that post.[137] By 1868, Shuvalov was able to wield considerable influence over several key ministries: Education, Justice, and Internal Affairs.

At the same time, Shuvalov contested with Miliutin the appointment of key officials at other levels. It appears that at one time he made some attempt to gain control over the Ministry of Finance, but he quickly abandoned these efforts.[138] Shuvalov apparently was able to dispose of governorships and other posts and was willing to use them as incentives for defection from the Miliutin camp and for loyalty to his own. The remaining obstacles to Shuvalov's triumph were the Ministries of State Domains, Foreign Affairs, and War; and Valuev succeeded in capturing the first of these in 1872.[139]

Shuvalov had his hand in just about everything. The planter party had resented the role played by the Miliutins in the settlement of the Polish revolt, and they particularly, feared the implications of the social program implemented there by the government.[140] Count M. N. Muraviev had been one of the objects of their hatred during and immediately after the insurrection, and when he was later appointed by the Emperor to head the special commission investigating the attempt on his life, Shuvalov intrigued against him again. There perhaps was as much personal animosity and fear of losing the initiative in Shuvalov's behavior as

135. Del'vig, II, 505.
136. Meshcherskii, II, 79.
137. Meshcherskii was most critical of Timashev's lack of qualifications for his post. He viewed Timashev as one of those young men who, like Shuvalov, looked elegant in uniform, waltzed divinely, and conversed brilliantly, but who neither knew Russia nor its administration. As far as he was concerned, Timashev had no political ideals whatever and instead had only political enemies. Meshcherskii, II, 77–78 and 143.
138. Valuev, II, 472.
139. Zalesov, "Zapiski," p. 537.
140. Valuev, I, *passim*. See the comments of K. N. Lebedev, "Iz zapisok senatora K. N. Lebedeva, 1867-i god," *Russkii Arkhiv*, No. 8 (1911), p. 492.

there was politics. But Shuvalov did side with the planters in their lament over the plight of their brother aristocrats in Poland, and it appears that the amnesty of May 17, 1867, was drafted by Shuvalov.[141]

But nothing equaled the Chief of Gendarme's intrigue against Miliutin himself. The War Ministry was the most important office beyond his control—particularly so since the social implications of the reforms conducted in the War Ministry cut across the interests of the gentry. In addition, the schools controlled by the War Minister could not be supervised in the same way as the national or ecclesiastical schools. Miliutin's insistence upon competence and individual merit as the overriding basis for the selection of officer candidates was a direct threat to gentry privileges. Therefore, the campaign by the planters quickly intensified after 1866.

These attacks rarely if ever came out into the open. They were often in the form of rumor campaigns and slights, mostly focusing on the large size of the military budget. When Miliutin invited open challenges to his policies in the presence of the Emperor, none was forthcoming,[142] but the backbiting and harassment continued as before. Miliutin's patience gave out. Despite the observation in the *Russkii Invalid* that the year 1867 had been a year of quiet and peaceful progress,[143] Shuvalov's intrigues led Miliutin in December of that year to complain against him to the Emperor. A tearful scene ensued in which it appears that Alexander was insensitive to his War Minister's plight; he probably was also pleased to be able to apply the old principle of divide and rule.[144] This may have been good politics, but it was poor statesmanship.

In the more public area of partisan debate, Miliutin's struggle with the planter party was carried on through the use of the *Russkii Invalid*. This official newspaper of the War Ministry carried on in its unofficial section a public dialogue with most of the important papers of the day. In the early days of Miliutin's administration, the *Russkii Invalid* rather self-consciously identified itself with other nationalist newspapers such

141. Valuev, II, 208.
142. Valuev, II, 481. This problem repeated itself often during the next several years. See, for example, *Dnevnik*, I, 82.
143. *Russkii Invalid*, No. 1 (1868).
144. Valuev, II, 228.

as Ivan Aksakov's *Den'* and Katkov's *Moskovskie Vedomosti*,[145] but this was short lived. The most bitter and lasting dialogue was with the obscurantist newspaper, *Vest'*, which was breathed into life from the corpse of the *Russkii Listok* only a few months after Miliutin took the *Russkii Invalid* in hand, and it survived the War Ministry's paper as a public paper by only a couple of years.

Vest' was a planter paper par excellence. Published by V. D. Skariatin and N. Iumatov, both close friends of Valuev, this journal saw the reformist view of the *Russkii Invalid* as its bête noir and attacked it incessantly throughout the decade. Its editorial policy was perhaps best summed up in a statement in the liberal newspaper *Golos* that the editors of *Vest'* and the planter party which it represented wanted to turn the clock back to February 18, 1861, the eve of the emancipation. They varied this attitude with the theme that they accepted the reforms in *principle*, that is that they accepted the *forms* of change as long as they had control.[146]

The attacks on the *Russkii Invalid* did not often provoke a response from either Miliutin or the editors. When at one time the assaults grew so intense and vitriolic that even Valuev asked the War Minister whether it were not time to muzzle *Vest'*, the latter replied that it was not necessary as far as he was concerned.[147] Nevertheless, the *Russkii Invalid* did occasionally reply. Finding a close bond of aristocratic unity between the planter party of Russia and the *szlachta* of Poland as a consequence both of the damage to aristocratic privilege inherent in the reforms and of the strong policy of "depolonization" in the western provinces (which in effect meant an assault upon the privileges of the land-owning nobility in favor of the peasantry), the *Russkii Invalid* noted that *Vest'* was so

145. S. P. Zykov, "Nabroski iz moei zhizni," *Russkaia Starina*, No. 7 (1910), p. 21, and *Russkii Invalid*, No. 213 (1863). Throughout most of the sixties, the support was reciprocal. See, for example, the editorial in *Moskovskie Vedomosti*, No. 92 (1863).

146. *Golos*, No. 198 (1872). *Golos* delivered this assault as an attack upon the newly established *Russkii Mir*, a newspaper which it saw as the heir and successor of *Vest'*. Among other things, *Golos* charged that the position of *Vest'* and *Russkii Mir* was sustained by the desire "to get rid of all that does not conform to class rule and the law of the whip."

147. S. P. Zykov, "Nabbroski iz moei zhizni," *Russkaia Starina*, No. 7 (1910), p. 495.

extreme in its attacks upon the policies of the Russian government that even the Polish newspapers were quoting it.[148]

Another editorial of the *Russkii Invalid* noted a charge by the editors of Vest' that it was an organ of "democracy and socialism." The *Russkii Invalid* saw in this only a wail for the abolition of serfdom and did not believe that anyone would ever believe such a charge.[149] In 1868, the editors in the War Ministry detected an interesting change in approach by *Vest'* which now undertook to defend the emancipation and all the other consequent reforms:

> But it itself hastens to explain the riddle, and its explanation is so curious that it would be a pity if it passed unnoticed. The situation, in its words, is this: every misfortune in those reforms is attributed to the participation of people whom *Vest'* calls "radicals." Radicals—they say—are quite able to initiate new problems, to promote new ideas which are rendered quite bankrupt as soon as they are put into practice. They—these supposed radicals—developed for the most part the details of those reforms; but no sooner had they fulfilled their purpose, than prudence demanded that they turn away from it in order that they not contaminate with their baneful influence the further course and development of the reform. It is necessary that the Tories occupy the place of these pernicious people. The *Vest'* assures us that this is the way it is done in all civilized countries and, by the way, in England where ordinarily the Whigs (the *Vest'* considers the radicals and the Whigs to be one and the same) stimulate the idea of reform, the Tories afterward take this reform into its hands.[150]

It was clear that the Miliutin party, the reform party, was considered unfit to implement the reforms it had helped to initiate and that only the planter party, which had resisted these reforms, had the capacity to run the country, reforms and all. *Vest'*, as did the planter party generally, overly reacted to the social and political posture of the War Minister and his party. To the planter party, he was a far more immediate danger than were any of the liberal and socialist publicists against whom the government from time to time took stern measures.

It is no wonder then that one of the chief objectives of the planters was

---

148. *Russkii Invalid*, No. 47 (1866). *Vest'* was most strongly motivated by a sense of corporate identity and saw fellow aristocrats in Poland as Russia's bulwark against Revolution. See, for example, *Vest'*, No. 1 (1863), p. 9.
149. *Russkii Invalid*, No. 47, (1866).
150. *Russkii Invalid*, No. 303, (1868).

to deny the War Minister the public voice he had in the *Russkii Invalid*. As early as 1863, Katkov began to complain in the *Moskovskie Vedomosti* about the general news coverage and editorial policies of official government newspapers,[151] and with the emergence and strengthening of the Shuvalov party, the time came to act.

The appointment of one of Shuvalov's creatures, A. E. Timashev, to the post of Minister of Internal Affairs helped to eliminate the last barriers. The planters in their extremity were apparently willing to sacrifice the official newspapers which they controlled in the other ministries, such as the *Severnaia Pochta*, in order to muzzle the *Russkii Invalid*. Shuvalov, Timashev and Valuev increased their attacks on the *Russkii Invalid*, saying that the articles published in it were not appropriate for the official organ of the War Ministry.[152]

At last they were able to persuade Alexander to close all the ministerial papers and to replace them with a single official government newspaper,[153] which of course would be put beyond the control of someone like Miliutin.

The matter reached its climax in the fall of 1868 with the Emperor issuing an order on October 27 closing the ministerial papers at the end of the year and the opening with the beginning of the new year of an official general newspaper by the government, the *Pravitel'stvennyi Vestnik*.[154] This decision did not completely close out the *Russkii Invalid*; it was allowed to continue publication as a purely military journal, and with the retirement of Men'kov as editor of the *Voennyi Sbornik* in 1872, the editorship of the two publications were joined.[155] The Emperor, with

151. *Moskovskie Vedomosti*, No. 270 (1863). *Russkii Invalid* was not the only official newspaper attacked in this manner. The suspicion that *Golos* was supported by the Minister of Public Instruction drew heavy fire from Katkov. See M. Lemke, *Epokha tsenzurnykh reform*, pp. 239–240.

152. S. P. Zykov, "Nabroski iz moei zhizni," *Russkaia Starina*, No. 7 (1910), p. 34. It should also be noted that Timashev hated *Moskovskie Vedomosti* and wanted to close it down. Valuev, II, 503–504.

153. S. P. Zykov, "Nabroski iz moei zhizni, . . . " pp. 34–35.

154. This newspaper survived until the Revolution. Its foundation was clearly understood in government circles to be an effort to undermine the position of Miliutin. Nikitenko, III, 134.

155. The new editor of the combined publications was General Alexander Ivanovich Lavrent'ev whose article in *Voennyi Sbornik* in 1862 had presented the War Minister's case for the creation of the military district system.

his characteristic lack of sensitivity and failure to understand the significance of the closing of the *Russkii Invalid* as a publication with any right to comment on social and political matters, commented to Shuvalov after the War Minister offered his resignation:

> I do not understand what has so enflamed Miliutin; does the newspaper really have such importance in his eyes that he seriously thinks to forsake the position over which he has labored so long. I assured him that he has my full trust. . . .[156]

The loss of the *Russkii Invalid* left Miliutin naked to his enemies; they could attack him and his policies in the press and he had no means of replying other than some occasional support from one or another of the liberal papers, particularly *Golos*.

156. Feoktistov, p. 350.

6

The Great Reform of 1874

THE BRIEF period from 1870 to 1874 saw Miliutin's greatest triumph but was also the time of his greatest trials. He succeeded with great effort in making all individuals in the Empire liable to military conscription, irrespective of class. Those who were exempted from service were granted this right on the basis of their individual life situations rather than their social origin. But this sharpened the already bitter conflict between Miliutin and the planter party at the time that party enjoyed its highest level of ascendancy, and the War Minister was able to succeed only because the issue was one of the survival of the Empire, enabling him to find some support among those who were normally on the other side.

At the root of the question, as was the case in so much of the reform activity in the War Ministry, was the still great problem of the budget. Despite all the best efforts of the War Minister, the army continued to be a heavy burden on the resources of the state. The constant need to provide the army with newer and more expensive arms was alone enough to cancel out savings in other areas.[1] The Minister of Finance, Reitern, more than once threatened out of frustration to resign because of the

---

1. In many cases, in fact, the savings accrued by more effective administration were used to augment salaries and to improve the quality of the soldiers' diet, and were not a net reduction in the budget of the War Ministry. See Bogdanovich, VI., 407–408.

increasing demands of the War Ministry,[2] and this same situation gave Miliutin's enemies yet another issue on which to attack him. The public press, whatever its political persuasion, tended to be permanently opposed to the high fiscal burden posed by the War Ministry.[3] By his own figures, Miliutin admitted that during the sixties his Ministry consumed more than a third of the entire state budget and was still unable to meet all of its obligations. Each year saw the figures rise: 129,687,000 rubles in 1866, 127,250,000 rubles in 1867, 136,700,000 rubles in 1868, and 147,702,000 rubles in 1869.[4] By 1871, this figure vaulted to 156,604,116 rubles.[5] The political and technological changes taking place throughout the rest of Europe, moreover, held out no promise of any end in sight to the rise in defense costs.

The intimate connection between the fiscal difficulties and the problem of recruiting for the army was made quite clear in an article appearing in the *Russkii Invalid* during 1864.[6] After reviewing the period since the Crimean War, the editorial noted that Russia had turned inward and, living only for herself, had been completely bound up in anticipation of the great domestic reforms of the sixties. The question of foreign wars and the consequent need for a large army were put aside, and the state sought only to reduce expenditures. For six years there had been no recruit levy while the army tried to reduce the great size to which it had grown during the war. There had even been proposals that the army be reduced by half and the savings used for railroad construction. But these peaceful aspirations had to give way before the shock of a renewed involvement in general European affairs with the outbreak of trouble in

2. See, for example, Valuev, II., 232.

3. See, for example; "Nel'zia li i etot raskhod sokratit'?" *Moskovskie Vedomosti,* No. 22 (1863); "Sravnenie voennykh raskhodov Rossii s germanskimi," *Moskovskie Vedomosti*, No. 145 (1872); the editorial in *Birzhevye Vedomosti,* No. 31 (1863); and the editorial in *S-Peterburgskie Vedomosti,* No. 32 (1873). *Golos* at different times both attacked and defended the War Ministry's budget policies (for a defense, see, No. 5, 1873). The budget seemed to be the one area, however, where Miliutin enjoyed the full and consistent support of the Emperor. See Valuev, II., 481, and *Dnevnik*, I., 125.

4. *Despatches*, March 6, 1872. Cf. Bliokh, II., 194–195n. The ratio of the expenditures of the War Ministry to the total state budget did tend to decline slightly.

5. *Journal de St.-Peterbourg*, January 10, 1871.

6. O., "1863-i god dlia russkoi armii," *Russkii Invalid*, No. 32 (1864).

Poland. New demands had to be placed on the army, and with its increasing responsibilities its significance also increased. The year 1863 began and ended with recruit levies, broaching again the question of how to devise the means for providing a sufficient number of men to guarantee the security of the Empire without greatly overtaxing its resources.

Miliutin had long wished for Russia to adopt a military system which allowed the army to be reduced to the smallest possible size in peacetime while remaining capable of rapid expansion in time of war. As early as 1856, he had drafted a plan incorporating this principle, but it had come to nothing.[7] Nevertheless, the idea still lived, and when he became the Minister of War it became an important part of his reform program. In his initial outline, submitted to the Emperor on January 15, 1862, he stressed the dangers inherent in retaining the current system:

Under present conditions, with the European powers each having a sizable standing army and a secure means for expanding their armed forces in the event of war, the relative political significance of Russia may not long endure. . . .[8]

At the very least, the Empire's position as a great power was at stake and, very possibly, much more. The War Minister recommended at this time a peacetime force of 765,532 men with sufficient trained reserves to expand the army to a total of 1,377,365 men in time of war.

He proposed to do this by adapting some of the practices of European powers to Russian conditions. A cadre or skeleton force would be maintained in peacetime, and this would provide the vehicle for the rapid expansion of the army at the outbreak of hostilities. Conscripts would be retained on active service only as long as necessary to train them; they would then be sent to the reserves and returned to their normal civilian occupations. In time of war they could be called up quickly, either to complement existing units or to form a battle reserve to train raw recruits also called up for the emergency.[9]

Later in the same year, Miliutin expanded upon these proposals in a memorandum which he introduced into the Council of Ministers. This called for a complete reappraisal of all contemporary recruiting statutes,

7. A. V. Fedorov, *Russkaia armiia v 50–70gg.* XIX v., p. 219.
8. *Doklad*, January 15, 1862, p. 74.
9. *Ibid.*, pp. 76–79.

not only because of fiscal requirements, but also because the emancipation had given the peasantry a new status. The elimination of seigneurial jurisdiction over the selection of recruits in particular meant that the state now had to set up new administrative machinery to perform that function. But far more critical from the point of view of guaranteeing the security of the state was the fundamental flaw in the relationship between the reserve system and the active army. The problem can perhaps best be illustrated by the fact that, while Russia maintained a larger peacetime army than any other European power, she did not have enough trained troops for wartime. An increase in the levy to offset this would, the War Minister argued, take hands away from the national economy and would weaken the state while weakening the army by siphoning off veteran troops to train the raw recruits.[10]

Varying slightly from his earlier estimates, Miliutin wanted a peacetime force of 798,194 men and a wartime strength of 1,410,027. At the time that this memorandum was prepared, there were only about 242,000 trained men on unlimited furlough who could be added immediately to the battle force, leaving a deficit of more than 370,000 men to be conscripted either after the outbreak of hostilities or the imminent danger of hostilities had forced mobilization. The War Minister considered it paramount that the army create a reservoir or *zapas* of trained men adequate to the minimum needs of the army in the event of mobilization.[11] This reservoir could only be created by holding annual levies to call sufficient numbers of men, giving them the necessary training, then releasing them to their usual civilian occupations.

This proposal raised the broader question of who should be obliged to serve. According to War Ministry statistics, there were 29,654,202 adult males in the Empire, exclusive of Poland and Finland, and, of these, only 23,588,121 were liable to conscription. Miliutin proposed that the annual levy ultimately be set at 70,000 men, but during the initial years while additional men would be needed to build up the reserve force this could be increased by as many as 25,000 men annually. He computed the yearly rate of conscription at about four out of each

10. "Novyia nachala voennoi povinnosti v Rossii," *Voennyi Sbornik*, No. 2 (1864), p. 220.

11. *Ibid., loc. cit.*

thousand male adults, but during those initial years the heavier demands might increase this to five or more per thousand.[12]

In the light of this heavy imposition upon the people, Miliutin felt that they should have some protection. The levy had to fall equally upon all parts of the Empire, and the army should ordinarily take only the younger men who had not yet acquired heavy responsibilities. Moreover, for reasons of economy and morale, the recruits should be trained as near to their homes as possible. But the most important way of mitigating the heavy burden of service would be to require that everyone serve, irrespective of his status. As it stood, only those who paid the poll tax or its equivalent were required to go into the armed forces, which in effect meant that only the several categories of peasants and the lower urban classes were liable to conscription. The grounds for exemption were many: one's social class, the region where one lived, level of education, colonists of foreign background residing in Russia, an individual's occupation, exiles, office-holders, particular family situations. The large number of exemptions cut the number of those liable to service by 20 percent with an even greater loss in quality. This 20 percent included most of the nation's educated and trained men and denied their services to the national defense.[13] Without doubt, this situation also adversely affected the morale of the armed forces to a marked degree. Miliutin and those about him looked upon this service as a sacred trust and therefore one that could not be allowed to stop at class lines or territorial limits. He wanted an acceptance of the *principle* that all men should serve, but noting the great changes already taking place in respect to the relation-

12. "Novyia nachala voennoi povinnosti v Rossii," *Voennyi Sbornik*, No. 4 (1864), pp. 258–259. The figures presented by the Ministry of Internal Affairs, headed at this time by P. A. Valuev, differed, claiming that the number liable to conscription was 24,285,807. Exclusive of Finland and Poland, the gentry class at this time was composed of 437,326 males. Other classes exempted from obligatory military service accounted for another half million. In this latter regard, see "Novyia nachala voennoi povinnosti v Rossii," *Voennyi Sbornik*, No. 3 (1864) p. 26, and "Novyia nachala voennoi povinnosti v Rossii," *Voennyi Sbornik*, No. 2 (1864), p. 221. Miliutin calculated that at the rate of four conscripts per thousand of population, it would take fourteen years to build up an adequate reservoir of trained men.

13. "Novyia nachala voennoi povinnosti v Rossii," *Voennyi Sbornik*, No. 4 (1864), pp. 258–259 and 265. Cf. the editorial in *Russkii Invalid*, No. 281 (1866).

ship of the gentry to the rest of society, he felt that any implementation of that principle would have to be deferred for the foreseeable future.[14]

The Emperor's response to the changing situation and the recommendations of the War Minister was to appoint a special commission under the chairmanship of State Secretary N. I. Bakhtin, an important figure in the reform of the court system. The broad significance of the study to be undertaken by the commission was reflected in the diversity of its composition. It included, in addition to representatives from the War Ministry, delegations from the Ministries of the Navy, Internal Affairs, State Domains, and Finance, as well as from the Second Section of His Majesty's Own Chancery. Alexander charged this body with the task of drafting a new general recruiting statute reflecting the changes that had taken place in Russian society, then presenting its study to the State Council.[15]

The subject was so large that the commission found it convenient to break itself down into a number of committees to examine the various dimensions of the problem. First, they wanted to study Russia's recruiting policies of the past and to examine contemporary practices elsewhere. Second, the commission wanted to review the entire question of exemptions from conscription and, third, to create the means for allowing those who so desired to volunteer for military service. Fourth, it wanted to explore the feasibility of setting limits upon the conditions under which individuals might purchase exemptions from the levy. In addition there was a whole range of other problems with which the commission had to deal, such as improvement in the quality of recruits and the special problems of recruiting in certain areas such as Poland.

The commission made rapid progress and submitted its report early in 1863, just as the Empire was undergoing a new recruit levy under the impact of the insurrection in Poland and in anticipation of a general European war. The results were in the main rather disappointing. The new legislation emerging from the studies by this body only established the administrative machinery for accepting voluntary enlistments and for implementing the annual conscription of recruits. Within these limits, the

14. "Novyia nachala voennoi povinnosti v Rossii," *Voennyi Sbornik*, No. 4 (1864), p. 265.

15. "Novyia nachala voennoi povinnosti v Rossii," *Voennyi Sbornik*, No. 2 (1864), pp. 179 and 221.

formula suggested by the War Minister was substantially adopted, and the levy throughout the sixties did tend to take recruits at the rate of four per thousand (or about 100,000 men a year).[16] The commission was not so successful in dealing with the broader issues, particularly those touching upon the privileges of the gentry.

The resistance of proponents of gentry interests was apparently enough to block the other aspects of Miliutin's program—even the relatively mild declaration of the principle that the gentry should be obliged to serve. They defended their privileges with such arguments as declaring that the right not to serve had been granted to them in perpetuity and that any change would mean that the crown had gone back on its word. They also argued that their numbers added to those obliged to serve would not make any significant difference since the gentry class only comprised about 5 percent of the population. Assuming an injured tone, they declared that the gentry had not in fact abused its privilege and in fact had continued to serve the state, with about 50,000 of their number currently serving in the armed forces. From another point of view, the gentry arguments suggested that because of the great differences between themselves and the other classes the rude conditions of army life meant that conscription for them would be a cruel form of punishment. To this last point, the War Ministry rather dryly remarked that military service was tough on everybody.[17] This resistance postponed any universal requirement of military service, but the question had been raised and remained an issue for the rest of the decade.

Miliutin was thwarted in yet another round during this early period of his administration. In September 1862 the Emperor had appointed yet another commission under the ungifted General P. A. Dannenberg. This group studied the tactical organization of the army with the aim of making organizational changes to facilitate rapid mobilization. The basis of

16. *Russkii Invalid*, No. 38 (1864), and Bogdanovich, III., *Prilozheniia*, No. 48. The *zapas* or reservoir of trained men in 1862 amounted to about 210,074, declined to 201,000 by early 1863, and by January 1865 was down to 122, 408. A year later, the figure was again up to 291,000. During the more normal years that followed the number increased rapidly and was up to 548,448 by the end of 1869. The number then held fairly constant. Cf. Bogdanovich, III., 118–119.

17. "Novyia nachala voennoi povinnosti v Rossii," *Voennyi Sbornik* No. 4 (1864), pp. 260–261.

their study was to be a proposal by Miliutin that the number of battalions in each regiment be increased from three to four, with the fourth battalion remaining inactive in peacetime. It would be activated upon mobilization and would be complemented by trained troops from the reserve. This would greatly speed the process of reform and would by itself allow the army to increase its own size by one third. But General Dannenberg did not attempt to deal with this proposal; instead he submitted to the Emperor a group of his own suggestions which bordered on the absurd. Dannenberg's personal intimacy with the Emperor made it difficult for Miliutin to attack him, but Miliutin was successful in preventing these counter-proposals from going very far. Dannenberg, together with a coterie of traditionally minded divisional commanders, was in this test of strength able to forestall and eventually to defeat this part of Miliutin's plans.[18]

Despite the harassment and the resistance to change, Miliutin did manage by the end of 1864 to solve the most immediate problems. On the basis of two general orders issued during this year, the War Minister set up the necessary machinery for inducting and training recruits. The levy was set at four per thousand, which during the sixties produced about 102,000 recruits annually, of which about 80,000 went into the infantry and the bulk of the balance into the cavalry. To train the infantry recruits, Miliutin created eighty reserve infantry battalions which were widely distributed throughout the Empire, so that recruits could be trained as near to their homes as possible.[19]

These battalions had no function other than the training of recruits. Each was composed of a permanent cadre and the transient recruits and was immediately subordinated to its respective provincial military chief and through him to the head of the military district. The cavalry system varied only slightly from this form, with a reserve squadron being created for each active regiment, although they were maintained separately and integrated into a reserve cavalry brigade.[20]

But this reform, although a step forward, was really merely mechanical and provided only the means for administering the annual levy and

18. A. V. Fedorov, pp. 71–74.
19. Bogdanovich, III., 36–38.
20. *Ibid.*, pp. 39–40.

the training of the recruits. The question of creating a numerically adequate reserve and its general relationship with the armed forces remained
and became the subject of intense debate, both public and private, which
increased in intensity after the dramatic events in Central Europe that
produced both the North German Confederation and a new power relationship in Europe. The debate exposed a wide variety of views, some
favoring a volunteer system like that of the recent American Civil War,
others finding their best model in the Prussian Landwehr, and some wanting the creation of a system conforming to the particular forms of Russia's own history and circumstances.[21]

The War Ministry adhered to the principle that whatever form the
reserve system might take, it was necessary to extend the obligation to
serve to all classes without exception. Assuming a tone of great urgency,
the War Ministry reminded the public of the significant changes taking
place in the other European armies and of the rapid course of developments in military technology. From this it concluded that Russia must
follow these examples, particularly those of France and Prussia, and
reduce the term of service to three years. By drastically increasing the
size of the annual levy and by maintaining a large number of noncommissioned officers on permanent service, it was hoped that the standing
army could be reduced to three or four hundred thousand men.[22] This
suggestion bore no fruit, however. Russia did not seem at the moment
to be threatened, and with the entry of Peter Shuvalov and his friends
into the government, the introduction of any reforms which would touch
the privileges of the gentry proved to be very difficult indeed.

The matter did not die, however, but remained a matter of much concern for those sensitive to the great changes taking place in western
and central Europe and who understood their importance for Russia. No
less a person than Miliutin's illustrious uncle, P. D. Kiselev, took him
to task for not moving more positively in this direction:

Dmitrii Miliutin came to talk with me . . . and spoke frankly about his
present position which he has held far longer than he would have imagined.
He very intelligently discussed the material situation of his Ministry, but he
views it just as we did forty years ago, not sufficiently appreciating the suc-

21. *Russkii Invalid*, No. 281 (1866).
22. *Ibid., loc. cit.*

cesses of the west and [our own] current isolated position in Europe. It is my conviction that we cannot remain in our present mode of recruiting, having before us entire armed nations. It is necessary to achieve parity in our defense and to achieve this to place under arms *all* people fit for this duty, and to retain them on duty for only a few weeks, as it is done in Switzerland, so that we might reach this goal . . . without overloading the people. In Switzerland, every canton has its arsenal which may arm a thousand men in the space of twenty-four hours. I saw in St. Moritz sixty modern cannon ready to fire in a campaign, together with the necessary weapons for the infantry. In the Swiss militia special attention is paid to target practice; marksmanship is held in high esteem in Switzerland.[23]

Clearly, Kiselev misunderstood Miliutin and failed to appreciate what he had been trying to do over the past several years, but his absence from Russia during much of the preceding decade would account for this. He did grasp the significance to Russia of the new popular armies in the west and saw the solution to Russia's dilemma in their imitation. He failed to take into account, however, the differences between the rude and uneducated peasants recruited into the Russian army and the relatively well educated Swiss or Prussian recruits. It simply took more than a few weeks to make a soldier out of a Russian peasant.

Some positive progress was made during these years, particularly in Miliutin's plan to reduce the size of the standing army while increasing the number of the reserves. The Polish Insurrection and the military operations in Central Asia had imposed heavy demands upon the army, but with the conclusion of the one and the occurrence of a lull in the other, a reduction became possible. A *prikaz* of April 16, 1866, allowed enlisted ranks who had entered active service before September 8, 1859, to go on extended leave.[24] Two years later, a similar order issued on May 20, 1868, placed all enlisted men with thirteen or more years of active service on unlimited furlough. In addition to this, some units having excess personnel received the right to furlough their senior men if they had ten or more years of active duty.[25]

But these efforts never really solved the problem. During the years 1862 through 1870, a total of 228,492 received outright discharges from

23. A. P. Zablotskii-Desiatovskii, *Graf P. D. Kiselev i ego vremia*, III., 411–412.

24. "Ofitsial'nyi otdel'," *Voennyi Sbornik*, No. 5 (1866), p. 103.

25. "Ofitsial'nyi otdel'," *Voennyi Sbornik*, No. 9 (1868), pp. 110–111, and Bogdanovich, III., 92.

the army, another 299,774 were placed on unlimited furlough, and 410,943 received temporary leave. But the net reduction over this period was only about 120,000 men, although the reservoir of trained men in reserve had been brought up to a level of 548,448.[26] This did reflect a numerical ratio between the active army and the reserve roughly in accordance with that prescribed by Miliutin nearly a decade before. But this achievement created an impasse; on the one hand, the net reduction of men on active duty was too small to offset rising costs in other areas, while on the other, further reductions could be achieved only at the risk of the security of the Empire.

The increasing gravity of the situation caused Miliutin to raise the question again with the Emperor in his annual official report on January 1, 1869. Miliutin suggested at this time that a reserve be created for the army by increasing the annual levy and by drastically reducing the terms of active service. He cited figures compiled by the General Staff indicating that an army of 1,150,000 men could be created in this way with another 875,000 men in reserve.[27] In his next report, submitted exactly one year later; he expanded upon this suggestion, noting that while changes had taken place in the army during his administration, changes were also taking place elsewhere:

In the meantime (since 1862), the results of the last war in Europe and the intense efforts of all the governments to develop their armed forces and to perfect their military technology, has forced us to the maximum development and perfection of our own army. In order not to be left behind, the War Ministry must satisfy the new labors, the new demands of the army.[28]

Miliutin pointed out that in the light of this, Russia's standing army was numerically deficient for any war involving the European powers and

26. *Ibid.*, III., 89, 95, 118–119, and *Prilozhenii*, Nos. 38 and 45. Between 1862 and 1870, 113,564 men died in service and 41,442 deserted, although more than half the deserters eventually returned. This death rate from noncombat causes should be compared with the number who died during the fifteen nonwar years preceding Miliutin's ministry, when a total of 389,420 perished, with the highest rate occurring in the late winter and early spring. This was attributed to their poor diet which left the soldiers vulnerable to disease. See L.Il'iashevich, "Statisticheskie izsledovanie smertnosti v nashei armii," *Voennyi Sbornik*, No. 2 (1863), pp. 372 and 412.

27. A. V. Fedorov, p. 219.

28. *Vsepoddaneishii doklad voennogo ministra*, January 1, 1870, pp. 1–2.

that the forces in reserve were not and under the present system could not be sufficient to bring the army up to the strength necessary to conduct such a war successfully:

will there be sufficient numbers in our army, even in its full composition in wartime, in view of the enormous armed forces which are being formed from among the masses of the armed peoples in all the European states, not excluding even Turkey?[29]

But just how many troops were enough? In this same report, he pointed out that the current standing army was composed of 727,000 men with another 533,000 in reserve, representing a total force of 1,260,000 men. Even two years later, the Empire had a standing army of 738,000 and a 620,000-man reserve.[30] What Miliutin had in mind was the achievement of a wartime capacity numerically equal to the combined armies of Austria and Germany, or a force of nearly two million men. He calculated that if Russia developed the ability to increase her army in wartime by the same ratio as Prussia, then the Empire would have to retain a peacetime force of only 692,000 men. This represented a substantial modification of his goals from a decade before, when necessity demanded only a peacetime army of 765,000 men which could be expanded in wartime to 1,377,365 troops.[31]

The arms race and the emergence of a new German Empire under Prussia represented a challenge that Russia had to accept. The Franco-Prussian War and the rapid victory by the Germans over a first-class power produced a profound effect in Russia. An editorial, for example, in the liberal *Vestnik Evropy* for November 1870 saw the German victory as the greatest fact of the year and concluded that it was a direct consequence of the Prussian military system. Couching its arguments in strong terms, the article declared that the time for illusions was past, and that Russia had no choice but to adopt the Prussian system. The army had to have a more national character based upon an all-class conscription and the reduction of the terms of active service.[32]

29. *Ibid.*, p. 17.
30. *Ibid.*, p. 9, and *Vsepoddaneishii doklad voennogo ministra*, January 1, 1873, pp. 9–10.
31. *Despatches*, March 6, 1872, and *Doklad*, January 15, 1862, p. 76.
32. "V. O.: Mneniia o voennom preobrazovanii," *Vestnik Evropy*, No. 11 (1870), pp. 372–374.

The pleas reflecting such opinions as these had already been anticipated in official circles and served to provide Miliutin with assistance from a completely unexpected quarter. While Count P. A. Valuev was a member of the Shuvalov clique and generally a member of the planter party, he often tried also to play the role of peacemaker and conciliator between his faction and the Miliutin group. In this case, Valuev had had an opportunity to see what the Prussian system really meant in practice. He had been abroad during the summer of 1870, had witnessed the clockwork mobilization of the Prussian army, and seen the devastating effects of that war machine. The impact of this experience led Valuev to pay a call upon Miliutin as soon as he returned to St. Petersburg. He described to the War Minister what he had seen and proposed the introduction of universal military service in Russia. Miliutin of course heartily agreed, but since he had been an unsuccessful advocate for this particular policy he suggested to Valuev that the proposition would have a much better chance for success if the latter brought the matter before the Emperor.

Valuev agreed and in response to Miliutin's suggestion drafted a memorandum entitled, "Thoughts of a Non-Military Person on Our Armed Forces." Before submitting it to the Emperor, however, Valuev showed it to Miliutin who generally concurred with its contents, since it differed little from the arguments he had been advocating for years. Valuev had pointed out the drastic shift that had taken place in the power relationships in Europe and had observed that Russia was in a state of decline unless proper measures were taken to redress the imbalance. Valuev had also analyzed the Prussian system of all-class military conscription, underlining the fact that while a large part of the Prussian population was required to serve, the standing army was relatively small. After relatively short periods of active service, the Prussian soldier entered the reserves and returned to his normal civilian occupation. Valuev's conclusion was that it was absolutely imperative that Russia adopt a similar system.[33]

The Emperor read and fully approved the memorandum in October 1870 and followed it up on November 4 with a public announcement

33. P. A. Zaionchkovskii, "Podgotovka voennoi reformy 1874 goda," *Istoricheskie Zapiski*, No. 27 (1948), pp. 172–173, and A. V. Fedorov, pp. 219–221.

in the *Pravitel'stvennyi Vestnik* of the government's intention to require military service of all classes in the Empire. The communique enjoined the War Minister, therefore, to:

compose and submit in statutory form for Imperial approval, proposals for the structure of reserve elements in the army, and for the extension of direct participation in the military conscription, in acordance with some general conditions, to all classes in the Empire.[34]

Miliutin considered this to be one of the most important acts of the reign, and the first step in a complete reorientation of the Empire's defense system:

The fourth of November of last year (1870) created a new epoch in the history of the development of our armed forces. The Imperial order concerning the extension of military conscription to all classes of the state, and concerning a reserve backing up the standing army, evokes a new basic reform for all parts of the War Office.[35]

A few days after the publication of the Imperial order, Miliutin responded by submitting to the Emperor two preliminary drafts. One dealt with the question of the necessary changes in the armed forces and the formation of the reserve and the other suggested basic guidelines for the system of universal military conscription. After reiterating many of his earlier arguments, the War Minister outlined in specific terms what he thought was necessary to guarantee the security of the Empire. He believed that Russia had to maintain a trained, battle-ready force of 500–600,000 troops in areas which were potential theaters of war. This army had to have the capacity to mobilize immediately to a strength of 1,653,393 enlisted men and 50,954 officers. To accomplish this, he calculated that the army would have to create thirty reserve divisions which would be complemented from the trained reserves in the event of war.

In order to provide the additional troops necessary for such an expansion of the army, Miliutin proposed increasing the rate of the annual

---

34. *Pravitel'stvennyi Vestnik*, No. 237 (1870). Actually considerable preparatory work had already been done. Not only did the many years of thinking and planning now find expression, but since early October 1870 the General Staff and a few of Miliutin's most intimate aides had been busy making studies and formulating principles. See P. A. Zaionchkovskii, "Podgotovka voennoi reformy 1874 goda," *Istoricheskie Zapiski*, No. 27 (1948), p. 173.

35. *Vsepoddaneishii doklad voennogo ministra*, January 1, 1871, p. 1.

levy from four to six out of each thousand inhabitants, raising the annual total to about 160,000 recruits. This larger number was possible
because the expansion of obligatory military service to all classes would
add five million more to the rolls of those eligible, besides adding to the
morale both of the army and the nation.[36] The national economy could
be expected to benefit as well, since the levy would fall more evenly
upon the productive elements of society. Miliutin pointed out, however,
that certain exceptions would have to be made for people living in very
remote or newly assimilated parts of the Empire and for the Cossacks.
These groups would be governed by legislation to be drafted at a later
date.

On the basis of Miliutin's memoranda, the Emperor, on November 17,
1870, appointed two special commissions.[37] The first of these was directed
to study the problems of reorganizing the army and creating the reserve;
the other was to study the question of conscription. While both of these
commissions were the direct responsibility of the War Minister, both
were chaired by the Chief of the General Staff, Count F. L. Heiden, in
whom Miliutin had the highest personal confidence. Moreover, the commission which was to prepare the legislation for universal military conscription included, besides representatives from the War Ministry,
delegates from other interested ministries and from several sections of
His Majesty's Own Chancery.

Miliutin drafted directives to guide the work of both commissions,
which, after their approval by Alexander, were released to both bodies
on December 20, 1870. These memoranda contained all that Miliutin
had already said in the previous analyses, but he now became more
specific about the direction he wanted to take. For example, he wanted
to divide the standing army into two parts: an active or field army and
the stationary force. In time of war, the field troops would retain their
existing structure and would act as the front-line battle force, while the
stationary troops would alter their status upon mobilization. These troops,
which in peacetime acted as the domestic watch, trained recruits, and
conducted the inspections and educational musters for those individuals
enrolled in the reserve, would be expected to continue these same func-

36. A. V. Fedorov, pp. 222–223.
37. Ibid., p. 224.

tions in the event of war while also acting as a battle reserve for the
infantry and artillery and as reinforcements for all branches of arms.[38]

The reserve forces themselves would form only in wartime. They
would be formed like any other troops into regiments and divisions (or
battalions and brigades in the artillery) in accordance with normal organizational tables. These reserve units would be kept separate from the
active army and would serve as a battle reserve, performing those secondary functions such as garrison and fortress duty or maintaining roads and
transportation, which would free the field forces for their basic combat
role. While not generally employable as first-line fighting troops, the
reserves would be able to perform all the support services necessary to
keep a modern army in the field. To retain their effectiveness as a battle
reserve, however, these troops would hold musters for short periods at
regular intervals during peacetime. In time of war they would form by
means of cadres drawn from among the stationary troops, with a sufficient proportion of the latter to assure the cohesiveness and effectiveness
of the unit. The stationary units would also be responsible for supplying
most staff personnel and for equipping the new formations.[39]

Miliutin's instructions concerning the conscription itself suggested that
the basic term of obligated service be set at fifteen years, of which seven
years were to be spent on active service with the balance in the reserve.
The annual levy would choose by lot about 25 percent of the young men
attaining the age of twenty-one. Since the increase in the size of the army
meant that the officer corps had to expand correspondingly, young men
possessing some education were to be encouraged to volunteer after
reaching the age of seventeen. Such volunteers would receive reduced
terms of active service, and should they succeed in passing the necessary
examinations they would be commissioned as officers in either the active
or reserve army.

The only acceptable reason for a dispensation not to serve was physical
incapacity. The army would, in addition to this, grant exemptions or
deferments to those who were necessary for the support of their families,
to those wishing to complete their education, and to those deemed es-

38. "Vsepoddaneishii doklad voennogo ministra, 20-go dekabria 1870 goda, No.
381," *Voennyi Sbornik*, No. 1 (1871), pp. 20–21.
39. *Ibid.*, pp. 23–28.

sential to the health of the national economy. Those receiving such exemptions would be enrolled in the levy on a general basis but would be called only under unusual circumstances. Those who actually entered the army would be chosen by lot to assure the fairness of the conscription. No one would be allowed to avoid military service by hiring a substitute as was formerly possible. Miliutin reinforced this strict injunction with the unqualified declaration that the defense of the fatherland was the sacred duty of every Russian subject.

The War Minister had already defined in an earlier proposal the precise situations in which exemptions and deferments might be granted. A young man could be excused from service if he were the son or grandson of a widow or widower, or if he were the brother of orphans. He might also be exempted if he were the sole surviving son after the death of his parents, providing that he had either a family, a home, or a business. Students enrolled in secondary and higher schools at the time their age group was conscripted would be deferred. It was clear that Miliutin wanted the obligatory military service to disturb the normal routine of national life as little as possible, a fact born out by his statement on principle that the conscripts would be kept on active duty only as long as it was necessary to make soldiers of them, provided that the standing army possessed a full complement of men.[40]

The two commissions began the active consideration of these proposals soon after the turn of the year. The more important of the two from the social and political point of view, the commission concerned with the conscription statute, met on January 5, 1871. Because of the wide importance of the deliberations of this body, it met with representatives of various interested classes and economic groups as well as with delegates from several of the provincial zemstva, all of which took part in the discussions.[41] In order to facilitate its work, the commission divided itself into four subcommittees, the most important being that charged with the study of privileges to be accorded to those possessing an education.

The first concern of this subcommittee was with those who were to be granted reduced terms if they volunteered. This was most important be-

40. *Ibid.*, p. 25, and P. A. Zaionchkovskii, "Podgotovka voennoi reformy 1874 goda," *Istoricheskie Zapiski*, No. 27 (1948), pp. 175–176.
41. P. A. Zaionchkovskii, *Voennye reformy 1860–1870 godov v Rossii*, p. 307.

cause it was to provide the incentives for potential officers to volunteer. If their general education was sufficient, these volunteers would be commissioned after passing the qualifying examination, or if their education was more limited they could become officers after completing the course in one of the junker schools. Volunteers were to be divided into three categories according to their educational backgrounds. The first category included those who had completed a university or its equivalent, and these would be obliged to serve only a period of three months on active duty. Those volunteers with a secondary education made up the second category; they would be required to serve for one year. The third category included those who had completed a primary education in a *progymnazium* or a district school who were expected to serve for two years.[42]

Since they were easier to train and were also of greater value to the national economy in their normal civilian occupations, the War Ministry also wanted to accord privileges to conscripts possessing an education. These were to take the form both of deferments and reduced terms of active service. The students were to be encouraged by this to stay in school as long as possible, and those who were conscripted were to be returned to civilian life as quickly as possible. The army needed to avail itself of the products of the nation's schools, but it did not want to do so at the cost of stagnating national development. The commission worked out a formula for deferring those students enrolled in school up to a maximum age, depending upon the level of the school. Conscripts with a university education would need to serve only six months, while those with a secondary education would be obligated to serve only eighteen months. Similarly, conscripts who had completed a *progymnazium* or a district school would be required to serve three years, and those with a primary education would be obligated for four years.[43]

Both commissions completed their work during 1872 and submitted their reports for consideration by the State Council. But the public storm of controversy that had begun with the Emperor's announcement that all classes would be required to serve in the armed forces continued unabated. The reaction was predictable: the "liberal" press was somewhat ambivalent but generally favorable, while the conservative and reaction-

42. *Ibid.*, pp. 308–309.
43. *Ibid.*, pp. 310–311.

ary press represented varying degrees of disapproval. Miliutin was at a severe disadvantage after the *Russkii Invalid* had been limited to the publication of purely official news or the narrowest of military subjects, and, as a consequence, he had to depend upon the good graces of well disposed editors to act as his advocates.

While at times critical and often at great pains to assure the public of its disapproval of certain of the War Minister's policies, the most important support came from the liberal paper *Golos*. This newspaper favored the principle of the all-class conscription from the beginning, viewing it as "a continuing development of the eternal manifesto of February 19, 1861,"[44] but it often disagreed with particular aspects of Miliutin's program, particularly over the question of the length of active service to be required of the conscripts. As time wore on and attacks upon the reform from the reactionaries became more bitter and insistent, the *Golos* became increasingly a partisan of the War Minister's program[45] and from time to time opened its pages to its defenders.

One of the loudest voices in opposition was that of Katkov, who delivered a series of broadsides in the *Moskovskie Vedomosti* seeking to mitigate the effects of Miliutin's program. Katkov concentrated particularly on the length of the term of active service to be required, desiring that it be shortened to the minimum, and on the privileges to be accorded to those possessing an education.[46] It is interesting to note at this juncture that the same questions and what appeared to be similar arguments also appeared in the journal *Vestnik Evropy*. This latter periodical was quite liberal and generally well disposed toward the proposed reform, so the essential difference between the two was their intent. The *Vestnik Evropy*, for example, wanted the terms of active service to be cut even more

44. See particularly *Golos*, No. 11 (1870). *Golos* was not disposed to be over optimistic, however, cynically expecting the gentry and the merchant classes would find some way to buy themselves free from the obligation to serve. *Golos*, No. 335 (1870).

45. *Golos* had often been one of the War Ministry's sharpest critics in the earlier years of Miliutin's administration, but after the closing of the *Russkii Invalid* as a general newspaper and the loss of its capacity to defend the interests of the War Minister, *Golos* in the early seventies began increasingly to undertake the defense of the War Ministry against the vitriolic attacks of its detractors. This reached its high point in 1873, although the editorship of *Golos* was especially sensitive to any charges that the views in their newspaper were anything other than their own. See, for example, *Golos*, No. 224 (1873).

46. See particularly, *Moskovskie Vedomosti*, Nos. 1, 28, and 227 (1871).

than the period proposed in Miliutin's instruction to the special commission, as did the *Moskovskie Vedomosti*, but it held this view because it wanted the patriotic duty of national service to be extended to the widest possible number of those in each age group.[47] Katkov was more concerned with finding means for the mitigation of service in order that the burden would be as light as possible for the better educated gentry.[48]

An even more strident voice than that of Katkov was that of R. A. Fadeev. His quixotic nature became increasingly evident in the attacks leveled at the new reform. The bitterness of his polemics and the opposition led him dangerously close to the extreme of public denunciation of the Emperor's will. His defense of the privileges of the gentry class was mystical in nature, and the proposals he advanced on their behalf were completely anachronistic.[49]

He had declared in the 1868 edition of the *Vooruzhennyia sily Rossii* that the gentry were the necessary foundation of the army and that the reforms promulgated up until that date had expelled that class from its natural role as the defenders of the fatherland. But he had gone farther than this and had said that military duty was the obligation of every Russian. The gentry were the natural bearers of the Russian spirit, and they, as the officer corps of the army, were bound by close moral ties with the ordinary soldiers drawn from the other elements of society. He was not so much interested in an officer corps which was technically competent as he was in one which provided moral leadership, thereby providing for Russia the true means for transforming the nation into the pre-eminent world power.[50] Fadeev clearly did not understand the significance of the Prussian sand tables and needle guns.

While Fadeev accepted (or appeared to accept) the principle of uni-

47. See, for example, *Vestnik Evropy*, No. 2 (1871), p. 828, and No. 5 (1871), pp. 406–409.

48. See particularly, *Moskovskie Vedomosti*, No. 28 (1871). Katkov wanted substantial privileges for the graduates of higher schools which were largely attended by the gentry, but on the other hand he did not want to see any advantages granted to those completing the course of a national primary school, warranting that they were too inferior to be accorded any privilege. See *Moskovskie Vedomosti*, No. 227 (1871).

49. Fadeev's social views were best expressed in his work entitled, *Russkoe obshchestvo v nastoiashchem i budushchem: (Chem nam byt'?)*. See particularly, pp. 249–250.

50. R. A. Fadeev, *Vooruzhennyia sily Rossii*, pp. 195–199 and 244ff.

versal conscription, he disagreed with its specific provisions. He was particularly concerned by the prospect of the gentry becoming submerged into the mass of the Russian population. The obligation to serve not only did not carry with it the assurance that the gentry would enjoy any special position in the army, but quite on the contrary it demanded that they serve their country on a basis equal to that of all other Russians.[51] Fadeev was in the awkward position of an anachronistic Starodum[52] whose sense of duty was mitigated by the knowledge that that duty was at variance with his concept of what it should be. In attacking the proposed conscription law, he used two basic approaches. On the one hand, he polemicized against all of Miliutin's reforms, concentrating on the Regulation of 1868, and on the other, he projected the War Minister's accomplishments and policies against his own concept of what Russian society should be. His polemics were often nothing more than excursions into semantics; at other times logic would give way to highly pitched screams born of impotent rage.[53]

The first installments of Fadeev's campaign were written only days after the Emperor had announced his intentions in the *Pravitel'stvennyi Vestnik* and were published in a series in the *Birzhevye Vedomosti* early in 1871. He began by reviewing the defeat of France by Prussia and suggested that the same flaws responsible for the French loss were inherent in the Russian system. While Russia had greater numbers of men than France, the latter at least had some reserves which could be brought into play while Russia had none.[54] Fadeev quite reasonably pointed out that there are two basic factors governing the size of an army: the tasks it has before it (the enemies it must face, the length of the frontiers, etc.) and the means available to the state (population, etc.) and that it is the reserve that allows the army to adjust to the demands of a particular situation.

But it became clear that Fadeev did not have in mind the usual kind

51. R. A. Fadeev, *Nash voennyi vopros*, pp. 183–215.

52. One of the principal characters in Denis Fonvizin's play, *Nedorosl'*.

53. Nowhere is Fadeev's angry style more evident than in his answer to a charge made in *Voennyi Sbornik* that he could not even pass the junior examination for admission to the War College. R. A. Fadeev, *Nash voennyi vopros*, pp. 10ff.

54. R. A. Fadeev, "Pereustroistvo russkikh sil," *Birzhevye Vedomosti*, No. 1 (1871).

of reserve force. He dreamed of some sort of mystical rising of the Russian nation, such as that of Minin and Pozharskii or Alexander Nevsky, as the real Russian reserve. Asking what kind of reserve was best for Russia, Fadeev did recognize, however, that something more than this was needed:

> In substance it comes down to the following: is it possible to trust the Russian people politically, to gather with their weapons in their hands in the same way that one trusts the standing army? I will answer another question: does there exist with us, did there exist formerly any form of differentiation, even any sort of shading in the general mood, in the views and conceptions, even in the habits, in one word, in the collective spirit of the mob,—between the army and the nation?[55]

Fadeev felt that the army should have a spirit different from that of the people in that the former was disciplined as a result of the training received from the officers. The officer corps represented the highest division of society, the gentry class, but together with the enlisted ranks they were fused into one great whole just as the gentry were an integral part of the nation.[56]

To Fadeev, the national or popular basis of the Russian army was in marked contrast to the armies of other countries, and any relationship other than the exclusive right of the gentry class to serve in the officer corps was held by him to be unnatural. The Russian people had never known any authority other than that of the Tsar, and the gentry were historically a service-nobility executing his will. This ancient relationship had produced a moral union of the several classes:

> The basis of this union does not of course lie in personal convictions, to which not all persons may arrive, but in the collective human feeling that is even stronger. Russia maintains the exclusive trust granted by the people to the sovereign power by the unshakeability of reciprocal trust. All this is clear as day.[57]

Translating all this into military terms, Fadeev rejected the French reserve system and the Prussian Landwehr as inappropriate for Russia and instead placed his faith in the ancient Russian military levy, the

55. R. A. Fadeev, "Pereustroistvo russkikh sil," *Birzhevye Vedomosti*, No. 2 (1871).
56: *Ibid.*
57. *Ibid.*

opolchenie,[58] as the best means of providing support for the standing

> The *opolchenie*—that is Russia; it is without cost and is inexhaustable, needing only arms and powder, both of which can be obtained without difficulty. The *opolchenie* would satisfy our goals in two simple ways: the use of rifles would be understood and it can be quickly mustered.[59]

Since this was to be a rising of the *nation*, the *opolchenie* like the Landwehr could be established only on soil not subject to any political shilly-shallying, where the popular mass considered itself to be Russian or sincerely wanted to be one with Russia. Fadeev, in questioning whether the proposed draft of 90,000 men or so a year would be sufficient, argued that in Russia it was necessary for the great bulk of the adult population to serve. The *opolchenie* needed less training, perhaps no more than three months. This training would be qualitatively different from that currently prescribed by the War Ministry:

> But the system of preparation must be different—no catechism, no grammar, no gymnastics—nothing other than the knowledge of how to handle a rifle and hit the target.[60]

Fadeev rejected every social implication of Miliutin's reforms, those of the past as well as those projected for the future. The gentry were to be the shepherds and the rest of the population the sheep. He refused to understand the significance of the nation in arms in modern European warfare; particularly, he failed to grasp the need for the kind of training necessary to make the nation in arms an effective fighting force. He disapproved of the army which left membership in the officer corps increasingly open to talent rather than to the gentry class exclusively, and he certainly had no use for the concept of the army as the school of the nation. Fadeev saw in the mystical rising of the nation, led by gentry, the means to defeat any of Russia's enemies. Russian national spirit was to him sufficient to overcome any technological or professional advantage of a potential enemy. But, perhaps most importantly, adherence to Fadeev's views would preserve the special position of the gentry class in

---

58. R. A. Fadeev, "Pereustroistvo russkikh sil," *Birzhevye Vedomosti*, No. 9 (1871).

army:

59. *Ibid.*
60. *Ibid.*

Russian society, leaving the execution of the Emperor's will in their hands as well as guaranteeing their supreme position over all other social classes.[61]

Fadeev continued to carp against the impending reform during the early seventies. He began to contribute regularly to the *Russkii Mir* and also continued his activity as a pamphleteer. The *Russkii Mir*, which began publication in 1871, replaced *Vest'* as the newspaper representing the most extreme gentry interest. Its editorials tended to be thoroughly vitriolic and were at times quite clumsy in the manner that Mark Twain referred to as "Arkansas journalism." Both Fadeev and the editorship began to refer to Miliutin's reforms sarcastically as the "system of 1862,"[62] and Fadeev argued that the lessons of the recent European wars dictated that the "system" be reversed.

His attacks upon the military reforms became more specific, centering chiefly upon the entire district system, education and the army, and the question of a battle reserve. His basic stand in all these matters was that the reforms violated morality. For example, he claimed that Russia already had enough educated men (!) and that the important qualification for an officer was his moral fitness.[63] He also disapproved of the district system because logistics were made a collegial responsibility rather than the exclusive preserve of an individual, and in the same vein he reacted violently to what he considered to be the subordination of tactical officers to the bureaucracy.[64] He fumed over the loss of the field commander's independence which left logistics and over-all strategy in the hands of the War Ministry and military district officials. The system to him was mechanical and caused the personal qualities of individuals to lose their significance.[65]

The concerted barrage by Fadeev and the editorship of the *Russkii Mir* was answered in part by a series of articles appearing in *Golos*. Many of

61. See, for example, R. A. Fadeev, *Russkoe obshchestvo v nastoiashchem i budushchem (Chem nam byt'?)*, pp. 132–134.

62. See, for example, *Russkii Mir*, No. 331 (1872).

63. R. A. Fadeev, *Vooruzhennyia sily Rossii*, p. 197, and R. A. Fadeev, *Russkoe obshchestvo v nastoiashchem i budushchem (Chem nam byt'?)*, pp. 138–139.

64. This is an almost constant theme. See, R. A. Fadeev, *Nash Voennyi Vopros*, pp. 109; 128–138; 153–154; 161; and 162–176.

65. *Ibid.*, pp. 183–185.

these were direct answers to specific items by Fadeev or the editors of
the *Russkii Mir* and were often written by officers or former officers with
practical general staff experience. One of the most interesting of these
was an article by one P. Ivanov, entitled, "On the Question of Discipline
in the Russian Army."[66] While the item itself was a competent refutation
of charges that the Miliutin reforms had served to break down the fabric
of discipline in the army, the most significant part was the publication
by *Golos* in a footnote of the cover letter accompanying the article when
it was received by the newspaper. In it, Ivanov asked that *Golos* find
some space in its pages for the article and then added,

> It is of interest to us not only because of the very subject itself, but also
> for its relationship to an organ of that obscurantist clique which with the end
> of the newspaper *Vest'* had apparently brought its cause to a conclusion.
> But, just as the darkness in the world never lifts, that clique about which I
> have just spoken has revived and started anew and has manifested itself in
> the newspaper *Russkii Mir*.
>
> It stands to reason that we do not oppose that which they have stated:
> let them say it. Their activity, although completely obscurantist and there-
> fore not without harm in literature, may for all that carry some benefit be-
> cause it acquaints one with the forces of the clique and with those stratagems
> which it resorts to for the achievement of its goals.
>
> We at first wanted to turn with our remarks to the *Russkii Invalid* but re-
> frained because the *Russkii Mir* considers the military journals to be entirely
> an incessant hymn "about the charms of the order established in the forces."
> What good would it do for *Russkii Mir* to consider that our article was writ-
> ten in defense of the War Ministry? We do not have any such pretensions
> nor do we desire any. . . . If our article achieves its purpose it will be for us
> far more important than any defense of the War Ministry: the public, at any
> rate the public which does not have the means to study seriously military
> problems, will otherwise be convinced by dishonesty, even by clever
> cheating.[67]

Aside from its commentaries on the methods of the opposition, this letter
serves to point up the essential issue in the quarrel—that it was not
merely a military problem nor a question of the national defense but

66. P. Ivanov, "Po voprosu o distsipline v russkom voiske," *Golos*, No. 313
(1871).

67. *Golos*, No. 313 (1871). In comparing *Russkii Mir* with *Vest'*, *Golos* declared
that the latter at least had been motivated by idealism, while *Russkii Mir* was
actuated only by practical desires. *Golos*, No. 25 (1873).

was in reality a social matter. The *Russkii Mir* represented just another chapter in the blind reaction of the more extreme planters who were unwilling to sacrifice any of their privileges for the sake of the preservation of the nation and who found in the War Minister the objectification of the cause of their declining position.

The planters in the government turned upon Miliutin in all their fury in an effort to unseat him. Their efforts were handicapped by the temporary defection from their ranks of Valuev who in this matter was an important ally of the War Minister. Count Peter Shuvalov manipulated the intrigue which developed, and used as his front man Miliutin's old friend and enemy, Field Marshal Bariatinskii. Shuvalov employed whatever means he could find in his hopes of overthrowing Miliutin, using his position to dangle the bait of high office and other rewards before those who would serve his purpose, and it appears that his behavior for a time at least bordered upon treason. Shuvalov formed an alliance with the German ambassador, Heinrich Reiss,[68] to work against Miliutin since the Germans disapproved of the growing strength and efficiency of the Russian army and the nationalist spirit of the War Minister.

Shuvalov's role was somewhat that of a grey eminence behind the throne, and rarely did he emerge to do battle openly with Miliutin, always prefering to use others. Miliutin was in no way deceived and noted in his diary that the prime force behind his enemies was Peter Shuvalov:

> Thus, even now, a majority of the members of the Committee of Ministers act as one with Count Shuvalov like an orchestra under the baton of a *capellmeister*. Timashev, Count Tolstoy, Count Pahlen, Valuev are the obedient instruments of Shuvalov.[69]

One of Miliutin's most observant contemporaries, A. V. Nikitenko, noted with keen insight the game being played by the Chief of Gendarmes:

> One must give Count Shuvalov his due; he has systematically shaped the system of the reaction. By subordinating to himself several of the chief administrators, especially the Minister of Internal Affairs and the Minister of

---

68. N. G. Zalesov, "Zapiski N. G. Zalesova," *Russkaia Starina*, No. 6 (1905), pp. 518–519. Zalesov's testimony further demonstrates that the Shuvalov clique was able, not only to use the promise of high office to win allies against the War Minister and his program, but that they were willing to ruin those who deviated.

69. *Dnevnik*, I., 119.

Public Instruction, he consequently goes from inhibiting and turning back one reform to inhibiting and turning back another and, in such a manner, welds into one block of strength the drive to lock Russia into an immobile position. What may come of this, of course, never enters his head. His intelligence is not the intelligence of a statesman but of a courtier.[70]

One of the most important of the tools of Shuvalov was D. A. Tolstoy, who also was under the influence of Katkov. Without doubt, the opposition considered the issue of education to be the War Minister's Achilles' heel, a view reinforced by their recent victory over him on the question of the right of *real* school graduates to matriculate in a university. Tolstoy's position as the Minister of Public Instruction and the nature of his own personality made him a perfect stooge for the machinations of Shuvalov and Katkov. Nikitenko, commenting on Tolstoy, wrote:

> As the motto of Count D. A. Tolstoy may serve the words: "all are fools except I alone." This man, intelligent and even kindly under normal conditions, does not know what it means to control and direct, but does know only one thing—he is powerful at court, how to strike to the right and to the left. . . .[71]

This negativism of Tolstoy was illustrative of the nature of most of the opposition to Miliutin; the planters had no really viable program but were bent on destroying whatever appeared to threaten their corporate interests.

The critical year was 1873 when the issues surrounding the extension of the obligation to serve to all social classes were taken from the ad hoc commissions and introduced into the State Council for general debate. Tolstoy, who had already gone for Miliutin's jugular in previous clashes, began the latest dialogue between the two or three days before discussion of universal military service in a special session of the State Council was to begin. Upon this occasion, he sent to all the members of that body a fifty-two-page memorandum, apparently written by Katkov, which had as its basic purpose the restriction for all practical purposes of the right to volunteer to the gentry. The effect of this would be to restrict again the officer ranks to all but a few from nongentry backgrounds.[72]

70. Nikitenko, III., 249.
71. *Ibid.*, III., 301.
72. A. I. Del'vig, II., 503.

This keynoted the tone of the Katkov press during the months in which the State Council debated the new law. Although the *Moskovskie Vedomosti* directed its attacks at several different issues—the military budget, the denial of the right to hire substitutes, and the long period of active service[73]—it concentrated its fire upon the question of deferments, particularly those granted in accordance with the level of an individual's education. Clearly, it was here that the opponents of the proposed law hoped to thwart the purpose of the new law; should those possessing a minimum of education receive especially advantageous treatment and should most education be limited to the gentry class, this would provide the gentry with the means for mitigating their obligation to serve, or might eliminate it altogether.

In one editorial, appearing in the *Moskovskie Vedomosti* on April 24, 1873, Katkov bitterly attacked Miliutin's position on the matter of privileges according to education. Katkov used as a means to undercut the War Minister's position the argument that the latter's proposals were at variance with the Prussian model and noted in particular that in Prussia only those with a university-level education were allowed reduced terms of service. Was not Prussia the most successful military state in Europe, and did it not follow that Russia should imitate her example? The best interests of the army and of the Empire would not be served if young men were allowed to defer their military service or if they could gain reductions in their tours of active duty merely by having attended a grammar school or a *gymnazium*. On the other hand, he asked, who would submit to the gruelling discipline of university study just to avoid or reduce his term of military service? Besides, he maintained, the army needed educated men and could not afford to release so quickly those who had some education.

It was not necessary for Katkov to remind his readers that the right to matriculate in a university had in 1871 been restricted to those possessing a certificate from a classical *gymnazium* and that his counterproposal would have narrowed the social base of those receiving deferments to the gentry class, since the merchant and other classes tended to favor the *real* schools. He did, however, support the merchant classes in another manner. He questioned the elimination of the right to

73. See above.

hire substitutes as proposed by the War Minister on the grounds that not all cases of hardship would be included so that family businesses might suffer.[74]

Under the guise of humanitarianism, Katkov wanted the creation of a privilege based upon wealth and position. The Moscow publicist, moreover, did not limit his activity on behalf of his views to publishing and to coaching Tolstoy from the sidelines. He personally came to St. Petersburg during the final weeks of the debate over the universal conscription law, and Miliutin was shocked to find him, together with Constantine Pobedonostsev, participating in one of the special sessions of the State Council.[75]

From the time that he introduced the draft legislation into the State Council on January 19, 1873, until the law was finally promulgated on January 1, 1874, Miliutin and the reform were under incessant attack. In the meetings of the State Council and the Committee of Ministers, Tolstoy was the usual spokesman for the opposition, with Shuvalov himself occasionally deigning to enter the lists. Tolstoy hammered away with great vigor but little imagination at the same points Katkov was attacking in the press, most particularly the demand that conscripts possessing an education below the university level be required to serve longer terms of active duty than those suggested by the War Minister.

Miliutin's own reasons for maintaining the views that he had toward the granting of privileges for education were best summed up in a statement he read into the record during a session of the State Council:

incomparably more important is the *general national* consideration, in that individuals receiving higher scholarly training need in peacetime remain on active service only for that period of time which is *absolutely necessary* for their acquaintance with the forms of military service and for the learning of a military occupation.[76]

He felt that the higher the level of education possessed by the conscript, the easier it was to train him, and he could therefore be released to civilian life that much earlier so that he could also help to make a contribution to the national economy. Moreover, this practice would serve

74. *Moskovskie Vedomosti*, No. 114 (1873).
75. *Dnevnik*, I., 110, and Nikitenko, III., 239–240.
76. G. Dzhanshiev, *Epokha velikikh reform*, eighth edition, p. 496.

as an incentive for young men to acquire as much education as possible.[77]

Miliutin's enemies found another way in which to attack him on the education issue. This dealt with the War Minister's admissions policies for the Medical-Surgical Academy, which was the institution for training physicians and surgeons for the army. Since 1871, when the Emperor had ruled that students wishing to enter institutions of higher learning had to have the *attestat* from a classical *gymnazium*, Miliutin had found that the number of candidates with such credentials were too few to meet the demands of the army, so he had chosen to admit candidates who had carried their studies only through the seventh form. Any other decision on his part would have meant that the army would soon have been without medical personnel. When he adopted this policy, Miliutin understood that sooner or later it would be called into question, and when his enemies raised the issue, he welcomed the opportunity to place the entire matter before an open forum.[78] There can be little doubt that he hoped to use this as a chance to raise the matter of classical and *real* schools again and to seek a revision of the Emperor's earlier decision.

But when the question did come up, he found an unexpected turn of events. In September 1873, during the height of the intense struggle to get his reform bill through the State Council, Miliutin received a penciled note from Alexander who was at that time relaxing at Livadia, his favorite watering place in the Crimea. The note simply ordered the War Minister to comply with the statutes.[79] When Alexander returned to the capital and spoke to Miliutin on the subject, his tone was sharp.

The Emperor categorically and ominously affirmed that all schools should be under the purview of the Ministry of Public Instruction, a view with which Miliutin would probably have concurred ten years earlier. But now he had to plead with Alexander that special institutions such as the Medical-Surgical Academy were another matter. The Emperor conceded only to the point of saying that the issue, as a matter of principle, would be put before a special committee composed of those ministers who had some type of school within their respective ministries. The Emperor topped this off with a tactless demonstration of hostility toward

77. *Ibid.*, pp. 496–497.
78. *Dnevnik*, I., 98.
79. *Ibid.*, *loc. cit.*

the military schools by pointing out the number of young officers who, as recent graduates of these schools, were acting as revolutionary agitators.[80]

When the committee was called to discuss this issue it was clear that the Emperor's mood had not changed. Miliutin's first witness was N. I. Kozlov, the Director of the Medical-Surgical Academy, who read to the meeting what Valuev referred to as "tactless memorandum."[81] This was basically an attack upon the system of classical education and a study of the general insufficiency of physicians in the Empire, particularly in the army. He supported his views with a variety of statistical information which also demonstrated that Russia was deficient in the means for overcoming the deficit. Of the 470 aspirants accepted into the Medical-Surgical Academy since the 1871 ruling, only ninety-five had received an *attestat* from a classical *gymnazium*, from which Kozlov concluded that the classical schools were a wholly inadequate source for complementing the institutions of higher learning.[82]

Alexander, who was often not capable of listening gracefully to opinions that differed from his own, grew impatient, sharply ordered Kozlov to finish, and by his manner made it quite clear that he had already decided to transfer the Academy to the Ministry of Public Instruction. The next day, however, the Emperor in a more private conversation with Miliutin softened his tone somewhat, saying that he only desired to link the Academy with the medical faculties of the universities. The War Minister, still smarting under the treatment of the day before, did his best to warn the Emperor of the dangers of pursuing the course laid down by Tolstoy.[83] Alexander was not immediately swayed, however, and the matter remained open for many months afterward as yet another subject for the harassment of the War Minister.

The military clique headed by Bariatinskii also applied its pressure. This group was especially dangerous for Miliutin because they also could lay claim to being military experts and could therefore challenge him on his own ground. In addition to those who wished to unseat the War

80. *Ibid.*, pp. 102 and 109–110.
81. Valuev, II., 285.
82. *Dnevnik*, I., 112–113.
83. *Ibid.*, p. 114.

Minister for political or personal reasons, there were a number of re-
spected military commanders who quite sincerely opposed one or another
aspect of the Miliutin reforms and whose prestige could be thrown into
the balance against him. Such generals as V. D. Krenke and the brilliant
military theorist and teacher, M. I. Dragomirov, whose personal dis-
positions toward Miliutin were quite friendly, disliked particulars of the
new military system[84] and their views were used to discredit the War
Minister. The clique was something of a front for the activities of
Shuvalov who aided it in many ways, but most particularly as the link
between it and the Emperor.[85]

Bariatinskii's opportunity for a new campaign came in February 1873,
when the Emperor convoked an *ad hoc* committee over which he personally presided. This body was convened at the suggestion of Miliutin
himself who had, in the summer of 1872 directly before the Emperor's
departure for the Crimea, raised the question of reviewing the armed
forces of the Empire in the light of recent European events:

I considered it my duty to turn the earlier attention of the Emperor to
those sacrifices which are demanded from a state in order to bring to fruition
those hypotheses based upon a belief in the need to increase the armed forces
of Russia in view of the enormous armaments of all Europe. It was in-
escapable to turn first to the matter of finances in connection with higher
considerations of strategy and tactics, and then to set forth the special
purposes of the organization of the army and its reserves. The resolution of
so important a question could not in my opinion be left to the responsibility
of the War Minister alone; it needed negotiation with other ministers and
their co-operation. Therefore, I proposed to the Emperor the idea of calling
into session some highly selected individuals and of using the benefits of their
expertise in both civil and military matters.[86]

The Emperor reacted favorably and appointed a committee which included besides Miliutin such members as Bariatinskii, Field Marshal
Count Berg, the Crown Prince, the Grand Dukes Nicholas Nikolaevich

84. See "Zapiski general-leitenanta V. D. Krenke: pervye gody S.-Peterburg-
skogo okruzhnogo intendantstva, 1864–1866 gg.," *Russkaia Starina*, No. 6 (1882),
p. 724, and No. 7 (1882), p. 137.

85. See, for example, N. G. Zalesov, "Zapiski N. G. Zalesova," *Russkaia Starina*,
No. 6 (1905), p. 517.

86. Quoted in P. A. Zaionchkovskii, *Voennye reformy 1860–1870 godov v Rossii*,
p. 288.

and Michael Nikolaevich, Reitern, Timashev, Shuvalov, the Chief of the General Staff Heiden, Count P. N. Ignatiev (the Chairman of the Committee of Ministers), and a number of the generals commanding military districts.[87]

This body met in the strictest secrecy from February 28 until March 31, 1873. The first session was quite calm while the general principles to be examined by the committee were read out. Miliutin himself with the advice of the Emperor had composed the agenda, but it soon became clear that the areas upon which most of the discussion was to center were the organization of the army, the quality of its composition, and finances. Bariatinskii attacked the War Ministry on these matters with a blistering assault upon what he called the bureaucratization of the army, provoking from Miliutin the comment:

There we heard anew the hackneyed charges that the bureaucracy has set itself up over the tactical element, that regimental commanders were formerly more important than now, that tactical commanders are burdened by paperwork and formalities. . . .[88]

But more importantly, Bariatinskii followed this up with a charge that there was no need to increase the budget of the War Ministry and that all that was necessary was a reduction both of waste and of unnecessary expenditures. The Minister of Finance, Reitern, followed this with the presentation of a study of the military and state budgets which indicated that defense costs had already reached levels which were the maximum tolerable for the fiscal survival of the state.[89]

After the presentation of some sentiments favorable to the positions of Bariatinskii and Reitern, Miliutin rose to defend his program and in this found some support from the side of the Emperor. The real issue here was Russia's ability to defend herself in the face of the enormous growth of power among the other European states, and it was clear that the national defense could not be sacrificed. But in an attempt to find positive ways by which to reduce the fiscal burden to the state, Alexander appointed a special subcommittee and named Bariatinskii as its chairman.

87. *Ibid.*, pp. 293–294, and P. K. Men'kov, II., 329.
88. *Ibid.*, p. 330, and P. A. Zaionchkovskii, *Voennye reformy 1860–1870 godov v Rossii*, p. 294.
89. *Ibid.*, pp. 294–295.

During the succeeding sessions the body discussed such matters as the means by which the army was to be mobilized and the related problems of organization. In the course of the debates, Miliutin had to defend his district system against renewed proposals for the reinstitution of the old corps system in some new form. This issue served to precipitate a marked coolness between Miliutin and the Emperor which came to characterize their relations during the rest of the year.[90]

Miliutin finally emerged with his reforms of the preceding decade intact and with general approval for the kinds of changes he had been advocating. The most striking achievement was that of increasing the number of tactical units and the adoption of the plan to

form in wartime above all *reserve elements* which would perform duties in the rear. . . . For complementing the forces in wartime, both active and reserve, there would be formed a *troop reservoir* without establishing any dependence between it and the active and reserve forces. . . . For the *reserve* and the *reservoir* troops, there would not in peacetime be any cadre. . . . For the performance of domestic duty there will be as before a sufficient number of *stationary troops* so that they might serve as the means and the partially prepared material for the [reenforcement] of the more durable structure in wartime of the cadres of the reserve and reservoir troops.[91]

In addition to the committee's decision to use the stationary forces as the means for mobilizing the army in the event of war, plans were also approved to expand the size of the army in wartime by increasing the number of regiments in each division to four, the number of battalions in each regiment to four, etc.[92]

The subcommittee of which Bariatinskii was chairman did not finish its work until some time afterward. Miliutin was understandably enraged over the Emperor's selection of a man who had been so much at the center of the intrigues against himself to head a committee empowered to examine every aspect of the War Ministry, and he was in no way mollified by Alexander's attempts to soothe his ruffled feelings:

Nevertheless, I have no illusions. I know that the intrigues waged against me are not to be taken lightly. . . . The commission of Prince Bariatinskii

90. *Ibid.*, pp. 295–301. Cf. Men'kov, II, 335–336.
91. P. A. Zaionchkovskii, *Voennye reformy 1860–1870 godov v Rossii*, pp. 301–302.
92. *Ibid.*, pp. 302–303.

remains as an ominous sign reminding me that the danger has not yet dissipated. It may be that the wind will again change and will again pick up some absurd phantasies which will completely force me to be diverted from further controlling the task of developing the structure of our army.[93]

Miliutin continued to live in suspense throughout the spring while the commission, with Imperial sanction, had a mandate to probe every corner of the edifice he had been ten years building. But the progress of the investigation was slow; the old Field Marshal was confined to bed for much of the period with an attack of the gout, and as time passed the matter began to recede from the War Minister's consciousness.[94]

Finally, in June 1873, the commission produced its report in the form of a pamphlet. The first draft was submitted for review to the General-Adjutant K. V. Chevkin, ostensibly because of his competence in economic matters but more likely because he was one of those who favored the overthrow of the War Minister. After Chevkin had reviewed the report, the commission met and signed the document in what was apparently the first and last meeting of the body.[95] It is entirely possible that the report, which clearly was not the work of the commission, was the work of one of Bariatinskii's intimates, most likely Fadeev.

Although Miliutin was fairly well informed of its contents, the Emperor did not show the report to him until late in July. Intended as a sweeping indictment of the War Minister, the pamphlet had four main points: It demanded a reduction and a simplification of official correspondence; it called for a corresponding reduction in administrative personnel. Thirdly, the suggestion was made that the savings effected by the implementation of the first two points should be used to augment the salaries of the remaining functionaries. The fourth and last demand was for greater economy by improving the morality of the administrative personnel. The report argued that these four goals had not been achieved even though the reforms were already more than ten years old.[96]

To support their conclusions and demands, Bariatinskii's group maintained that the War Ministry had been increasing its personnel rather than reducing them. As evidence, they stated that the War Ministry, during

93. *Dnevnik*, I., 78.
94. *Ibid.*, pp. 81–82.
95. *Ibid.*, p. 87.
96. Zisserman, III., 255.

the years 1871 and 1872, had increased its administrative strength by 808 persons. Miliutin, in his response to the report, countered by pointing out that despite the addition of the huge new Turkestan Military District, the administration of the army had 846 fewer men than it had had in the pre-reform era, and, furthermore, the figures cited by the commission were erroneous because of a misprint in the lithographed version of the War Minister's official report of January 1, 1873.[97]

The commission's report, in an effort to support the charge of the over-bureaucratization of the War Ministry, claimed that the volume of administrative correspondence had increased as well, leading to bottlenecks and expensive delays. The War Minister rebutted this with statistical information demonstrating that between the years of 1863 and 1871, administrative correspondence within the Ministry had actually declined by 41 percent and that the figures provided by the commission for the years 1861, 1862, and 1863, were incorrect.[98] In the main, Miliutin found quite in error the evidence produced by the commission to support its claims that costs had risen in the War Ministry as a result of administrative inefficiency.

The fears of the War Minister were in no way justified by the findings of the commission. Despite the fact that they had possessed a mandate to comb through the War Ministry to discover any flaws in the system created by Miliutin, they in their overconfidence had contented themselves with superficial assessments which were relatively easily disposed of. Miliutin began to sense his own victory as it became clearer that the intrigue against him had lost a golden opportunity:

there was hardly a line of the commission's journal which remained without refutation. Together with this, I submitted a reply to the report of the State Controller (S. A. Greig), giving rein to an extremely offensive charge against the War Ministry. . . .[99]

Although the Emperor questioned Miliutin closely on each item in the commission's report, the incident soon blew over with no more harm done than the anxiety caused the War Minister. In fact, as Miliutin himself remarked, it was a source of personal satisfaction that a group pos-

97. *Ibid.*, p. 256.
98. *Ibid.*, pp. 257–258.
99. *Dnevnik*, I., 95.

sessing so much ill will toward him and who had the perfect opportunity
to strike a telling blow against him, had been able to find no more damning
evidence. After twelve years of service, his enemies were able only to
level empty charges at him.[100] The missed opportunity also spelled the
end of Bariatinskii's influence, and he began to cease to be useful in the
intrigue against Miliutin. Noting in his diary two years later the decline
in the Field Marshal's fortunes, Valuev commented that he was now
"zero" in the government and like a foreigner at Court.[101] When Bariatinskii made a gesture toward reconciliation, Miliutin refused the proffered
hand.[102] The brilliant conqueror of the Caucasus and his former Chief
of Staff no longer shared any common ties.

The year 1873 saw the planters step up the press campaign against the
War Minister, with the sharpest clashes occurring between the *Russkii
Mir* and *Golos*. The *Russkii Mir* continued to echo the charges made
elsewhere against the military reforms, concentrating a considerable proportion of its attack against the district system of administration and on
its corollary, the Regulation of 1868. *Golos*, which still shied away from
any suggestion that it was the spokesman for the War Ministry,[103] nevertheless, did yeoman service in pleading its case before the public. Not
only did it continue in this period to make space available for the publication of articles by advocates of the War Ministry, but the editorial page
itself was often devoted to taking issue with specific charges brought
by the *Russkii Mir*.[104]

But the real debates on the new law took place in the special sessions
of the State Council convoked by the Emperor for the drafting into final
form of the universal military conscription law. When Miliutin presented
the conclusions of the two commissions to the special session of the State
Council and to the ministers in January of 1873, the response was quite
varied, including some opposition. The War Minister had anticipated this
and, a gradualist at heart, had sought to mitigate some of the sharpness of
the reform by tempering it with at least some period of transition:

it would be useful with the implementation of the proposed statute to allow

100. *Ibid.*, p. 92.
101. Valuev, II., 321.
102. *Dnevnik*, II., 71.
103. See above. *Golos*, No. 224 (1873).
104. For example, see *Golos*, Nos. 25, 39, 69, and 196 (1873).

the War Ministry to try to find some administrative measures which possibly would relieve individuals of the privileged classes entering military service by conscription from the fulfillment of service obligations. For example, measures would be included for the enlistment of individuals of these classes in such units of the forces which they themselves may choose or which in general dispose of better quarters, [or even] freeing them from the obligation to live in barracks, etc.[105]

Despite Miliutin's efforts to meet the advocates of gentry interest half way, D. A. Tolstoy was especially sharp in his initial criticism. He in particular opposed all phases of the program to grant privileges according to education, seeing in it the dilution of the special position of the gentry in the officer corps by artisans and merchants.[106]

Miliutin did not agree and wrote in reply:

We have at the present time in the army only a few officers not from the gentry, the sons of priests, bureaucrats, merchants, etc.; without doubt, individuals from the merchant and even the townsman classes, achieving a sufficient level of education, will be in the body of the officer corps, but with the introduction of universal military conscription there is no reason to suppose that they will constitute a predominant element in the army.[107]

Miliutin of course felt that the planters were overdrawing the matter of nongentry elements gaining control of the officer corps, which of course they were. But privileged groups faced with the loss of some of their exclusive privileges rarely behave rationally nor do they often objectively face the broader issues.

The first meeting of the special session of the State Council took place only a few days after the conclusion of Alexander's *ad hoc* committee which examined the organization of the army. Convened on April 2, 1873, this body was charged with discussing the proposed conscription law itself and therefore included besides representatives from the War Ministry the responsible persons from a wide variety of ministries and bureaus. Included were the War Minister, the Crown Prince, the Grand Dukes Nicholas and Michael Nikolaevich, the chairmen and members of the Departments of Law and of State Economy, the Field Marshals Prince Bariatinskii and Count Berg, General Adjutant N. P. Ignatiev, Prince

105. A. V. Fedorov, pp. 225–226.
106. *Ibid.*, p. 227.
107. *Ibid.*, *loc. cit.*

A. A. Suvorov, Baron V. K. Lieven, Valuev, and the Ministers of the Court, Finance, Internal Affairs, Justice, Public Instruction, Shuvalov, the Chief of His Majesty's Own Chancellory for the Affairs of the Kingdom of Poland, and Gorchakov.[108] While a significant part of the complexion of this body was the same as that of the recent *ad hoc* committee, there was at least one significant difference and that was that the chair was now held by the Grand Duke Constantine. This had the appearance of being, and in fact proved to be, favorable to Miliutin's cause.

The first session, like those that followed, was stormy and marked by the deep cleavages between the opposing factions. The old State Chancellor, Gorchakov, who was by this time bordering on senility, sought both to pour oil on troubled waters and to mitigate some of Miliutin's program by urging a gradualness in implementing the reform. He pointed out that the evolution of a similar reform in Prussia took more than a decade. He also argued that it was necessary to raise Russia's educational level before acting, and he further suggested, although on what grounds is not clear, that the introduction of large numbers of men into the army might be deleterious to morale. Miliutin replied that any postponement until the educational level of the lower classes equalled that of the higher orders of society would be highly dangerous, since it would require several decades, and by that time Russia would be outstripped by all the armies of Europe. Nor could the War Minister see any danger to discipline and morale as a result of introducing large groups into the army. Gorchakov found little support and his proposals failed.[109]

The first subject to be debated actively was the general issue of privileges to be accorded to those possessing an education and the related topic of service by volunteers and Jews. Count Shuvalov personally began the debate by assuming the posture that the radical theories espoused by the educated youth would serve as a corrupting influence among the innocent soldiers. Those possessing a modicum of education should, or so he maintained, be put into special student units in order not to contaminate the mass of the army. These special student units should be

108. P. A. Zaionchkovskii, *Voennye reformy 1860–1870 godov v Rossii*, p. 320n.
109. P. A. Zaionchkovskii, "Podgotovka voennoi reformy 1874 goda," *Istoricheskie Zapiski*, No. 27 (1948), p. 189.

concentrated in the larger cities where they could be more effectively supervised.

Shuvalov of course found support for these views among his political following, but Miliutin successfully parried the thrust by pointing out that the army was already critically short of educated personnel and could not allow so valuable a resource to be wasted.[110] Turning to the matter of service by Jews, Miliutin succeeded in gaining support for enrolling them in the levy on a general basis and then leaving it to the War Minister to determine in which units Jews would be allowed to serve as officers.[111]

But the real hatchet man of the opposition was Count Tolstoy, and it was he who took up the cudgel on the issue of education and privileges. He argued, first of all, that the assignment of various types of schools into categories for purposes of assigning privileges to those entering military service was the prerogative of the Ministry of Public Instruction. He cited Prussia as a precedent in this regard, and he further, rather strangely for a minister responsible for the educational establishment of the Empire, claimed that the granting of privileges to those possessing an education was discriminatory. Miliutin replied to this in a special memorandum which he read to the assembly. He based his refutation on the need to be practical and upon the need to retain some meaning in the concept of granting reduced terms of active service to those having an education. But the War Minister went beyond this and viciously attacked Tolstoy and the failures of Russian education under his administration, pointing out that the basic cause of all this was the general lack of schools, the deplorable condition of those that did exist, and the wholly impractical curricula.[112]

During the third sitting of the special session on April 11, heated debates took place over the matter of privileges to be granted according to special family situations. For example, Prince P. G. Ol'denburgskii, the head of the Fourth Section of His Majesty's Own Chancellory, opposed categorically the liberation of only sons from military service. During the next session, held three days later, Miliutin and Tolstoy again locked in a

110. *Ibid.*, p. 190.
111. *Ibid.*, p. 191.
112. *Ibid.*, p. 186.

bitter quarrel, with the latter persisting in his demands on the matter of the educational institutions. His fierce outburst hardly allowed Miliutin time to speak in rebuttal, but the War Minister was on this occasion nobly assisted by the chairman, the Grand Duke Constantine, who hotly defended Miliutin's views.[113] Moreover, when the points of debate became technical and devolved upon military usages, the opposition was at a serious disadvantage.[114]

The state visit of the Emperor William of Germany took its toll from the session that met on April 26, with the Grand Duke Constantine and Count Berg going to Gatchina where the German Emperor was being entertained. The chair was occupied temporarily by Bariatinskii who was at this time a very sick man and unable to exploit his position. Moreover, the subject for debate was the administrative structure and procedure for the implementation of the conscription and, as Miliutin observed, it proved to be "a subject too dry for our raging orators." The subsequent sitting also proved fruitful with the passage of a great many articles of the draft law including those prescribing the conditions for volunteering. This progress was not uncontested, however, and had to be accomplished despite the obstructionism of Tolstoy and his two supporters, Pahlen and Ignatiev.[115]

By early May, the work was ready to be referred to the regular session of the State Council in the fall. The War Ministry then turned to making its final plans for the conscription for 1874 under the old law, but it now had hopes of making the transition to the new system during the course of the year. The special session of the State Council had resulted in solid achievement despite the bitterness of the opposition. Except for minor changes, the entire War Ministry program had survived intact. The most important of the changes were these: the general term of service in the navy and among troops serving in remote areas was again set at ten rather than nine years, seven of these years to be spent on active duty and the remaining three on a standby status; the term of service for individuals completing institutions of higher learning was raised from six to nine months; the term of service for graduates of secondary schools

113. *Dnevnik*, I., 78–79.
114. *Ibid.*, p. 80.
115. *Ibid.*, pp. 81–82.

was set at one and a half years; the maximum age for retention in the levy was raised from thirty-eight to forty years of age; and special regulations governing the statutory service of Jews were established.[116]

When the general session of the State Council convened in the fall for a final review of the universal service statute, Miliutin wryly noted that "Again on the scene is Count D. A. Tolstoy, and again there are peevish, jaundiced, obstinate disputes."[117] Tolstoy took advantage of the first session to vent his spleen upon the military *gymnazia*, which were particularly annoying to him. Despite his conduct, however, the draft law went through the State Council without a hitch and the members gathered on November 16 to sign the journal of the proceedings. A week later the draft was in the hands of the Emperor. The Imperial Manifesto embodying the new law had its first reading before the State Council on November 28, at which time Gorchakov made a few final but vain attempts to alter those provisions affecting the privileges of the gentry.[118]

A few days later, on December 3, Alexander gathered about himself an informal group of his advisers, including Miliutin, the Grand Duke Constantine, Admiral N. K. Grabbe, State Secretary D. M. Sol'skii, and the Crown Prince. Alexander made clear to them his approval of the Universal Military Service Statute, but warned that not everyone saw matters this way: "There is strong opposition to the new law; many are frightened, seeing in it a democratization of the army."[119]

This probably was the motive for Alexander's calling of this meeting. He wanted to make his position clear amid all the intrigues and to remind the proponents of the reform that in this matter they possessed his fullest confidence. When this small group withdrew from the presence of the Emperor, they attended a session of the State Council at which the manifesto was given a second reading.

The opposition to the reform and to Miliutin's program had not given up, however, and during this session Tolstoy was back singing his old refrain. He had circulated a few days earlier a lengthy memorandum, probably drafted by Katkov, in which he reasserted his abhorence of the

116. P. A. Zaionchkovskii, *Voennye reformy 1860–1870 godov v Rossii*, p. 324.
117. *Dnevnik*, I., 105.
118. *Ibid.*, pp. 106–107.
119. *Ibid.*, pp. 107–108.

principle of granting privileges according to education. But the chair was occupied by the Grand Duke Constantine, who conducted affairs in such a manner as to leave Tolstoy to fume in silence. When Miliutin talked to the Emperor on the following day, it appeared that someone had again been trying to prejudice him against the reform. [120]

At the next reading of the manifesto, on December 11, the issue of volunteer service was debated. This aspect of the reform was understandably opposed by the "aristocratic clique" because it would tend to make entry into the officer corps much easier for nongentry elements. For this session, Shuvalov and Tolstoy had very carefully gathered their forces and made the meeting ring with meaningless proposals.

Miliutin contemptuously viewed the whole affair as a tempest in a teapot, but it was clear that the planters had chosen this occasion for a showdown. The argument employed this time was that no volunteers should be accepted unless they were in the first or second category (i.e., that they had completed a secondary or higher school), which would have the effect of limiting the social base of those becoming officers.

Constantine Pobedonostsev, who was later the grey eminence of the reign of Alexander III, spoke at length in defense of class privileges, thereby bringing into the open the fact that the debate over education and the privileges accorded to it had really been a struggle by the planters for the retention of their special position in society. The opening of such careers as that of an army officer to talent rather than class privilege spelled the inevitable doom of the gentry as a privileged order. But Pobedonostsev found no support outside his own little circle. Miliutin felt, nevertheless, that many had sympathized with him but had themselves feared to come out into the open, fearing that he had gone too far.[121]

Shuvalov himself had already recognized defeat and had moved to salvage what he could by reaching a compromise with Miliutin. The Chief of Gendarmes successfully proposed in the Council, on the basis of a prior agreement with the War Minister, that volunteers from the third category (i.e., those having completed a primary school of six years) would, should they become officers, be accorded the privileges of the

120. Ibid., p. 109.
121. Ibid., p. 111.

gentry only upon the completion of no less than three years of active service.[122]

One last minor question arose during this session. This was the question of whether the War Ministry in commissioning officers from among the volunteers would accept the *attestat* granted by the secondary schools as the criterion for commissioning, or whether it should continue to require the normal officers' examination. The matter was quickly dropped, but Miliutin noted with some good humor that it was Pahlen rather than Tolstoy who hotly supported this issue. The War Minister mused to himself that perhaps Pahlen's own son stood in fear of the officers' examination.[123]

When the Council reconvened a few days later, only some minor issues remained. There were a few discussions of the role to be played by the Jews and Mennonites and other nonassimilable groups. Tolstoy and his associates again employed some polemical rhetoric, but again the Grand Duke Constantine kept matters under close control and invited only those opinions pertinent to the specific matter at hand.[124] On December 24, the journal of the State Council was read for the last time, and on January 1, 1874, the Emperor promulgated the Universal Military Service Statute by decree.

Emotionally exhausted and resentful of his enemies, Miliutin wearily sat down to his diary on that last evening of the year of 1873 and recorded the anguish of his frustration. The year had been one of constant trial and strain. Within the Committee of Ministers the majority acted according to the wishes of Shuvalov and on behalf of the entrenched privileged orders of society, even to the detriment of the national good. The War Minister looked ahead to the next year with a heavy heart.[125] But, despite his low spirits, the victory did belong to Miliutin. The manifesto issued by Alexander on the following day capped years of labor by the War Minister, and the new law represented in itself a sufficient achievement to make Miliutin one of the great statesmen of the period. Moreover, this

122. Heretofore, all officers on active service were accorded the rank of personal nobles.
123. *Ibid., loc. cit.*
124. *Ibid.*, p. 115.
125. *Ibid.*, pp. 119–120.

was accomplished against the concerted opposition of his personal and political enemies.[126]

Even though it dawned in victory, the new year began badly. The events of the preceding months had been tough on the relations between Miliutin and the Emperor, and when the awards and commendations were passed out to those who had participated in the drafting of the new statute, the War Minister did not even receive a word of thanks from Alexander.[127] But just as the darkness is supposed to be greater before the dawn, Miliutin's fortunes began to change.

The first hint of his success was early in the year when Miliutin's candidate for the governor-generalship of Poland, General-Adjutant P. E. Kotzebue, was selected by the Emperor to fill that post over the candidate supported by Shuvalov.[128] A day or two later, Miliutin was quite surprised to receive an Imperial rescript in recognition of his role in the drafting of the universal military conscription law,[129] and almost simultaneously his daughter was honored by being named a lady-in-waiting to the Empress.[130] Alexander himself gave Miliutin his warm thanks, saying, "I thank you for this matter, just as for all else. Now may God allow *us* to bring it to fruition."[131]

These incidents symbolized the beginning of a warming trend between Alexander and his War Minister, and by March Miliutin began to notice a definite change.

In a more cordial atmosphere, he took the occasion to pour out to the Emperor, without sparing any details, his own side of the story of all the intrigues that had been directed against him. The Emperor, for a change, listened quietly and thoughtfully.[132] The reasons for this did not become clear until summer when Count Shuvalov was unexpectedly removed

126. The entire statute and its later modifications may be found in V. Gorlov, *Ustav o voinskoi povinnosti.*

127. *Dnevnik*, I., 122. The Emperor had, however, granted Miliutin an Imperial rescript two years earlier, on January 29, 1872, thanking him for his services and his work on behalf of the reforms. This rescript was published in *Golos*, No. 31 (1872).

128. *Dnevnik*, I., 129–130.

129. *Ibid.*, pp. 130 and 132.

130. *Ibid.*, p. 130.

131. *Ibid.*, p. 132. Italics in the original.

132. *Ibid.*, p. 144.

from his post as Chief of Gendarmes and sent to England as ambassador. There can be little doubt that the arrogance Shuvalov had begun to display with an increasing abrasiveness was at least partly responsible for the Emperor's acting deliberately to remove him from his influence at court.[133] While many enemies yet remained, the departure of so powerful and dedicated a foe as Shuvalov made Miliutin's life much easier.

The changing climate around the Court enabled the War Minister to resolve one of the lingering controversies engendered by the bitter fight over universal military conscription. This was the question of incorporating the Military-Surgical Academy into the Ministry of Public Instruction, a move that was to have been the first step in taking away all functions of education from the War Ministry. The struggle had cooled with time, and Miliutin had let it be known that he accorded the matter sufficient significance to resign if this design were fulfilled and the Academy detached from the War Ministry.[134] After much time and difficulty, the matter was finally brought to a vote in the Committee of Ministers on May 20, 1875. Miliutin was victorious by a margin of twenty votes to three,[135] and a month later the Emperor was pleased to uphold the decision of the majority.[136] Before the removal of Shuvalov, the decision very likely would have gone the other way, but without him the planter party had no leverage in the government and no leadership.

From this time forward, Miliutin's relationship with the Emperor was much closer and, although he was not spared further difficulties, they never achieved the levels of those years from 1868 to 1874. His importance as an adviser to the Emperor and his influence on the affairs of state rose to the highest levels. It is not easy to explain Alexander's change in attitude in those first months in 1874. Perhaps it was a natural consequence of his decision to remove Shuvalov or the results of a genuine realization of the worth of his War Minister. The stir that the later reforms caused in foreign capitals was without doubt a source of pleasure. Or he may have come to appreciate that Miliutin was only interested in a strong and healthy Russian state, just as he himself was.

133. *Ibid.*, pp. 159–161, and Valuev, II., 311–312.
134. *Dnevnik*, I., 155.
135. *Ibid.*, pp. 198–202.
136. *Ibid.*, p. 207.

From the moment of his victory in creating an all-class system of military conscription and the subsequent fall of Shuvalov until his own resignation early in the reign of Alexander III over the issue of the Loris-Melikov constitution, Miliutin stood as one of the most important statesmen of the Empire. He was the Emperor's most trusted adviser on a wide range of issues and his voice bore great weight in the resolution and formulation of policy. His own personal loyalty to the Emperor and proven ability, together with the ineptness of his enemies, allowed him in the end to play the very role the planters had sought to deny him. The War Minister remained subject to harassment and was forced from time to time to see the Emperor fall under the temporary influence of one or another of his enemies, but it never reached the proportion of the years 1867 to 1874.

Miliutin's path from the beginning of his administration had never been easy. Despite his own gradualist and practical outlook, he was associated in the minds of the more conservative and reactionary elements in the Imperial government with the circle about his brother Nicholas, whom they considered be be a "red." Consequently, the planters viewed the War Minister's attitudes and policies as much more democratic than they really were. With the rise of Dmitrii Miliutin and the dismissal and virtual exile of his brother, the friends and associates of the latter grouped themselves about the War Minister, forming what was in effect the reform party. This grouping tended to reinforce the conviction on the part of the reactionaries that Miliutin was an extreme democrat, particularly when the War Minister out of his need for capable administrators turned to such men as General N. N. Obruchev, whose earlier association with Chernyshevskii tainted him for life. Moreover, Miliutin was faced with the natural resistance to change met by every reformer. The new patterns constructed by the War Minister implied not only the ultimate diminution of the privileges of the gentry class but also eliminated the offices and restricted the expectations of individuals. Miliutin tried at one and the same time to open the officer corps to talent while continuing to recognize the historical role of the gentry class. While essentially a practical man, the War Minister was motivated in part by ideology. He was a convinced and passionate Great Russian nationalist who believed that there was no place in Russia for any special privileged group, whether social class or ethnic minority, and who consistently strove for the organic unity of the nation.

Miliutin's reforming activity was in the first instance made possible by the near bankruptcy of the state and in subsequent years was sustained by it. The initial goal was to create an administrative system which would allow Russia to live within her means without sacrificing the national security. The failures within Russian society itself forced the War Ministry to go much farther, most particularly by providing the basic general education for both officers and enlisted men while making their military training more practical. The reforms progressed much more rapidly than Miliutin had anticipated, largely because of the insurrection in Poland and the threat of a general European war. In subsequent years he was able to modify and add to his original creation as experience and conditions dictated. Most importantly, the radical shift in the European power balance following the Prussian victories over Austria and France allowed Miliutin to implement a long-cherished dream. This was the system of universal military conscription, which as the most direct threat to gentry class privileges produced some of the sharpest attacks upon the War Minister and the basic principles of his previous reforms. Miliutin was able to bring this latest project to fruition only because one of the most important of the planter party, P. A. Valuev, momentarily defected and persuaded the Emperor that the national security was at stake. The four years before the final promulgation of the statute embodying the principle that all classes were equally liable to conscription were among the most difficult in Miliutin's entire career and were not made any easier by the general coolness and insensitivity of the Emperor.

Certainly Miliutin's path would have been much easier if Alexander II had been a more consistent and a wiser man. The War Minister's own conviction that the autocracy was the absolutely necessary agency for Russia's progress was based upon the principle that the autocrat was the partner of the Russian people, and, standing above the interests of all groups, he was able to assure the organic unity and the equality of the entire nation. Quite on the contrary, Alexander allowed himself to be insulated from reality by Shuvalov and the planter party and in those years often served the interests of the gentry. Certainly one gets the impression that Alexander was never really a reformer except for his conviction that the serfs had to be freed and that all subsequent reforms were dictated by circumstances.

It is a tribute to Miliutin that, given the situation, he was able to accomplish so much. His own personal integrity, his passionate belief in the justice of what he was doing, and his indispensibility to the Emperor as an administrator all contributed to his success. In the course of achieving this success he was forced to suffer the slings and arrows of an entrenched and privileged gentry and the frustration derived from the lack of understanding and sensitivity on the part of the Emperor whom he so faithfully served. One cannot help asking the question, what would the reform period have been like had it not been for the personal sacrifices and constructive policies of Dmitrii Miliutin? Russia would surely have declined as a Great Power. It is even possible that the Empire would have drifted toward becoming an aristocratic oligarchy with all of its social and economic implications. One fact is without doubt. Dmitrii Miliutin stood among the greatest statesmen of the Russian Empire.

Selected Bibliography

A. E. K. "Mikhail I. Dragomirov i voenno-uchebnye zavedeniia," *Russkaia starina*, No. 10, 1908.

A. P., P. B., and the Editor. "Graf Dmitrii Alekseevich Miliutin vo vremia upravlenie ego voennym ministerstvom, 1861–1881 g.g." *Russkaia Starina*, Vol. XLIX (1886). [An interesting and laudatory article on Miliutin's reforming activities.]

Apolev, M. "Neskol'ko myslei po povodu stat'i, pomeshchennoi v No. 10 'Voennogo Sbornika' za 1859g., pod zaglaviem: 'Ob armeiskikh pekhotnykh ofitserov.' " *Voennyi sbornik*, No. 5, 1860.

Arnol'dov, F. A. "Sovremennoe znachenie voinskoi povinnosti." A supplement to the periodical *Niva*, No. 6, 1902.

Askew, William C. "Russian Military Strength on the Eve of the Franco-Prussian War." *The Slavonic and East European Review*, Vol. XXX (1951).

Babet, N., "Voisko i narodnoe khozaistvo." *Russkii Invalid*, No. 125, 1863.

Baiov, A. K. *Graf Dmitrii Alekseevich Miliutin.* St. Petersburg, 1912.

Barabash, Ia. "Neskol'ko myslei o gramotnosti v voiskakh." *Voennyi sbornik*, No. 2, 1866. [An argument in favor of the establishment of soldiers' libraries.]

Baranius, praporshchik L.-gv. Litovskogo polka "Polkovyia unter-ofitserskiia shkoly." *Voennyi sbornik*, No. 7, 1865.

Bariatinskii, A. I. "Perepiska." *Russkii arkhiv*, No. 1, 1891.

Barsukov, N. P. *Zhizn' i trudy M. P. Pogodina.* 22 volumes. St. Petersburg, 1888–1910.

Bartenev, A. "Biografii generalissimusov i general-feldmarshalov Rossiiskoi

Imperatorskoi armii: Graf Dmitrii Alekseevich Miliutin." *Voenno-istoricheskii sbornik*, No. 1, 1914.

Bermanskii, K. L. "Konstitutsionnye proekty tsarstvovaniia Aleksandra II." *Vestnik prava*, No. 9, 1905.

Bilderling, A. "Graf Dmitrii Alekseevich Miliutin." *Voennyi Sbornik*, No. 2, 1912.

Bliokh, I. *Finansy v Rossii XIX stoletiia*. 2 volumes. St. Petersburg, 1882.

B[obrovskii], P. "Dvadtsatipiatiletie iunkerskikh uchilisch (20-go sentiabria 1864–1889gg.)." *Voennyi sbornik*, Vol. CXC (1889).

Bobrovskii, P. O. *Iunkerskiia uchilishoha: Istoricheskoe obozrenie ikh razvitiia i deiatel'nostri*. 3 parts. St. Petersburg, 1872–1876.

Bobrovskii, P. "Ob uchrezhdenii iunkerskikh uchilisch." *Voennyi sbornik*, No. 11, 1864.

[Bobrovskii, P.] "R.V.O.: sostoianii iunkerskikh uchilishch." No. 7, 1866.

Bobrovskii, P. "Uchilishche podpraporshchikov, byvshee v Voronezhe s 1856 po 1863 god." *Voennyi sbornik*, No. 7, 1864. [An important study of the school that was the model for the Military and junker schools.]

———. "Vzgliad na gramotnost' i uchebnuia komandy (ili polkovyia shkoly) v nashei armii," *Voennyi sbornik*, Vol. LXXVI (1870), Vol. LXVIII (1871), Vol. LXXIX (1871).

———. "Vzgliad na iunkerskiia uchilishcha, ikh razvitie i sostoianie so vremeni ikh uchrezhdeniia (1864 goda)." *Voennyi sbornik*, No. 3, 1869. [A very useful article, providing a background and a contemporary evaluation of the junker schools.]

———. "Vzgliad na obrazovanie v iunkerskikh uchilishchakh." *Voennyi sbornik*, No. 3, 1870.

———. "Zametki o sostoianii nekotorykh iunkerskikh uchilishch." *Voennyi sbornik*, Vol. LXXVI (1870).

Bogdanov, I. M. *Gramotnost' i obrazovanie v dorevoliutsionnoi Rossii i v SSSR*. Moscow, 1964.

Bogdanovich, M., general ed. *Istoricheskii ocherk deiatel'nosti voennogo upravleniia v Rossii v pervoe dvadtsati-piatiletie blagopoluchnogo tsarstvovaniia Gosudaria Imperatora Aleksandra Nikolaevicha (1855–1880 g.g.)*. 6 vols. St. Petersburg, 1879–1881. [A basic study, indispensable for the study of the reform period.]

———. "O sredstvakh k rasprostraneniiu prosveshcheniia v armii." *Voennyi sbornik*, No. 1, 1863.

———. "Voennaia politika i voennyia uchrezhdeniia v sovremenom ikh sostoianii." *Russkaia starina*, Vol. XXI (1878).

Borodkin, M. *Graf D.A. Miliutin v otzyvakh ego sovremennikov*. St. Petersburg, 1910.

Bykov, P. V. "D. A. Miliutin - Biograficheskii ocherk." *Sever*, No. 46, 1903.

"Chego ne nedostaet eshche iunkerskim uchilishcham." *Voennyi sbornik*, No. 8, 1872.

Ch-ov, P. "Neskol'ko slov na stat'iu g. M.Apoleva." *Voennyi sbornik*, No. 8, 1861.

Chubinskii, M. "Pamiati D. A. Miliutina," *Vestnik evropy* (September 1912).

Constantine Nikolaevich, Grand Duke "V kn. 'iz dnevnika.' " *Krasnyi arkhiv*, Vol. X (1925).

Curtiss, John Shelton. *The Army of Nicholas I, 1825–1855*. Durham, N. C.: Duke University Press, 1965.

———. "The Army of Nicholas I: Its Role and Character." *The American Historical Review*, Vol. LXIII, No. 4 (1958).

"D.A.Miliutin."*Niva*, No. 10, 1872.

"D.A.Miliutin." *Zhivopisnoe obozrenie*, No. 22, 1876.

"D.A.Miliutin i Nikolaevskaia Akademiia general'nogo shtaba." *Russkii invalid*, No. 248, 1908.

"D.A.Miliutin v 1863–1864g. Zametka (Pis'mo v red.). *Russkaia starina*, Vol. XXXVIII (1883).

"D.A.Miliutin - voennyi ministr." *Narodnaia shkola*, No. 10, 1874.

"D.A.Miliutin, voennyi ministr;Biografiia." *Narodnaia shkola*, No. 10, 1874.

Danilov, N. A. *Istoricheskii ocherk razvitiia voennogo upravleniia v Rossii.* St. Petersburg, 1902.

Del'vig, A.I. *Polveka Russkoi Zhizni: Vospominaniia A.I.Del'viga, 1820– 1870*. 2 volumes. Moscow-Leningrad, 1930.

Despatches from U.S.Ministers to Russia. 1808–1906. National Archives.

D'iakov,V.A., and I.S.Miller, *Revoliutsionnoe dvizhenie v russkoi armii i vosstanie 1863g.* Moscow, 1964.

"Die Russische Armeereform und Deutschlands Militarische Zukunft." *Das Ausland*, No. 5, 1876.

Diugamel, A.O. "Avtobiograiia A.O.Diugamelia." *Russkii arkhiv*, No. 2, 1885.

Dragomirov, Mikhail Ivanovich. *Sbornik original'nykh i peredovnykh statei, 1856–1881*. St. Petersburg, 1881.

———. *Zapiski taktiki dlia voennykh uchilishch.* St. Petersburg 1866.

Dzhanshiev, G. *Epokha velikikh reform.* Moscow, 1896. [This contains a chapter devoted to the Universal Military Service Statute of 1874.]

Fadeev, Rostislav Andreevich. *Nash voennyi vopros.* St. Petersburg, 1873.

———. *Russkoe obshchestvo v nastoiashchem i budushchem(Chem nam byt'?)*. St. Petersburg, 1874.

———. *Vooruzhennyia sily Rossii.* Moscow, 1868.

Fedorov, A.V. *Russkaia armiia v 50–70gg.* XIXv. Moscow, 1959. [A very uneven Marxist work; generally of doubtful value.]

Fedorov, Prince V. *Vooruzhennye sily russkoi armii v XIX stoletii.* St. Petersburg, 1911.

Feoktistov, E.M. *Vospominaniia E.M.Feoktistova. Za kulisami politiki i literatury, 1848–1896.* Leningrad, 1929.

Garmiza, V.V. *Podgotovka zemskoi reformy 1864 goda.* Moscow, 1957.

Gazenkampf, M. *Moi dnevnik 1877–1878gg.* St. Petersburg, 1908.

Glinoetskii, N. *Istoricheskii ocherk Nikolaevskoi Akademii general'nogo shtaba.* St. Petersburg, 1882.

Glinoetskii, N. "Istoricheskii ocherk russkogo general'nogo shtaba." *Russkii invalid,* Nos. 112 and 116, 1872.

Gololobov, A. "Nasha Akademiia General'nogo Shtaba." *Voennyi sbornik,* Vol. LXXIX (1871).

Gorlov, B. *Ustav o voinskoi povinnosti dopolnennyi vsemi pozdneishimi izmeneniiami po l centiabria 1912 goda.* St. Petersburg, 1913.

Grabbe, P. "Iz dnevnika i zapisnoi knizhki." *Russkii arkhiv,* No. 6, 1904.

Grierson, Captain J. M. *The Armed Strength of Russia.* Prepared in the Intelligence Branch of the War Office. London, 1886.

Il'iashevich. "Chisloviia danniya o sostave korpusa ofitserov nashei armii po vospitaniiu i sosloviiam." *Voennyi sbornik,* No. 11, 1863.

Insarskii, V.A. "Zapiski V.A.Insarskogo." *Russkaia starina,* No. 9, 1897.

Iordanskii, N.I. *Konstitutsionnoe dvizhenie 60-kh godov.* St. Petersburg, 1906.

"Iubilei gr. D.A.Miliutina." *Istoricheskii vestnik,* No. 1, 1884.

"Iunkerskiia uchilishcha." *Voennyi sbornik,* No. 10, 1868.

"Iunkerskiia uchilishcha v 1867 godu." *Voennyi sbornik,* No. 2, 1868.

Jelavich, Charles. "The Diary of D. A. Miliutin, 1878–1882: A Review Article." *The Journal of Modern History,* Vol. XXVI, No. 3 (September 1954).

Kachakov, B.M. *Pedagogicheskie kadry voenno-uchebnykh zavedenii v tsarskoi Rossii.* 2 volumes. Leningrad, 1947.

Katkov, M.N. *Sobranie peredovykh statei Moskovskikh Vedomostei, 1863–1887 gg.* 25 volumes. Moscow, 1897–1898.

Kernosovskii, A. *Istoriia russkoi armii.* 3 parts. Belgrade: Tsarskii Vestnik, 1934.

"Khod preobrazovanii v nashei armii." *Russkii Invalid,* No. 276, 1863.

K-ii,M. "Neskol'ko slov o voennykh shkolakh dlia obrazovaniia unterofitserov." *Voennyi sbornik,* No. 11, 1879.

"K istorii voenno-uchebnoi reformy imperatora Aleksandra II-go: 1856–1870." *Russkaia starina,* Vol. LIV (1887).

"Komplektovanie armii ofitserami." *Voennyi sbornik,* No. 7, 1869.

"K 75-letiiu v ofitserskikh chinakh gr. D.A. Miliutina." *Russkii invalid,* No. 245, 1908.

Kornilov, [A.A.]. "Graf D.A.Miliutin." *Rech,* No. 40, 1912.

Krenke, Lt. General V. D. "Gramotnost' v armii." *Voennyi sbornik,* No. 5, 1868.

Krivenko, V. S. *Iunkerskie gody. 25 let nazad.* St. Petersburg, 1898.

Kuropatkin, A. N. *Zadachi Russkii armii.* 3 vols. St. Petersburg, 1910.

Lalaev, Major-General M. *Istoricheskii ocherk Voenno-uchebnykh Zavedenii podvedomstvennykh Glavnomu ikh Upravleniiu: Ot osnovaniia v Rossii voennykh shkol do iskhoda pervogo dvadtsatipiatiletiia blagopoluchnogo tsarstvovaniia Gosudaria Imperatora Aleksandra Nikolaevicha, 1700–1880.* St. Petersburg, 1880.

Lavrent'ev, A. "Territorial'naia sistema voennogo upravleniia." *Voennyi sbornik*, No. 7, 1862.

Leer, G. "Glavnyia kharakteristicheskiia cherty frantsuzkoi i prusskoi uchebno-vospitatel'nykh sistem sravnitel'no s nasheiu." *Voennyi sbornik*, Vol. LXIII (1868).

Lemke, M.K. *Politicheskie protessy v Rossii 1860-kh godov.* Moscow-Petrograd, 1923.

Leroy-Beaulieu, A., *Un homme d' État Russe.* Paris, 1884.

Levshin, D.M. *Pazheskii korpus za sto let.* St. Petersburg, 1902.

L.K. "Vzgliad na stepen' obrazovaniia russkikh ofitserov v armii." *Voennyi sbornik*, No. 1, 1858.

Lokhvitskii, A. "Unichtozhenie telesnykh nakazanii." *Russkii Invalid*, No. 87, 1863.

Makeev, Colonel N. N.G.Chernyshevskii - redaktor"Voennogo sbornika"- Moscow, 1950.

Maslov, N. "Iunkerskiia shkoly v armii." *Voennyi sbornik*, No. 6, 1861.

Mart'ianov, P. "Eshche neskol'ko slov po povodu predpolozheniia ob otkrytii dostupa nizhnim chinam k proizvodstvu v ofitsery." *Voennyi sbornik*, No. 10, 1863.

Mart'ianov, P. "O rasprostraneniia v voiskakh voenno-iuridicheskogo obrazovaniia." *Voennyi sbornik*, No. 5, 1866.

Men'kov, P.K. *Zapiska Petra Kononovicha Men'kova.* 3 volumes. St. Petersburg, 1898. [Volume two contains Men'kov's diary, which is interesting, useful, but unreliable.]

Meshcherskii, Prince V.P. *Moi Vospominaniia.* 3 volumes. St. Petersburg, 1897–1912.

———. *Ocherki nyneshnei obshchestvennoi zhizni v Rossii.* St. Petersburg, 1868.

"Mestnyia voiska." *Voennyi sbornik*, No. 7, 1864.

M.G. "Ustroistvo i sluzhba general'nogo shtaba." *Voennyi sbornik*, No. 7, 1873.

Miliutin, Graf D. A. *Dnevnik D. A. Miliutina.* Introduction by P. A. Zaionchkovskii. 4 volumes. Moscow, 1947–1950. [This is an extremely valuable primary source, and basic to any study of Miliutin.]

Miliutin, D.A. *Istoriia voiny Rossii s frantsiei v tsarstvovanie Imperatora Pavla I v 1799 godu.* 5 volumes. Moscow, 1851.

———. "Kriticheskoe issledovanie znacheniia voennoi geografii i statistiki." *Voennyi Zhurnal*, No. 1, 1846.

————. *Pervye opyty voennoi statistiki.* 2 volumes Moscow, 1847.

————. *Rukovodstvo k s'emke planov.* Moscow, 1832.

————. "Suvorov kak polkovodets." *Otechestvennye Zapiski,* No. 4, 1839.

[Miliutin, D.A.] "Voennyia reformy Imperatora Aleksandra II." *Vestnik evropy,* No. 1, 1882. [The first of a proposed series by the former War Minister. Due to the action of the censors only this one ever appeared. Although it is an apologia, it is an indispensable source for Miliutin's views.]

Miller, F.A. "Dmitrii Miliutin: Liberal or Conservative?" *Jahrbücher für Geschichte Osteuropas,* No. 2, 1965.

M. J. "Die Reformen der Heeresorganisation in Russland seit 1867." *Preussische Jahrbucher,* Vol. XXVIII, Part 3 (1871).

M.M.Stasiulevich i ego sovremenniki v perepiske. 4 volumes. St. Petersburg, 1911–1912.

M.R. "Znachenie novogo distsiplinarnogo polozheniia." *Voennyi sbornik,* Vol. LXVII (1869).

"Nashe finansovoe polozhenie." *Russkii Invalid,* Nos. 228, 229, 230, 232, 234, 235; 1866.

N.D.N. "Obshchii obzor' preobrazovanii po chasti ustroistva vooruzhennykh sil Rossii s 1856 po 1860 god." *Voennyi sbornik,* Nos. 1, 2, and 3. 1861.

Nemirovich-Danchenko, Vasilii. "Sei ostal'noi iz stai slavnoi." *Russkoe slovo,* January 26, 1912.

"Neskol'ko slov po povodu Vysochaishogo poveleniia 4-go noiabria. *Russkii Invalid,* No. 258, 1870.

Nevedenskii, S. *Katkov i ego vremia.* St. Petersburg, 1888.

Nikitenko, A.V. *Dnevnik v trekh tomakh.* 3 volumes. Leningrad, 1955.

"Novyia nachala voinskoi povinnosti v Rossii." *Voennyi sbornik,* Nos. 2, 3, and 4, 1864.

O. "Biudzhet voennogo ministerstva i potrebnosti armii." *Russkii Invalid,* No. 81, 1865.

————. "1863-i god dlia russkoi armii." *Russkii Invalid,* Nos. 32 and 59, 1864.

Obzor deiatel'nosti ministerstva narodnago prosveshcheniia i podvedomstvennykh emu uchrezhdenii v 1862, 63, 64 godakh. St. Petersburg, 1865. [Contains excellent tables for a study of the costs, types, and enrollments of schools maintained by Ministry of Public Instruction.]

"Obzor deiatel'nosti voennogo ministerstva." *Voennyi sbornik,* No. 10, 1865.

"Ofitsial'nyi otdel':Prikaz voennogo ministra, February 20, 1868, No. 42." *Voennyi sbornik,* Vol. LXII, 1868. [Regulation for training artillery officers.]

Ol'shevskii, M.Ia. "Kavkaz s 1841–1866 god." *Russkaia starina,* Vols. 78, 79, 81, 82, 83, and 84 (1893–1895).

————. "Kniaz' A.I.Bariatinskii na Kavkaze v 1859g." *Russkaia starina,* Vol. XXIX, 1880.

"O novom poriadke voiskogo khoziaistva v armii." *Voennyi sbornik*, Vol. LXVII, 1869.

"O rekrutskoi reformy." *Russkii Invalid*. Nos. 96, 97, and 105, 1864.

"Otdel' ofitsial'nyi; Prikaz voennogo ministra, March 10, 1866, No. 85." *Voennyi sbornik*, No. 6, 1866. [This act reformed the Corps of Pages.]

Parensov, P. "Iz proshlogo." *Russkaia Starina*, No. 11, 1908.

————. *Iz proshlogo: Vospominaniia ofitsera general'nogo shtaba.* 2 volumes. St. Petersburg, 1904.

Patrakov, V. "O gramotnosti nizhnikh chinov i o vedenii otchetnosti po etomu predmetu." *Voennyi sbornik*, Vol. LXXIII, 1870. [An interesting inquiry into methods of determining the degree of literacy of army recruits.]

Pavlovskii, N.F. "Aleksandr Vasilievich Golovnin, ego uchastie v preobrazovanii voenno-uchebnykh zavedenii," *Russkaia starina*, No. 9, 1887.

P.B. "Neskol'ko slov o general'nom shtabe." *Voennyi sbornik*, No. 5, 1874.

P.B[obrovskii]. "K voprosu o razvitii sposobov dlia komplektovaniia armii ofitserami." *Voennyi sbornik*, No. 10, 1870.

"Pervye gody Sankt Peterburgskogo okruzhnogo intendantstva 1861–1866: Zapiski gen. leit. V. D. Krenke." *Russkaia starina*, Vols. XXXIV and XXXV (1882).

Petrov, A. *Russkaiia voennaia sila.* 2nd edition. 2 volumes. St. Petersburg, 1892.

Petrovich, M.B., "Russian Pan-Slavists and the Polish Uprising of 1863," *Harvard Slavic Studies*, Vol. I., 1953.

Platov, A., and Kirpinev, L. *Istoricheskii ocherk obrazovaniia i razvitiia artillericheskogo uchilishcha, 1820–1870 g.* St. Petersburg, 1870.

Pogoskii, A. "O gramotnosti v voiskakh." *Voennyi sbornik*, No. 6, 1866.

"Po povodu byvshogo i predstoiashchego rekrutskikh naborov." *Russkii Invalid*, Nos. 235, 236, 242, and 244, 1863.

"Po povodu obshchei voinskoi povinnosti." *Delo*, No. 12, 1870.

"Predpolozhenie predostavit' unter-ofitseram obshchogo sroka pravo prokhodit' iunkerskiia uchilishcha." *Voennyi sbornik*, No. 2, 1867.

"Preobrazovaniia novovedeniia po voennomu vedomstvu za poslednyia 10 let(1856–1866)." *Nedelia*, Nos. 13 and 14, 1866.

"Prikaz po voennomu vedomstvu o mestnykh i rezervnykh voiskakh." *Voennyi sbornik*, No. 11, 1874.

"Prikaz voennogo ministra, January 11, 1868, No. 5; Pravila dlia postupleniia ofitserov v voenno-iuridicheskuiu Akademiiu," *Voennyi sbornik*, Vol. LX, 1868.

Public Record Office; Reference 65/662.

Riasanovsky, N.V. *Nicholas I and Official Nationality in Russia, 1825–1855.* Berkeley; University of California Press, 1959.

Rieber, A.J., ed., *The Politics of Autocracy: The Letters of Alexander II to Prince A.I. Bariatinskii.* New York: Humanities Press, n.d.

Rittikh, A. F. *Graf D. A. Miliutin.* St. Petersburg, 1912.

Rogov, G.A. "Istoricheskii ocherk pozhertovanii v pol'zu voenno-uchebnykh zavedenni." *Pedagogicheskii sbornik*, Nos. 7, 8, 9, and 10, 1871.

Rozental', V.N. "Ideinye tsentry liberal'nogo dvizheniia v Rossii nakanune revoliutsionnoi situatsii: Peterburgskii kruzhok K.D. Kavelina v 1855–1857 gg." *Revoliutsionnaia situatsiia v Rossi v 1859–1861 gg.* Moscow, 1963.

Rustow, W. *Die Russische Armee.* Wien, 1876.

"R.V.O.: Deistviia komiteta dlia razsmotreniia zamechanii po proektu o vzyskaniiakh po pravilam voennoi distsipliny; Zametka o deistviikh komiteta dlia sostavleniia proekta ustava o voennom sudoproizvodstve i sudoustroistve." *Voennyi sbornik*, No. 6, 1863.

"R.V.O.:Iunkerskiia uchilishcha v 1867 godu." *Voennyi sbornik*, Vol. LIX (1868).

"R.V.O.: Kommissariatskoe i proviantskoe dovol'stviia." *Voennyi sbornik*, No. 2, 1863.

"R.V.O.: Komplektovanie rezervnykh voisk." *Voennyi sbornik*, No. 7, 1865.

"R.V.O.:Lichnyi sostav ofitserskikh klasov pri auditorskom uchilishche." *Voennyi sbornik*, No. 11, 1866. [This study analyzes the branch of service, age, rank, years of service, etc. of officers entering the auditor's school.]

"R.V.O.:Novoe polozhenie o polevom upravlenii voisk v voennoe vremia." *Voennyi sbornik*, No. 6, 1868.

"R.V.O.:Novyi voinskii ustav o nakazaniiakh." *Voennyi sbornik*, No. 6, 1868.

"R.V.O.:Novyia postanovleniia o proizvodstve nizhnikh chinov v ofitsery." *Voennyi sbornik*, Vol. LXVII (1869). [This contains a copy of the regulations covering the commissioning of noncommissioned officers.]

"R.V.O.: Novyia priemnyia programy dlia ispytaniia ofitserov, postupaiushchikh v Nikolaevskuiu Akademiiu general'nogo shtaba." *Voennyi sbornik*, Vol. LXIV (1869).

"R.V.O.:Obshchii obzor' novoi organizatsii armii." *Voennyi sbornik*, No. 1, 1863.

"R.V.O.:Obzor preobrazovanii, sostoiavshikhsia v techenie 1874–1875 godov v organizatsii nashikh voisk." *Voennyi sbornik*, No. 1, 1876.

"R.V.O.:Ofitserskie klasy pri auditorskom uchilishche." *Voennyi sbornik*, No. 10, 1866.

"R.V.O.: Osnovnyia polozheniia preobrazovaniia voenno-sudnoi chasti." *Voennyi sbornik*, No. 12, 1865.

"R.V.O.:O zaniatiiakh pekhotnogo otdela komiteta ob izmenenii organizatsii armii." *Voennyi sbornik*, Nos. 3 and 5, 1863.

"R.V.O.: Polozhenie o glavnom upravlenii general'nogo shtaba." *Voennyi sbornik*, No. 12, 1863.

"R.V.O.: Predpolagaemyia izmeneniia v poriadke proizvodstva iunkerov i vol'noopredeliaiushchikhsia." *Voennyi sbornik*, No. 4, 1863.

"R.V.O.: Predpolozhenie o poriadke proizvodstva v ofitsery nizhnikh chinov unter-ofitserskogo zvaniia." *Voennyi sbornik*, No. 4, 1863.

"R.V.O.:Preobrazovanie uchilishch voennogo vedomstva." *Voennyi sbornik,* No. 8, 1866. See also *Russkii invalid,* No. 139, 1866.

"R.V.O.:Prikaz po voennomu vedomstvu o mestnykh zapasnykh i rezervnykh voiskakh." *Voennyi sbornik,* No. 11, 1874.

"R.V.O.:Programy dlia iunkerskikh uchilishch." *Voennyi sbornik,* No. 2, 1867.

"R.V.O.: Rekrutskii nabor nastoiashchogo 1863 goda i ego kharakter; deistviia komiteta dlia peresmotra rekrutskogo ustava; pervonachal'noe obrazovanie rekrut." *Voennyi sbornik,* No. 4, 1863.

"R.V.O.:Russkaia armiia v 1864 godu." *Voennyi sbornik,* Nos. 8, 9, 10, 11, and 12, 1866. [Reviews a most critical year in the reform of the various parts of the military system.]

"R.V.O.:Sovremennoe sostoianie iunkerskikh uchilishch." *Voennyi sbornik,* No. 7, 1866.

"R.V.O.:Staticheskiia svedeniia o iunkerskikh voennykh uchilishch za 1863–1866g." *Voennyi sbornik,* No. 12, 1866.

"R.V.O.:Svod zamechanii na proekt ob ustroistve voennogo upravleniia po okrugam." *Voennyi sbornik,* Nos. 3 and 5, 1863. [Extremely valuable, this article discusses and analyzes the various attitudes in regard to the War Ministry's plans for a military district system.]

"R.V.O.: Uchrezhdenie voennykh okrugov i preobrazovanie v ustroistve mestnkyh voisk." *Voennyi sbornik,* No. 9, 1864.

"R.V.O.: Russkaia voenno-administrativnaia sistema." *Voennyi sbornik,* No. 10, 1864.

"R.V.O.:Voenno-feldsherskiia shkoly." *Voennyi sbornik,* Vol. LXVIII (1869).

"R.V.O.:Voenno-nachal'nyia shkoly, uchitel'skaia seminariia voennogo vedomstva i voenno-chertezhnaia shkola." *Voennyi sbornik,* No. 2, 1867.

"R.V.O.: Voennyia progymnazii," *Voennyi sbornik,* No. 7, 1869. [Includes the text of the act creating the *progymnazii.*]

"R.V.O.: Zametki o proizvodstve nizhnikh chinov v ofitsery." *Voennyi sbornik,* No. 7, 1863.

Sbornik pravitel'stvennykh rasporiazhenii po vvedeniiu obshchei voinskoi povinnosti. St. Petersburg, 1874.

Schneidler, Dr. M. F. C. *Das Russische Reich unter Kaiser Alexander II.* Berlin, 1878.

Schuyler, Eugene. "Letter book," December 31, 1873–January 9, 1879. Manuscripts Division, Library of Congress.

Selivanov, V.V. "Koe-chto o rekrutskoi povinnosti." *Sel'skoe Blagoustroistvo,* No. 2, 1859.

Semenov-Tian Shanskii, P.P. *Epokha osvobozhdeniia krest'ian v Rossii (1857–1861).* 4 volumes. Petrograd, 1913–1916.

Seredonin, S. M. *Istoricheskii obzor deiatel'nosti Komiteta Ministrov.* Vol. III, part 2. St. Petersburg, 1902.

Shatilov, D.V. "Mysli po povodu unichtozheniia telesnogo nakazaniia v voiskakh." *Voennyi sbornik*, No. 10, 1863.

———. "Preobrazovanie nashei armii i komplektovanie eia ofitserami." *Otechestvennyia zapiski*, Nos. 5 and 6, 1865.

Shavrov, K. "Gramotnost' v voiskakh." *Voennyi sbornik*, No. 5, 1892.

Shchetinina, G.I. "Novyi dokument po istorii vnutrennei politiki Rossii epokhi vtoroi revoliutsionnoi situatsii (Proekt A.A. Saburova - D.A. Miliutina)." *Problemy Istochnikovedeniia*, Vol. IX. Moscow, 1961.

Shklarevich, V. "O sostave uchebnogo kursa, tseli i kharakter prepodavaniia nauk v voennykh uchilishchakh." *Pedagogicheskii sbornik*, No. 5, 1865.

"Shkoly i uchebnyia komandy v armii." *Voennyi sbornik*, No. 6, 1862.

Siminov, I.S. "Graf D.A.Miliutin," *S-Peterburgskie Vedomosti*, No. 97, 1904.

———. "Gr. D.A.Miliutin i voenno-uchebnoe vedomstvo." *Pedagogicheskii sbornik*, No. 2, 1912.

———. *Na pamiat' o general-feldmarshale russkoi armii graf Dmitrii Alekseevich Miliutin*. Izdanie *Pedagogicheskii sbornik*. St. Petersburg, 1912.

Skalon, D. A., general ed. *Stoletie voennogo ministerstva, 1802–1902*. 13 volumes. St. Petersburg, 1902–1914. [An absolutely indispensable source—this work is a goldmine of documents and materials.]

Sladkevich, N.G. *Ocherki istorii obshchestvennoi mysli Rossii v kontse 50 - nachale 60-kh godov XIX veka*. Leningrad, 1962.

"S.O.: Po voprosu o preobrazovanii real'nykh gymnazii." *Zhurnal ministerstva narodnogo prosveshcheniia*, No. 155, May 1871. [Sums up the views of the Tolstoy-Katkov party in the classical versus real school controversy.]

Sol'skii, D. *Otchet po Gosudarstvennomu Sovetu za 1870 god*. St. Petersburg, 1871.

———. *Otchet po Gosudarstvennomu sovetu za 1873 god*. St. Petersburg, 1875.

Stankevich, A.V. *T.N.Granovskii i ego perepiska*. 2 volumes. 2nd edition. Moscow, 1897.

Svatikov, S.G. *Konstitutsionnoe dvizhenie pri Aleksandre II*. Moscow, 1916.

Tatishchev, S. S. *Imperator Aleksandr II, ego zhizn' i tsarstvovanie*. 2 volumes. St. Petersburg, 1911.

"Tekst 'Polozheniia' o proizvodstve nizhnykh chinov v ofitsery." *Voennyi sbornik*, No. 5, 1869.

[Terner, F.G.] "Vospominaniia zhizni F.G. Ternera." *Russkaia Starina*, Nos. 1, 2, 6, 1910.

Trubnikov, Sh.K. "R.V.O.:Zapiski nachal'nyi voennoi administratsii dlia iunkerskikh uchilishch." *Voennyi sbornik*, No. 7, 1867.

"Trudy komiteta, vysochaishe utverzhdennogo dlia opredeleniia dovol'stviia armeiskikh voisk." *Voennyi sbornik*, Nos. 9, 10, 11, and 12, 1862.

"Uchebnaia chast' iunkerskikh uchilishch po otchetam za 1867–1868 uchebnoi god." *Voennyi sbornik*, No. 10, 1869.

V.A. "R.V.O.: Predpolozhenii o preobrazovanii prodovol'stvennoi chasti (s prilozheniiami)." *Voennyi sbornik*, No. 5, 1866.
V.A. "Smeta voennogo ministerstva na 1863 god." *Russkii Invalid*, No. 130, 1863.
Valuev, P.A. *Dnevnik P.A.Valueva: Ministra vnutrennikh del.* 2 volumes. Moscow, 1961.
Velinskii, A. "Voina i Rossiia." *Grazhdanin*, No. 44, 1876.
Veniukov, M.I. "Istoricheskie ocherki Rossii v tsarstvovanie Aleksandra II." *Golos minuvshogo na chuzhoi storone*, Nos. 1, 2, and 3, 1926.
Verigin, F. "Zametka na osnovanii polozheniia preobrazovaniia voenno-sudnoi chasti." *Voennyi sbornik*, No. 9, 1863.
Vitte, Baron N. "Vsesoslovnaia voinskaia povinnost' chetyre goda spustia po vvedenii eia v deistvie." *Voennyi sbornik*, Vol. CXXII (1878).
"Vnutrenee obozrenie: Obshchaia voennaia povinnost' i nashe real'noe obrazovanie." *Vestnik evropy*, December 1870. [A liberal view of the relationship between the question of national education and universal military service.]
"Vnutrenee obozrenie: Osnovaniia proekta o voinskoi povinnosti; Voenno-okruzhnaia sistema i eia protivniki." *Vestnik evropy*, March–April, 1873.
"Voenno-sudnaia reforma." *Voennyi sbornik*, No. 8, 1867.
"Voennyi ministr, g.a. Dmitrii Alekseevich Miliutin." *Vsemirnaia illiustratsiia*, Vol. V, No. 105 (1871).
"Voennyi obzor 1871 goda." *Russkii invalid*, No. 6, 1872.
"Vopros o vooruzhenii Rossii (Peredovaia stat'ia)." *Golos*, No. 280, 1867.
Vsepoddaneishii doklad voennogo ministra. January 15, 1862. [Although a lithographed copy of the original report is deposited in the New York Public Library, the citations in the text are taken from *Stoletie voennogo ministerstva: Prilozheniia k istoricheskomu ocherku razvitiia voennogo upravleniia v Rossii, 1802–1902*, I., as it reproduces the marginal comments of the Emperor.]
———. January 1, 1870.
———. January 1, 1871.
———. January 1, 1872.
———. January 1, 1873.
"Vsepoddaneishii doklad voennogo ministra ot 20-go dekabria 1870g., No. 381; Obshchiia rukovodiashchiia osnovaniia dlia komisii o lichnoi voennoi povinnosti; Obshchiia rukovodiashchiia osnovaniia dlia komisii ob organizatsii voisk." *Voennyi sbornik*, No. 1, 1871.
Vsepoddaneishii otchet voennogo ministerstva za 1863 god. St. Petersburg, 1865.
Vsepoddaneishii otchet voennogo ministerstva za 1864 god. St. Petersburg, 1866.
Vsepoddaneishii otchet voennogo ministerstva za 1865 god. St. Petersburg, 1867.

Vsepoddaneishii otchet voennogo ministerstva za 1866 god. St. Petersburg, 1868.

Vsepoddaneishii otchet voennogo ministerstva za 1867 god. St. Petersburg, 1869.

Vsepoddaneishii otchet voennogo ministerstva za 1868 god. St. Petersburg, 1870.

Vsepoddaneishii otchet voennogo ministerstva za 1869 god. St. Petersburg, 1871.

V-skii, S. "Ob ofitserov armeiskikh pekhotnykh polkov, po povodu stat'i, pomeshchennoi v 'Voennom Sbornike' za 1858 god: 'Stepen' obrazovaniia ofitserov v armii. 'L.K." *Voennyi sbornik*, No. 10, 1859.

Wessel, N. "Voennyia uchilishcha i voennyia gymnazii." *Pedagogicheskii sbornik*. No. 1, 1867.

Witte, S.Iu. *S.Iu.Vitte : Vospominaniia.* 3 volumes. Moscow, 1960.

Zabelin, A. "Vospominaniia ob Imperatore Aleksandre II-om." *Voenno-istoricheskii vestnik*, Paris. No. 8, 1956.

Zablotskii-Desiatovskii,A.P. *Graf P.D.Kiselev i ego vremia*, 4 volumes. St. Petersburg, 1882.

Zaionchkovskii, A. M. *Vostochnaiia voina 1853–1856 gg., v sviazi s sovremennoi ei politicheskoi obstanovkoi.* 5 volumes. St. Petersburg, 1908.

Zaionchkovskii, P. A. "Arkhiv D. A. Miliutina," *Voprosy istorii*, No. 5–6, 1946.

————. "Perevooruzhenie russkoi armii v 60-70-kh godakh XIX v." *Istoricheskie zapiski*, Vol. XXXVI (1950).

————. "Podgotovka voennoi reformy 1874 goda." *Istoricheskie Zapiski*, Vol. XXVII. (1948). [A valuable work, due to the inclusion of materials not elsewhere available.]

————. *Voennye reformy 1860–1870 godov v Rossii.* Moscow, 1952. [This is the closest thing to a fundamental secondary work on the military reforms. Most valuable because it contains materials from documents not available elsewhere.]

————. "Voennye reformy Miliutina." *Voprosy istorii*, No. 2, 1945.

Zalesov, N.G. "Zapiski N.G.Zalesova," *Russkaia starina*, No. 11, 1903, and No. 6, 1905.

Zeddeler, Baron L.L. "Neskol'ko slov o naznachenii voennykh uchilishch." *Pedagogicheskii sbornik*, No. 12, 1868.

Zherve, N. *Graf D. A. Miliutin.* St. Petersburg, 1912.

Zisserman, A. *K istorii pokoreniia Kavkaza, 1726–1880.* 3 volumes. St. Petersburg, 1881.

Zisserman, A.L. *Fel'dmarshal kniaz' Aleksandr Ivanovich Bariatinskii, 1815–1879.* 3 volumes. Moscow, 1890. [Extremely disposed in favor of Bariatinskii, this work is nevertheless indispensible; in it are published much of Miliutin's correspondence and some documents of importance.]

Zykov, S.P. "Nabroski iz moei zhizni." Nos. 4, 6, 7, 9. *Russkaia Starina*, 1910.

Index